Dyslexia, Dysgraphia, OWL LD, and Dyscalculia

Second Edition

Dyslexia, Dysgraphia, OWL LD, and Dyscalculia
Lessons from Science and Teaching

Second Edition

by

Virginia W. Berninger, Ph.D.
University of Washington
Seattle

and

Beverly J. Wolf, M.Ed.
Slingerland® Institute for Literacy
Bellevue, Washington

·P A U L·H·
BROOKES
PUBLISHING CO ®

Baltimore • London • Sydney

Paul H. Brookes Publishing Co.
Post Office Box 10624
Baltimore, Maryland 21285-0624
USA

www.brookespublishing.com

Typeset by Progressive Publishing Services, Emigsville, Pennsylvania.
Manufactured in the United States of America by
Sheridan Books Inc., Chelsea, Michigan.

The individuals described in this book are real people whose situations are masked and are based on the authors' experiences. In all instances, names and identifying details have been changed or deleted to protect confidentiality.

SLINGERLAND® is a registered trademark of the Slingerland® Institute for Literacy. This book is not endorsed or approved by the Slingerland® Institute for Literacy.

Clip art in Figures 13.2 and 13.3 ©istockphoto.com.

Library of Congress Cataloging-in-Publication Data

The Library of Congress has cataloged the print edition as follows:

Names: Berninger, Virginia Wise. | Wolf, Beverly J. | Berninger, Virginia Wise. Dyslexia, dysgraphia, OWL LD, and dyscalculia.
Title: Dyslexia, dysgraphia, OWL LD, and dyscalculia: Lessons from science and teaching / Virginia W. Berninger, Ph.D., University of Washington, Seattle, Washington and Beverly Wolf, M.Ed., Bellevue, Washington.
Description: Second edition. | Baltimore, Maryland : Paul H. Brookes Publishing Co., [2015] | Revised edition of: Teaching students with dyslexia and dysgraphia | Includes bibliographical references and index.
Identifiers: LCCN 2015021980 | ISBN 9781598578942 (pbk.) | ISBN 9781557669346 (pbk.) | ISBN 9781681250106 (pdf ebook) | ISBN 9781681250120 (epub ebook)
Subjects: LCSH: Dyslexic children—Education. | Children with disabilities—Education. | Reading disability | Learning disabilities. | Remedial teaching. | Dyslexia. | Agraphia.
Classification: LCC LC4708 .B47 2015 | DDC 371.9—dc23
LC record available at http://lccn.loc.gov/2015021980

British Library Cataloguing in Publication data are available from the British Library.

2019   2018   2017   2016   2015

10   9   8   7   6   5   4   3   2   1

Contents

About the Authors

Virginia W. Berninger, Ph.D., Professor and Research Affiliate, Educational Psychology, Center on Human Development and Disability, University of Washington, Box 353600, Seattle, Washington 98195

Dr. Berninger received her Ph.D. in psychology at Johns Hopkins University and has had a career informed both by translation science (bridging basic research and application to practice) and interdisciplinary contributions to assessment, diagnosis, and treatment, including instruction. As a professor at the University of Washington, Dr. Berninger has been the principal investigator of research grants on typical language development and specific learning disabilities funded by the *Eunice Kennedy Shriver* National Institute of Child Health and Human Development and also the co-investigator of a research grant on math development and instruction funded by the U.S. Department of Education. This interdisciplinary research has been informed by Dr. Berninger's prior teaching experience (in urban, suburban, and rural settings in general and special education and at the elementary and secondary levels); training in clinical psychology and experience as a licensed psychologist (in assessment of developmental and learning disabilities); and ongoing consultation with schools, teachers, and parents for more than 30 years. Her current efforts focus on evidence-based, treatment-relevant differential diagnosis of specific learning disabilities and professional development for teachers and other professionals in schools and outside schools who influence school practices.

Beverly J. Wolf, M.Ed., Director, Slingerland® Institute for Literacy, 12729 Northup Way, Suite 1, Bellevue, Washington 98005

Ms. Wolf received her M.Ed. in education at Seattle Pacific University and brings to this collaborative effort experience as a classroom teacher, a principal of an elementary school for children with dyslexia, Dean of Faculty for the Slingerland® Institute for Literacy, and an educational consultant providing professional development nationally and locally on structured language teaching. She has authored articles and books about dyslexia, creative activities for the classroom, and language-related guides for teachers. Ms. Wolf is a member of the Council of Advisors of the International Dyslexia Association (IDA), a past secretary and board member of IDA, the recipient of the John and Beth Slingerland Award from the Slingerland® Institute, the Beth Slingerland Award from the Washington State Branch of the International Dyslexia Association (WABIDA), and the Outstanding Educator Award from the Renton School District. Through her professional experiences she has had the good fortune to hold the hands of teachers whose professional expertise and experience helped shape her own work as she in turn shared with them. Ms. Wolf is inspired by her ongoing work with the next generation of teachers. They stimulate her and motivate her to continue to develop materials that make teaching and learning exciting and fun. As she does, she reminds others that students with learning disabilities benefit from the collaboration of many professionals sharing with each other and learning from each other.

Foreword

One may wonder how Virginia W. Berninger and Beverly J. Wolf could improve upon the first edition of their text, but they have done so with a highly readable and enjoyable second edition written primarily for teachers. This book, however, will assist anyone working with children with specific learning disabilities (SLDs) as long as he or she believes that students learn differently—especially those who come from atypical backgrounds (e.g., culturally and linguistically diverse, poverty, military families, and the like)—and therefore will benefit from differentiated instruction (Mascolo, Alfonso, & Flanagan, 2014).

Berninger and Wolf weave a masterful tapestry of science and best practices to provide teachers with just the right amount of information to be effective with students who experience learning difficulties with handwriting, spelling, reading and listening comprehension, oral expression, written expression, math computations, and math problem solving (IDEA 2004). They do so by tapping diverse fields of study such as genetics, neuroscience, cognitive science, linguistics, and education.

In an era when our educators are held to levels of accountability that surpass that of many other disciplines and where there is great disagreement about how best to identify SLDs (Flanagan & Alfonso, 2011) and whether or not specific learning disabilities exist (Shaywitz, Escobar, Shaywitz, Fletcher, & Makuch, 1992), it is heartening to read a volume that does not blame but rather supports and values those working on the front lines to teach our students so they may be successful. Berninger and Wolf begin their tome with an excellent treatise on the present, past, and future of SLDs via Chapters 1 and 2, which constitute Section I. In Section II they provide four chapters on translating research lessons into teaching tips for students K–12. Each chapter addresses different areas of study or subject matter and links assessment to instruction via instructional resources, assessment of the academic domain, and teacher resources. This design works well and should make it easy for teachers and others to find their way to what they need most for specific students. Next, in Section III, the authors move beyond individual assessment and instruction to what may be even more important to assist students—a better understanding of the multiple systems involved in educating students. Whether one subscribes to Bronfenbrenner (1977), Ramey and Ramey (1998), Sarason (1996), or Clinton (2006) to name a few, there is no doubt that systems play a critical role in the education of all students, including those with and without disabilities. Finally, in Section IV Berninger and Wolf recognize that there is continued need for professional development and cross-disciplinary communication and collaboration. The three chapters in Section IV may have to be read more than once, as they challenge the status quo and call upon all educators to work together in an integrated fashion rather than in silos or discrete disciplines that provide only part of the solution (Berninger, 2015).

As a dean of a school of education where individuals are prepared to become general education teachers, special education teachers, educational administrators, school counselors, and school psychologists, I am delighted to have been given the opportunity to write a foreword for my colleagues' latest volume. I have no doubt that their comprehensive, authoritative, and useful addition to best practices in teaching students with SLDs will be read by many and become a landmark in the field.

Vincent C. Alfonso, Ph.D.
Dean
School of Education
Gonzaga University

REFERENCES

Berninger, V.W. (2015). *Interdisciplinary frameworks for schools: Best professional practices for serving the needs of all students.* Washington, DC: American Psychological Association.

Bronfenbrenner, U. (1977). Toward an experimental ecology of human development. *American Psychologist, 32,* 513–531.

Clinton, H.R. (2006). *It takes a village* (10th anniversary ed.). New York, NY: Simon & Schuster.

Flanagan, D., & Alfonso, V.C. (Eds.). (2011). *Essentials of specific learning disability identification.* Hoboken, NJ: Wiley.

Individuals with Disabilities Education Improvement Act (IDEA) of 2004, PL 108-446, 20 U.S.C. §§ 1400 *et seq.*

Mascolo, J.T., Alfonso, V.C., & Flanagan, D.P. (Eds.). (2014). *Essentials of planning, selecting, and tailoring interventions for unique learners.* Hoboken, NJ: Wiley.

Ramey, C.T., & Ramey, S.L. (1998). Early intervention and early experience. *American Psychologist, 53,* 109–120.

Sarason, S.B. (1996). *Revisiting "The culture of the school and the problem of change."* New York, NY: Teachers College Press.

Shaywitz, S.E., Escobar, M.D., Shaywitz, B.A., Fletcher, J.M., & Makuch, R. (1992). Evidence that dyslexia may represent the lower tail of a normal distribution of reading ability. *The New England Journal of Medicine, 326,* 145–150.

Foreword

Reading and writing difficulties have been studied by various professionals, such as neuropsychologists, cognitive psychologists, and educators. Though much progress has been made in our knowledge of the nature of reading and writing problems, our understanding of how to incorporate instructional procedures, especially writing, has lagged far behind. In this second edition, Virginia W. Berninger and Beverly J. Wolf provide the science and teaching of reading and writing skills to individuals with varying needs. I am delighted to see additional information in this edition based on recent research, making this volume a very valuable resource for anyone interested in teaching reading and writing skills.

Reading and writing skills are basic for survival. Various studies have shown that a child who has difficulty learning to read by the end of first grade may have greater difficulty acquiring these skills later on, and these difficulties can affect not only academic achievement but also social and personal skills (Snow, Burns, & Griffin, 1998). For instance, Juel (1994) found that students who did not have the knowledge of letter names and the common sounds of the letters by the end of first grade had a very high probability of having reading difficulties by fourth grade. Conversely, students who knew the names of the letters and their common sounds by the end of first grade had an equally high probability of being good readers by fourth grade. Thus, it is imperative that children be provided with systematic, explicit, and sequential instruction in reading and writing from very early grade levels in order to stop the vicious cycle of failure in reading and writing.

With their combined knowledge in neuropsychology, learning disabilities, and instruction, Berninger and Wolf provide a scientific, yet written in an easily understandable fashion, resource on overcoming the difficulties of reading, writing, and oral language. The volume clearly outlines how to help children with difficulties in basic literacy skills, not only from the teacher-instructional perspective but also from classroom management, the role of parents, and teacher education. This second edition is much expanded with new information on technology, content area reading, and preparation of preservice teachers, as well as professional development for in-service teachers. I have used the previous edition of the book in my courses on reading and writing, and I definitely plan to use the new edition as a textbook in my graduate and under-graduate classes. I very much enjoyed reading this new edition, and my hat's off to both Berninger and Wolf for producing such a useful volume.

R. Malatesha Joshi, Ph.D.
Professor of Literacy Education, ESL, and Educational Psychology
Texas A & M University

REFERENCES

Juel, C. (1994). *Learning to read and write in one elementary school.* New York, NY: Springer Verlag.

Snow, C.E., Burns, M.S., & Griffin, P. (1998). *Preventing reading difficulties in young children.* Washington, DC: National Academy Press.

Foreword

In this second edition, Virginia W. Berninger and Beverly J. Wolf deepen their commitment to translation science, which they define as the conversion of "research findings into treatment-relevant, evidence-based diagnoses" (Chapter 1, p. 16). Translation science is appropriately considered as the basis for assisting educators in systematically asking the right instructional questions to achieve two ends: optimizing the academic achievement of students with specific learning disabilities (SLDs) and maximizing their cognitive and social engagement in the learning process. The translation science that serves as the cornerstone of this volume is an outcome of two interrelated research strands that Berninger and colleagues implemented over the past 2 decades. These strands include: 1) similarities and differences in the neurobiological and behavioral profiles of the four SLDs featured in the book and 2) strategic intervention studies that focused on the integration of content knowledge at multiple levels of language across the four language systems combined with self-regulatory procedures for internalizing new information.

However, from the professional perspective of a speech-language pathologist long concerned with school-age students struggling with oral language and literacy learning (which the authors refer to as oral and written language learning disability, or OWL LD), this second edition deserves another accolade in the primacy now given to language. For example, the four functional language systems (language by ear, language by eye, language by mouth, and language by hand) and the multiple levels that comprise this communication system, from the subword to the discourse level, serve as the volume's conceptual framework. When one or two of the four language systems fail to coordinate in expected ways with one another, the behavioral consequence may be one or more of the SLDs. The conceptual prominence allocated to language systems and levels is then transformed into practical applications through two major and intersecting dimensions of the volume's organization: the differential diagnosis of the specific learning disabilities and, in this Common Core era, the design of relevant instructional approaches that advance student learning across content areas consistent with individual diagnostic needs. Hence, the salience of language that the authors render in this edition should not be underestimated. Although it may seem obvious that language is at the heart of all academic learning, including mathematics, the complexity of language can seem overwhelming to many educators and to some education researchers as well. A frequent result is simplification. The synergistic levels and functions of language oftentimes are relegated to a single construct, such as "vocabulary" or "syntax," and student learning is then premised on minimal understanding of how this synergy routinely affects the variability of comprehension and expression in speaking, listening, reading, writing, and spelling activities for individual students. In sum, we can look into the "language mirror" but may not see our reflection.

The great contribution of this new edition is to empower educators to look more often into the language mirror and understand how the four functional language systems may or may not work in concert for individual students and how dissociations can be reflected at different levels of language in both the oral and written domains. In this sense, Berninger and Wolf have transformed the opaque into a more transparent plan for the differentiation of profiles among the SLDs, as well as the tailored treatment of each student's diagnostic profile consistent with his or her developmental and instructional needs for implementation within the general education classroom.

Elaine R. Silliman, Ph.D.
Professor Emeritus
Communication Sciences & Disorders
University of South Florida

Preface

At a time when research on specific learning disabilities (SLDs) is rapidly expanding and parental and professional concern is growing about whether SLDs are being diagnosed and treated sufficiently and consistently, this second edition provides an update on research and practice issues. The second edition has a revised title because research is documenting that multiple kinds of SLDs exist and may even co-occur. These include dysgraphia, dyslexia, oral and written language learning disabilities (OWL LD), and dyscalculia.

As in the first edition, the importance of collaborations between researchers and teachers will be emphasized. We call attention to the emerging field of translational science, in which researchers and teachers are encouraged to form partnerships that address the challenging issues of translating research findings into educational practice. A new feature in the second edition is the inclusion in Section II of numbered Research Lessons, which call attention to new findings from research that are relevant to teaching, and numbered Teaching Tips, which call attention to educators' voices of experience in teaching students with and without SLDs. The challenges of translating research into practice are related in large part to the enormous diversity among students in any given classroom. Such diversity has not yet been addressed in the standards adopted by states or the annual tests given to assess whether individual students meet the standards. One source of diversity is specific kinds of SLDs, which occur in students from a variety of socioeconomic, cultural, and language backgrounds. A major focus of the second edition is evidence-based assessment–instruction links for preventing SLDs and monitoring response to instruction for students with SLDs in Grades K–12.

To meet the needs of all students with SLDs, this second edition expands the applications of lessons from research and teaching. First, because teachers are educating students in the digital era, we discuss how technology can be used not only for accommodations but also for ongoing explicit instruction. Second, we broaden the scope to lessons from research and teaching to interdisciplinary teams within schools and in the community that work with school-age children and youth. Third, we offer guidelines for preservice teachers and in-service preparation for teachers and other educational professionals on an interdisciplinary team who work with students with SLDs in school settings. Fourth, we discuss the applications of these lessons to educating those who make educational policy, pass laws, and regulate government implementation of policy and laws so that the Common Core Standards and related assessment are more appropriate for students with SLDs.

This second edition is substantially revised from the first edition and contains much new content. Many chapters feature appendices that include assessment resources, instructional resources and programs, and teacher resources. In addition, Appendix 12A presents a model for preservice teacher education in colleges of education and also for in-service professional development to prepare teachers and members of interdisciplinary teams to work with students with and without SLDs. Appendix 14A proposes Common Core Standards for the policy makers, lawyers, legislators, and government officials who make or implement regulations regarding education. Most important, we propose moving beyond an overly legalistic approach to a more proactive, best professional practices approach to educating students with SLDs in general education that reflects current understanding of translation science, promotes more positive home–school relationships, and is ultimately more cost effective.

Translating research into educational practice and informing research by the realities of educational practice will require team efforts. The whole story of the value of research–school partnerships will ultimately be told by readers who translate this book, and other sources of knowledge, into their own professional practice on behalf of all students, including but not restricted to those with SLDs.

Acknowledgments

Preparation of this book was supported, in part, by HD P50HD071764 from the *Eunice Kennedy Shriver* National Institute of Child Health and Human Development (NICHD) at the National Institutes of Health (NIH). The opinions and assertions presented in this book are those of the authors and do not purport to represent those of the *Eunice Kennedy Shriver* NICHD, the NIH, or the U.S. Department of Health and Human Services.

*To the children and youth who struggle to
learn oral language, reading, writing, and math despite otherwise
typical development and the many teachers committed to helping them
learn successfully based on lessons from science and teaching experience*

Translation Science

Situating the Present in the Past and Future for Specific Learning Disabilities

If ye don't know the past, then ye will not have a future.
If ye don't know where your people have been,
then ye won't know where your people are going.

The Education of Little Tree (Carter, 1990, p. 40)

Section I guides a journey from the pioneering, early contributions to the present field and its challenges. This section offers a vision of how students with specific learning disabilities, including but not restricted to dyslexia, can be educated more effectively.

Historical Context for Current Issues in Specific Learning Disabilities

Current issues are best understood in the context of the history of the field of learning disabilities.

EARLY HISTORY OF SPECIFIC LANGUAGE DISABILITY DIAGNOSIS AND TREATMENT

Systems for translating ideas into written symbols that represent speech syllables and phonemes have existed for more than 5,000 years. These symbols have been used for many purposes, ranging from sacred religious texts to everyday business transactions (Aaron & Joshi, 2006). Only recently in the history of human civilization, however, did societies attempt to teach all of their citizens to read and write. In the process, we have discovered that some struggle more than others in learning written language.

In the late 19th and early 20th centuries, two emerging fields—psychology and neurology—provided clues as to why some children struggle to acquire language. Psychologists used the experimental method to identify the mental processes involved in reading (e.g., Huey, 1968). Neurologists learned about brain function and behavior by observing individuals who had lost a language function before death and performing autopsies on their brains after death. Clinical neuropsychologists and neurologists observed children who struggled in acquiring language functions. Together, psychologists and neurologists introduced the idea that individual differences in the mind or brain might make it difficult for some students to learn from instruction that is adequate for most students.

Groundwork for studies in oral language disorders began in the 19th century when Paul Broca, a French surgeon and neuroanatomist, examined the brain of an individual who had lost speech with apparently no other impairments. When the individual died, an autopsy showed that a lesion in the left side of the brain in the front was the cause of that speech disability. This section of the brain is now named *Broca's area* in his honor. Although Broca assumed that this brain area controlled speech output and, if injured, caused speech difficulty, contemporary research has shown that this region is involved in more than speech. Broca's area has been shown to house executive functions for all language systems—listening, speaking, reading, and writing (see Mesulam, 1990).

German neurologist Carl Wernicke studied an individual who could speak but had lost the ability to understand oral language. During the autopsy, Wernicke found a lesion in the left side of the brain near the back, which is now understood to be the area of the brain involved in language comprehension. This section of the brain is now named *Wernicke's area* in his honor. According to contemporary brain imaging research, structural and functional differences occur between typical readers and writers and individuals with specific learning disabilities (SLDs) in both Broca's and Wernicke's regions (for a review, see Berninger & Richards, 2002).

Modern understanding of SLDs, such as dyslexia, began at the end of the 19th century. The first report of "word blindness" in a child came from W. Pringle Morgan, an English doctor. In an 1896 article in the *British Medical Journal*, Morgan described a bright student who knew his letters but was unable to read; he also spelled bizarrely. Because his visual memory for words was defective or absent, he was described as "word blind," a term introduced by Kussmaul (see Henry, 1999). Morgan believed that the problem was genetic because the student's father had similar problems and learned to read only with great difficulty. In 1917, James Hinshelwood, a Scottish ophthalmologist, summarized thirteen cases of word blindness and concluded that it was not as rare as once thought. Hinshelwood pointed out how symptoms of word blindness were similar to those of adults with brain injuries who lost the ability to read. He was the first to advocate a specific mode of instruction for students with written language disorders who were unable to read by sight alone: an alphabetic method that involves multiple brain regions (see Richardson, 1989).

In 1925, Samuel T. Orton, an American psychiatrist and neuropathologist, began to expand the early work on dyslexia. As chair of the University of Iowa's Department of Psychiatry, he created the Mobile Mental Hygiene Clinic to provide multidisciplinary services to communities in rural Greene County, Iowa. He studied a 16-year-old boy who could not read even though he seemed bright. Orton (1937/1989) discovered a number of other students with similar difficulties and was impressed by how their personality development was adversely affected by this handicap. Based on clinical observation, Orton noted five different kinds of learning disorders:

1. Developmental alexia (without word reading) or word blindness—the inability to read in a way consistent with mental age or other academic skills that is not due to visual or motor disturbance in seeing or copying letters or words

2. Developmental word deafness—the inability to identify sounds correctly and understand spoken language despite adequate hearing

3. Special disability in writing

4. Motor speech delay

5. Stuttering

The first disorder corresponds to dyslexia, the second to the listening comprehension problems of oral and written language learning disability, the third to dysgraphia, and the fourth and fifth to the speech problems that may interfere with oral expression (see Chapter 2).

Working with Lauretta Bender, who studied the physiology of animal brain anatomy, Orton noted important neurological differences between children whose language problems were related to brain injury, which led to loss of previously acquired language functions, and those with developmental problems who struggled with acquiring language functions. Like Hinshelwood, Orton recognized that dyslexia was neurologically based but that its treatment must be educational (Richardson, 1989). He proposed instructional procedures for reading, handwriting, and spelling that were informed by the neurological organization of the brain—namely multiple primary zones for sensory input including somatosensory (touch), kinesthetic (movement detection), visual, and auditory. He advocated for drawing on all these sensory input and sensory-integration brain regions in teaching phoneme–grapheme correspondence. Additional information on the pioneering medical professionals can be found in Richardson (1989).

At the same time, pioneering educators were also developing teaching methods for treating written language disorders. In 1932, Anna Gillingham joined Samuel Orton in the Language Research Project of the New York Neurological Institute to take charge of organizing teaching procedures based on Orton's findings (Childs, 1968). Gillingham and her colleague Bessie Stillman developed the Orton-Gillingham method, emphasizing the structure of language and understanding of its principles. The instruction was direct but always involved teacher–student interactions to learn a concept. Phonology, sound–symbol association, syllables, morphology, syntax, semantics, and comprehension of written language were taught. Techniques used were diagnostic, structured, sequential, systematic, and cumulative, and they provided simultaneous association of auditory, visual, and kinesthetic sensory channels. Many editions of the Gillingham-Stillman manual, *Remedial*

Training for Children with Specific Disability in Reading, Spelling, and Penmanship, have been published.

Marion Monroe, psychologist and educator, and member of Samuel Orton's mobile clinic, conducted a laboratory school. Monroe was responsible for the examination of errors in oral and silent reading in experimental and control groups. She developed the *Reading Aptitude Tests* (Monroe, 1936). Her influence extended to all classroom teachers and their students as the primary author of many of the *Dick and Jane* reading books.

Grace M. Fernald pioneered one of the first multisensory teaching approaches (visual, auditory, kinesthetic, tactile) for teaching sight words using all four modalities of input. Using this approach, students see a word, trace it with their finger, and say each word as they trace it. Progress with this sensory-motor integration approach was slow because only three or four words were presented at a time. This look-say-do method is described in Fernald's (1943) *Remedial Techniques in Basic School Subjects.*

Katrina de Hirsch applied much of Orton's information to children with developmental speech problems and contributed to a greater understanding of the interrelationships between reading disabilities and speech and language problems. With Jeanette Jansky and William Langford, she published *Predicting Reading Failure* (1966). She and Jansky also published *Preventing Reading Failure* (1972), which included the Predictive Index, a valuable diagnostic instrument in early identification and intervention for learning problems.

June Lyday Orton established a clinic for reading and speech disorders at Bowman Gray School of Medicine in North Carolina. She worked on the diagnosis and educational treatments of individuals. She also trained remedial teachers and taught students in medicine and psychology.

The pioneering educators worked with teachers as well as students with learning problems. Gillingham expected teachers to understand and defend their rationales for instruction (Slingerland, 1980). Bessie Stillman taught them to plan a succeeding lesson based on student performance during the current lesson (Slingerland, 1980). Together, Gillingham and Stillman trained many who continued to develop teaching approaches for students who struggled in learning to read and write. After being trained herself, Sally Childs went on to train teachers, assisted in revisions of the Gillingham-Stillman manuals, and published her own teaching materials, including a systematic program of phonics for the classroom (Childs, 1962).

Beth Slingerland, also trained by them, built upon their training and took the methods in new directions. Slingerland was convinced that her contribution was to provide preventive measures for students with specific language disabilities—in particular, dyslexia. She concluded that "one-to-one teaching" could never reach all of the students who were not learning (Slingerland, 1980, p 5). Slingerland taught a graduate-level class that included lectures on background, rationale, phonics, and language structure, as well as daily demonstrations and a practicum in which the teachers-in-training tutored individual students using the approaches modeled for them each morning.

Interest in the Slingerland® teaching approach—a structured, sequential, and systematic adaptation of the Orton-Gillingham approach—spread to public school districts throughout the country. The total language arts program included daily work with handwriting, as well as practice of automatic association of sounds and symbols, encoding (sounds to written symbols), decoding (written symbols to sounds), writing (expressive written language), and reading (receptive written language). Slingerland's unique contributions included teaching strategies for developing sight recognition of words students could not decode and for applying the structure of language to reading comprehension.

Like Slingerland, Aylett Cox found that the need for teacher training was too great for a one-to-one approach and instead worked with groups of teachers. She gradually refined and added to the Orton-Gillingham approach and published a textbook (Cox, 1992), materials, and criterion-referenced evaluations. Her Alphabetic Phonics training program is still in use in many clinics and schools across the country.

Other contemporary teachers have continued to carry on the work of the educational pioneers who trace their roots to Orton and multisensory methods, such as Wilson Anderson, Judith Birsh, Sandra Dillon, Tori Greene, Marcia Henry, Arlene Sonday, Nancy Cushen White, Barbara Wilson, and many more. See Birsh (2011) and Rawson (1973) for examples of their work and the contributions of others to teaching students with SLDs and teaching teachers to teach them. This field has been and continues to be a field in which professionals build upon the contributions of others and expand them with their own unique contributions. Unfortunately, many of these contributions were made outside public school systems, which were not always open to this approach to instruction.

Other pioneers, coming from other disciplinary traditions, also made contributions to basic and applied knowledge about understanding and teaching students who may struggle with language learning, both oral and written. Some of these pioneers were clinicians who trained other clinicians or teachers. For example, faculty members at the Temple University Psychology of Reading Program, such as Gilbert Schiffman, trained many of the teachers and clinicians who provided assessment and intervention in Pennsylvania and surrounding areas. Likewise, Rutgers Learning Clinic, headed by Edward Fry, provided training for both students struggling with language learning and the professionals who then worked in school settings in New Jersey and surrounding areas. Syracuse University, under the leadership of Benita Blachman and colleagues, trained many of the classroom teachers and teacher leaders in reading in New York and surrounding areas. Classic texts often used in preservice and in-service teacher education programs included *The Improvement of*

Reading (Gates, 1947), *The Teaching of Reading and Writing* (Gray, 1956), and *Reading Difficulties: Their Diagnosis and Correction* (Bond & Tinker, 1967).

Many states had requirements for teacher certification to teach in the public schools that required a course or two in the teaching of reading and the language arts at the preservice level to obtain initial certification and additional courses at the graduate level to obtain permanent teaching certification. Methods were developed for identifying instructional levels for the accuracy of word identification without and with passage context; accuracy and rate of oral reading; and passage comprehension based on factual and inferential questions and passage recall. These levels were used for grouping students for differentiating instruction and monitoring progress for flexible regrouping throughout the year.

Some schools had reading specialists with 60–90 graduate credits in reading who were available for assessment, consultation, and small-group instruction in local buildings. In schools with reading specialists, decisions about whom to test and teach and about how to work with teachers were left to these specially trained professionals who were allowed to function in a flexible manner without burdensome regulations and paperwork. However, not all schools had access to such professionals. Although these approaches had impact in some regions, they were not available in all schools in every area of the country or in all teacher education programs.

EVOLUTION OF SERVICES
FROM PRIVATE TO PUBLIC SECTORS

By the early 1960s, parents were increasingly frustrated because they could not get educational services in public schools for their children with a variety of disabling conditions. These conditions ranged from intellectual and developmental disabilities (development outside the normal range) to specific learning disabilities (development within the normal range except for struggles with specific oral and/or written language skills). Parents did not understand why schools would not enroll their children with intellectual and developmental disabilities and why schools could not teach students who were otherwise developing normally to read and write. Many parents came together and organized a landmark conference in 1963 in Chicago where Samuel Kirk gave a keynote address. Kirk proposed the generic label *learning disabilities* for children whose development was normal except for a struggle with reading, writing, and/or math. The parents took a strong position that a multidisciplinary team approach was needed to meet all of their children's educational needs.

After the conference, parents of children with learning disabilities partnered with parents of children with intellectual disabilities to mount a national political movement to gain services and rights for students with these and other educationally disabling conditions. That parent-initiated effort in the United States culminated in the Education for All Handicapped Children Act of 1975 (PL 94-142), which guarantees free appropriate public education (FAPE) for all students with educationally disabling conditions. Unfortunately, an agreement could not be reached on how to define a learning disability based on *inclusionary* criteria—defining what the disability is. Rather, *exclusionary* criteria were adopted to specify what a learning disability is not. These exclusionary criteria informed both federal and state laws: A learning disability is not due to intellectual disabilities, sensory acuity or motor impairments, a lack of opportunity to learn, or cultural differences.

Importantly, the learning disability category in the special education law is not based on diagnostic criteria for defining the nature of a specific learning disability—what it is and how it is differentiated from other kinds of specific learning disabilities in an instructionally relevant way. Rather, an umbrella category is used to determine if a student qualifies for special education services. Moreover, these eligibility criteria for qualifying for special education services under the category of learning disabilities vary widely from state to state. Many parents and educational professionals find the system confusing. See Torgesen (2004), Johnson and Myklebust (1967), and Kirk and Kirk (1971) for further discussion of these issues and more information on the history of the field of special education.

Also, "appropriate" instruction in special education laws was not defined on the basis of evidence from developmental, learning, instructional, and brain sciences. Meta-analyses show that special education for students with learning disabilities may not be effective for reading (e.g., Bradley, Danielson, & Hallahan, 2002; Vaughn, Moody, & Schumm, 1998). Special education services may not have been effective for many reasons, including lack of teacher knowledge of effective practices for designing, implementing, and evaluating differentiated instruction. Simply legislating special education services appears not to be sufficient. While progress has been made in some ways, there is need for change and more effective ways for multidisciplinary teams to deliver assessment services linked to instructional services. Solutions will require moving beyond blaming teachers and teacher education programs, and avoiding parents due to fear of lawsuits, to finding realistic, evidence-based, and cost-effective approaches given limited resources. Such solutions need to take into account the perspectives of all involved—students, teachers, and parents.

EMERGING APPROACHES TO RETHINKING AND TRANSFORMING EDUCATIONAL PRACTICES

As explained earlier, there is a difference between diagnosis (identifying what is wrong and why a student might struggle) and eligibility (determining if a student qualifies for special services). Moreover, there has been longstanding confusion over how to determine eligibility for services. Initially, and still in some states, discrepancy between a full-scale score on a cognitive measure and achievement in specific domains such as reading, writing, and math is used. However, researchers could never validate the amount of discrepancy that identified an SLD versus a non-SLD. Subsequent reauthorization of the original PL 94-142 introduced response to intervention (RTI) so that students were not excluded simply because they had not had an opportunity to learn. However, RTI does not specify the kinds of evidence-based instruction that should be used for different SLDs, each of which involve different impaired skills. For example, some students may have an SLD in handwriting. Other students may have an SLD in word decoding and spelling. Yet other students may have an SLD in listening comprehension, reading comprehension, oral expression, and/or written expression of ideas. Still others have an SLD in specific areas of math. In some cases a student may have more than one SLD.

The opportunity to learn may be related to socioeconomic, cultural, and language differences, all of which should be taken into account when planning and implementing appropriate instruction instead of being used as exclusionary criteria for specialized instruction. SLDs occur in all socioeconomic, cultural, racial, and language groups. Furthermore, many parents are seeking diagnoses to explain why their children struggle in specific ways and instructional approaches that may transform their children from struggling to successful learners. They are not necessarily seeking eligibility for their child to be pulled out of the classroom and miss instruction relevant to Common Core Standards or other standards.

GENERATION OF INTERDISCIPLINARY BASIC RESEARCH KNOWLEDGE ON SPECIFIC LEARNING DISABILITIES

In 1989, the Interagency Committee on Learning Disabilities recommended in a report to the U.S. Congress that more research be funded on SLDs. Considerable basic research from multiple disciplines (e.g., genetics, neuroscience, linguistics, cognitive, instructional, and developmental science) has resulted from this initiative.

Twin studies (e.g., Kovas, Haworth, Dale, & Plomin, 2007; Olson, Wise, Connors, Rack, & Fulker, 1989; Willcutt, Pennington, & DeFries, 2000) have provided evidence that dyslexia has both genetic and environmental influences. Family aggregation studies showed a probable genetic basis for specific phenotypes (measures of the behavioral expression) of dyslexia and related learning disabilities: accuracy and rate of pseudoword reading and real-word reading; spelling; and related phonological, rapid naming, and supervisory attention/executive function (e.g., Hsu, Wijsman, Berninger, Thomson, & Raskind, 2002; Raskind, Hsu, Thomson, Berninger, & Wijsman, 2000). The genetic basis of dyslexia may be heterogeneous, meaning many different chromosomes and gene locations on the chromosomes are involved; specific chromosome linkages tend to be related to the phenotype studied (Brkanac et al., 2007; Cardon et al., 1995; Grigorenko et al., 2001). For example, different chromosome linkage has been reported for real-word and nonword reading (Chapman et al., 2004; Igo et al., 2006) and for accuracy and rate of nonword reading (Raskind et al., 2005). Spelling, which many think of as a purely visual or orthographic process, also has a genetic pathway from phonology in dyslexia (Wijsman et al., 2000).

The locations of genes on chromosomes have also been studied. Two specific gene locations associated with dyslexia have replicated across research groups—one on chromosome 15 and one on chromosome 6. Based on case-control studies involving individuals who had the specific allele (variant gene) on chromosome 15, the research team at the University of Washington found that the mean score on a phonological phenotype (nonword repetition) was lower for individuals with than without the variant gene in the same location. Also, individuals with the gene variant on chromosome 6 scored lower on an executive function phenotype (rapid alternating switching attention) than did individuals without the gene variant in the same location (Berninger, Raskind, Richards, Abbott, & Stock, 2008).

Collectively, these genetic findings have educational implications. Genes may influence learning in at least three ways. First, genes may affect how the brain is wired during early fetal development. Second, genes may affect maturation of the brain after birth by guiding the process of forming sheaths of myelin, a white fatty substance, which form around axons that transmit electrical signals from one neuron to another neuron and thus connect spatially separated neurons functionally in time with greater speed and efficiency of neural conduction. One reason some students fail to respond to instruction may be that parts of the brain needed to learn from instruction have not yet undergone myelination, but they may in the future. Third, regulatory genes may influence the protein chemistry in the cell bodies of neurons in the brain that regulate their moment-to-moment operating systems, which in turn influence the learning process (see genetics primer in Berninger, 2015). In addition, genes may contribute to two core types of impairments typically found in children with dyslexia: phonological (Morris et al., 1998; Rack, Snowling, & Olson, 1992; Stanovich & Siegel, 1994) and executive function (Lyon & Krasnegor, 1996; Swanson, 1999). Genetic variation in processes affecting reading and writing acquisition may make it more difficult, but not impossible, for affected individuals to learn to read and write if taught in a way they can learn.

Advances have also been made in understanding the brain bases of SLDs (see brain primer in Berninger, 2015). Differences have been observed between proficient readers and students with dyslexia in the word-form regions in the back of the brain in lower temporal and related parietal regions where spoken and written words are coded into memory for further processing (e.g., Eckert et al., 2005; Pugh et al., 1996). Children with and without dyslexia differ not only in phonological coding in the left Broca's area but also in orthographic coding in the right Broca's area (Aylward et al., 2003); they also differ in the right cerebellum involved in timing of language processing (see Eckert et al., 2003). Both common and unique neural brain signatures have been observed for phonological, orthographic, and morphological word-form coding tasks (Richards, Aylward, Raskind, et al., 2006). Following instructional treatment aimed at phonological, orthographic, and morphological coding (see Chapter 4) rather than to phonics practice alone, chemical activation in the brain (Richards et al., 2002) and blood oxygen level-dependent activation (Richards et al., 2005) normalized, and the rate of phonological decoding and orthographic coding on behavioral measures improved (see Unit I lessons in Berninger & Wolf, 2009b).

Venezky (1970), a linguist, made pioneering contributions in showing that both morphology and phonology are represented in English orthography; spelling is more predictable than claimed by the playwright George Bernard Shaw, who complained, perhaps in jest, that English is hopelessly irregular. A grasp of the predictable patterns requires four fundamental insights. First, the predictability is often not at the single-letter level. Graphemes are one- or two-letter units that correspond to phonemes. In English, these graphemes often involve two-letter spelling units such as *th* in *thing* or *this, or* as in *fork* or *word,* or *ng* as in *sing* or *ring,* which stands for a different sound than either the letter *n* or the letter *g* alone. Also, blends such as the *bl* in *blend* are best treated as two-letter spelling units because the corresponding sounds have to be produced faster in time than the single sounds for each of the single-letter constituents in order to avoid an unwanted vowel sound intrusion, such as a schwa in between the /b/ and /l/ in /bul-end/ instead of /blend/. Therefore, students should be taught to parse written words into the one- or two-letter units that correspond to a phoneme rather than to try to decode words or spell words one letter at a time in left-to-right order.

Second, the predictability does not involve one-to-one mapping of letters onto sound or sound onto letters but rather alternations, which are permissible options. Some letters have more than one sound associated with them, such as the letter *c,* which can stand for the /k/ or /s/ sound. Note that the /th/ in *thing* and the /th/ in *this* are alternations (a different phoneme is associated with this common spelling unit). Likewise, /or/ in *fork* and /or/ in *word* are alternations for the common *or* spelling. Teaching alternations provides an alternative strategy to use when decoding or encoding written words (see Berninger, 1998a).

Third, the alternations add predictability at the level of word families (see Berninger, 1998a). For example, the alternations for the *ough* word family are /long o/, /aw/, /short u/, or /oo/, respectively, for *though, thought, rough,* and *through.* Those four-to-one odds are reasonably predictable considering that no one complains about the many sound–meaning associations that English speakers handle all the time with ease in implicit memory. Consider the pronunciation /t/ /oo/, which can mean *also,* a quantity more than one but less than three, moving in the direction toward, and so forth. That is why dictionaries often list so many meanings for the same word spelling and pronunciation (see Stahl & Nagy, 2005).

Fourth, pronunciations and spellings are often predictable when morphology as well as phonology and orthography are taken into account, such as *tion* in nation or *sion* in session. See Nunes and Bryant (2006) for research evidence and translation of research findings into instructional practices that support the predictability of English morphophonemic orthography.

When these insights were pointed out to a child in the summer between third and fourth grade, she began to bloom in reading and spelling and told the neighborhood and extended family that she could not believe that her teachers had never told her about these secrets of English spelling. If George Bernard Shaw had a teacher who taught him these insights, he might have better appreciated the predictability of English spelling!

Little research has been done on *polysemy*—a term used by linguists for the ability to map multiple meanings onto the same sound form (Stahl & Nagy, 2005). However, reflection about variable meanings for the same spoken word could be an important part of the literacy program as students add on spelling knowledge to the sound–meaning–spelling relationships (see Beck, McKeown, & Kucan, 2008). Such knowledge can enhance vocabulary development as well as phonological decoding in reading (pronouncing written words) and phonological encoding in spelling (writing spelling units to stand for sounds in spoken words).

Self-regulation of attention may be particularly relevant when orthographic symbols are involved in literacy learning (Thomson et al., 2005). Some individuals with dyslexia appear to have difficulty self-regulating their attention across the letters in a left-to-right direction within written words to identify the spelling units that correspond to phonemes (Richards et al., 2007). This impairment can interfere with phonological decoding as much as phonological awareness problems can. For strategies to help students improve their attentional focus to letters and spelling units within written words during the decoding process, see Chapter 4 and Berninger and Wolf (2009a, Unit II lessons).

The National Reading Panel (NICHHD, 2000) did not consider the importance of orthographic or morphological coding or executive functions for supervisory attention or the kinds of learning differences in beginning literacy identified by Connor, Morrison, and Katch (2004). Conner's team showed that beginning readers differ greatly in the literacy knowledge they bring to school and the amount of explicit, teacher-directed instruction they require. Teachers need to differentiate instruction according to an individual student's need for teacher-guided, other-regulation in learning compared to self-regulated learning. Students who have biologically based attention or executive function impairment require more other-regulation from adults, who provide guidance and serve as their executive functions, so they can learn self-regulation of their language learning. Those who have attention and executive functions that fall within the normal range are better able to engage in self-directed learning (see Connor et al., 2004). Students with SLDs may require explicit instruction in language and math skills throughout schooling, but not all students in the classroom require the same degree of explicit, teacher-directed instruction. Neither do the Common Core Standards or other state standards consider adaptations needed in teaching academic skills to students who vary in self-regulated learning.

Thus, in keeping with the goal of translating basic interdisciplinary science into educational practice, Part II of this book covers strategies for providing explicit, teacher-guided instruction in handwriting, decoding and spelling, aural or oral comprehension, oral and written production, and math. Special education is not the only option for providing such explicit instruction for students who need more of it than their classmates do; however, it is advisable to document a diagnosis of an SLD and specify the nature of specialized instruction needed in the least restrictive environment (general education classroom) and an appropriate progress monitoring plan to evaluate if the student is responding to that specialized instruction.

Accommodations alone are seldom sufficient for students with significant executive function impairments who also need systematic and multilevel language instruction by ear, eye, mouth, and hand or multicomponent math instruction. The curriculum requirements in school change after the primary grades when the primary literacy tasks are learning to read orally (pronounce written words), identifying words during silent reading, and associating meaning with the sounds, spelling, and morphology of words. In later grades, students are expected to complete longer, more complex written assignments, which often require them to write about what they read—that is, integrate reading and writing (Altemeier, Abbott, & Berninger, 2008). Students who had problems in phonological decoding earlier in development may now have trouble with completing written assignments and integrating writing and reading unless given specialized instruction in the executive functions for integrating reading and writing. Although a meta-analysis (Graham & Perin, 2007a, 2007b) showed that students in fourth grade and above generally require explicit and strategic writing instruction, many schools do not yet provide such instruction (see Chapters 3, 4, and 5 in this book, as well as lesson sets in Berninger and Wolf, 2009b). Chapter 6 in this book addresses the writing requirements of math.

Also, toward the goal of translating science into classroom practice, Sections II and III of this book emphasize the importance of systematic, structured, sequential instruction in oral and written language for translating research knowledge into instructional practice. If students who have dyslexia do not see words as wholes, they must be taught to process constituent letters in each word from left to right. Many students do not fixate on the beginning of the word and may look at any part of it, sometimes randomly. As a result, word recognition is erratic. The teacher must guide them in learning left-to-right progression for decoding single words as well as for reading across the page. These students may have particular difficulty with sight words. They can use some decoding skills to begin access to a word such as *the*, in which the *th* corresponds to a phoneme but the *e* corresponds to a schwa or reduced vowel rather than a full phoneme, with predictable spelling. Automatic recall requires many, many exposures—sometimes as many as 200—in isolation and in phrases. Fortunately, the word *the* occurs at a very high frequency, so students will have many exposures. When students have mastered words in isolation, they need to learn to "chunk" groups of words into meaningful phrases for reading with fluency and comprehension. Some strategies for chunking are offered in Chapter 5. However, introduction of too many elements in too short a time can result in confusion and frustration. Teachers need to pace the introduction of each new element so that the student can feel success with both single words and sentences.

Finally, synthesis of interdisciplinary research findings across many research groups supports a multicomponent working memory architecture that supports language learning (Berninger & Richards, 2010; Berninger & Swanson, 2013). This language learning system has the following components:

1. Three-word-form coding units for storing and processing heard/spoken words, viewed/written words, and base words with and without affixes (phonological, orthographic, and morphological, respectively) and a syntax buffer for accumulating words

2. Two loops for cross-code integration of internal codes and output codes through mouth or hand (phonological loop and orthographic loop, respectively)

3. A supervisory attention panel for focusing attention, switching attention, sustaining attention, and self-monitoring

Students with the SLDs covered in this book have been shown to have impairments in these supervisory attention components of working memory. Whether components are impaired for word forms, syntax buffer, and loops can depend on the nature of the SLD. The working memory components of a system must work in concert—that is, be orchestrated in time like the musical instruments in an orchestra (see Posner, Petersen, Fox, & Raichle, 1988)—for individuals to learn to read and write easily and fluently (quickly with smooth coordination). Impairments in any of the components can interfere with the efficiency and timing of the whole language system.

The important issue for translation science is that this multicomponent working memory system supporting language learning is internal. Thus, these SLDs are invisible disabilities (not visible to others), and they are not due to lack of motivation or effort. Students with dyslexia or other SLDs report having to expend more mental effort to accomplish what those without dyslexia or other SLDs may do with ease. For example, students with dyslexia

stayed slow or became slower across rows in sustaining mental effort for naming letters or letters and numerals, whereas those without dyslexia stayed fast
(Amtmann, Abbott, & Berninger, 2007). Therefore, students with SLDs view
themselves as less competent. Teachers can help students to identify their own
strengths and talents despite their invisible disability interfering with language
and/or math learning, while helping them to feel pride in their accomplishments. Although they may not produce the same products as peers, these
students may be working harder than anyone else in the class. One high school
student told Beverly Wolf, "Having dyslexia is like climbing the mountain on
your hands and knees while everyone else rides the chair lift."

EVIDENCE-BASED ASSESSMENT–INSTRUCTION
LINKS FOR SPECIFIC LEARNING DISABILITIES
AND THE PROMISE OF TRANSLATION SCIENCE

Much remains to be done to translate research findings into treatment-relevant, evidence-based diagnoses that are implemented with consistency across
states and schools within states. One challenge for translation science is the
frequency with which SLDs occur in the general population of school-age
children and youth. Research studies at the Mayo Clinic have shown that
one in five students have some kind of SLD with or without attention-deficit/
hyperactivity disorder, and SLDs affect writing as well as reading (Colligan &
Katusic, 2015). With this number of affected students, pull-out models for special education are not cost effective nor time efficient for the delivery of a full
educational program. Thus, translation science should direct its efforts to how
teachers can more effectively implement appropriate, specialized instruction
for the various SLDs in the general education classroom. Despite the way the
special education laws have been written, the solution is not to remove the student from the general education classroom, but rather to provide individually
tailored, differentiated instruction within general education; other members
of the interdisciplinary team provide support services for the teacher and students. Other chapters in this book will offer practical suggestions for doing so.

Another challenge is that basic research is generally based on designs that
compare groups. Research findings based on group designs can be helpful in
validating conceptual frameworks and effective treatments in general, but they
do not generalize in a simple way to all individuals, especially those who may
have different learning profiles and are learning in different social contexts than
those in which the research was conducted. Further complicating matters is the
fact that research has the luxury of focusing on a single variable at a time, holding all other variables constant to the extent possible. In contrast, educational
practitioners who are charged with implementing the research findings in
classroom instruction face the enormous challenge of taking multiple variables
into account in providing developmentally appropriate, individualized instruction for multiple diverse learners (typically between 25 to 30 in a classroom).

This service delivery model contrasts dramatically with that of most kinds of delivery of professional services, such as by physicians and psychologists, who typically work with one client at a time or at most a small group.

To summarize, effective teaching also requires the artful and skillful combination of multiple instructional components in an organized fashion. On the one hand, research has advanced understanding of the nature of different kinds of SLDs and validated conceptual frameworks for diagnosis and instruction. On the other hand, much professional teamwork remains to validate translation science on how to best implement research findings in real-world classrooms and schools.

Preparing and Supporting General Education Teachers to Teach Students with Specific Learning Disabilities

A Lebanese-Scottish immigrant homesteader's son, Samuel Kirk, was inspired by his own experiences in teaching illiterate farmhands on a wheat farm how to read. These experiences led him to pursue a career that brought educational opportunity to all. Both before and after serving as director of the Federal Office of Education of Handicapped Children (1963–1964), he was founding director of the Institute for Research on Exceptional Children at the University of Illinois. Samuel Kirk's most visionary contribution to public policy occurred in 1964. Recognizing that laws granting FAPE were necessary, Kirk also realized law is not sufficient. Thus, in 1964, he persuaded the federal government and the U.S. Congress to begin to fund teacher training to provide the specialized instruction students with SLDs needed.

Since Samuel Kirk's visionary legal and educational contributions as a psychologist, much progress has been made, but there is still a long way to go to provide sufficient teacher training for FAPE. Moreover, much also remains to be done to educate interdisciplinary teams, policy makers, and government officials to understand that FAPE requires more precise, treatment-relevant definitions of the specific kinds of SLDs so that assessment and instruction can be meaningfully linked throughout K–12 for each of them. Such an effort will require preservice and in-service professional development, not only for teachers but also all members of an interdisciplinary team.

International Collaboration

After Samuel Orton's death, a group of friends and colleagues founded the Orton Society, which was dedicated to disseminating Orton's work and encouraging and promoting research, diagnosis, treatment, and professional development of practitioners regarding developmental oral and written language disorders (Columbia University Health Sciences Library, n.d.). The Orton Society evolved into the International Dyslexia Association (IDA), with many branches throughout the United States and the world. Other organizations, such as the Council for Exceptional Children, Learning Disabilities

Association, and National Institute of Language Development, have been formed to support the education of individuals with SLDs, their teachers, and parents, as well as research efforts. Other countries have passed laws and instituted initiatives to deal with SLDs, but the laws and implementations vary somewhat from country to country. Nevertheless, there is increasing interest in how SLDs may be defined in similar ways across countries for research and practice.

Creating More Positive Home–School Relationships

One of the unfortunate consequences of a legal approach to FAPE has been the resulting adversarial relationships between some parents, empowered to advocate for their children, and schools. Such advocacy often has involved lawyers and lawsuits. Schools have had to devote a sizable amount of their limited financial resources to existing or potential lawsuits. Throughout this book, practical, cost-effective suggestions will be made for nurturing more positive and less adversarial home–school relationships. Both school and home contribute in important ways to a student's language and math learning.

When educators work with students with SLDs, they may be working with parents who also may have biologically based SLDs. Parents' memories of personal struggles at school, which possibly continue into the present, can complicate communication between the school and the home. Parents who are sensitive to their own learning problems may find a diagnosis for their children comforting because they are relieved to have a name, finally, for their own problems. The label also gives them powerful empathy for their children's struggles. Educators should be sensitive to these cross-generational experiences that may influence parents' relationships with their children's schools and teachers.

All children are most likely to optimize their learning if schools and parents work together collaboratively. Therefore, the assessments described in Chapters 3–6 begin with recommendations for reaching out to the parents beginning in kindergarten, and then keeping parents in the communication loop throughout their child's K–12 school years.

Current and Future Directions in Defining and Differentiating Specific Learning Disabilities

Disabilities cannot be identified only on the basis of symptoms, for example, difficulty in learning to understand and construct oral or written language or learn math. Rather, they have to be identified in the context of an individual's profiles of developmental and learning skills.

SPECIFIC LEARNING DISABILITIES DIFFER FROM DEVELOPMENTAL DISABILITIES

Not all disabilities affecting language and/or math learning are the same. Some occur in individuals who are outside the normal range in all five domains of development (pervasive developmental disability) or one or more but not all domains of development (specific developmental disability): cognitive and memory, heard and spoken language, sensory and motor, social and emotional, and attention and executive function. Batshaw, Roizen, and Lotrecchiano (2013) provided an overview of these developmental disabilities of neurogenetic origin, as well as acquired disabilities that occur in childhood due to brain injuries or toxins that result in development falling outside the normal range.

Individuals with such developmental disabilities require specialized instruction aimed at their current developmental levels, but they have different instructional needs and developmental trajectories than those with specific learning disabilities (SLDs)—the topic of this book. See Chapters 7–10 in

Berninger (2015) and Silliman and Berninger (2011) for diagnosing and treating students with pervasive and specific developmental disabilities.

In this book, we present numbered Research Lessons and associated numbered Teaching Tips. In Chapter 2, three Research Lessons are presented together followed by three related Teaching Tips. Then a fourth Research Lesson is provided followed by a Teaching Tip that is yoked to it. Just as the first step in algebra is to define the variables in an equation, we define the four SLDs on which this book focuses—dysgraphia, dyslexia, oral and written language learning disability (OWL LD), and dyscalculia—in Research Lesson 2-3.

 # Research Lessons

SPECIFIC LEARNING DISABILITIES ARE PLURAL
Research Lesson 2-1

Language is not a single, homogeneous function. Multiple motor output systems, as well as multiple sensory input systems, are relevant to language learning. There are four functional language systems—language by ear, language by eye, language by mouth (Liberman, 1999), and language by hand (Berninger, 2000). These functional language systems may develop at the same rate and learn to work together in concert, or one or more of these functional language systems may develop at a different rate so that the four systems do not work in concert (Berninger & Abbott, 2010). Moreover, each of the four functional language systems is multi-leveled, ranging from *subword* units to *word* units to *multiword clausal/syntax* units to multisyntax *discourse* (Berninger, 2015).

Research Lesson 2-2

Math is also not a single, homogeneous function. Longitudinal studies showed that there are quantitative (number) skills, visual spatial skills, and language skills contributing to math learning (Robinson, Abbott, Berninger, & Busse, 1996). Thus, SLDs that impair language may interfere with math learning.

Research Lesson 2-3

Not all SLDs are the same. Interdisciplinary research evidence is accumulating that SLDs interfering with language learning can be defined in evidence-based ways, based on where the impairment is in cascading levels of language—subword, word, and syntax/discourse (Berninger, 2008;

Berninger & Richards, 2010; Berninger, Richards, & Abbott, 2015). In this cascading model, an impairment is not associated with an impairment at a higher level of language than the level of the primary impairment, but there may or may not be a co-occurring impairment at a lower level of language.

Dysgraphia is a word of Greek origin that means the condition of having impaired graph (i.e., letter) production. Dysgraphia is an SLD in students for whom developmental motor coordination disorder (outside the normal range) can be ruled out, but those with dysgraphia have unusual difficulty with subword letter formation—producing legible letters others can recognize and doing so automatically in a consistent way that does not drain limited working memory resources. Put another way, dysgraphia is a written language disorder in serial production of strokes to form a handwritten letter and involves not only motor skills but also language skills—finding, retrieving, and producing letters, which is a subword level language skill. The impaired handwriting may interfere with spelling and/or composing, but individuals with only dysgraphia do not have difficulty with reading.

Dyslexia is a word of Greek origin that means the condition of having impaired lexicon (i.e., word) skills. As often happens when a suffix is added to a base word in English, the spelling of the base word is transformed—in this case, *lexicon* is shortened to *lex*. Dyslexia is an SLD for which both pervasive and specific developmental disabilities can be ruled out and only word level skills in word reading and spelling are impaired—not syntactic skills in listening and reading comprehension or oral or written expression. In the early grades, problems in oral reading are readily observable, but these problems may persist into the upper grades. In some cases, both the accuracy and rate of oral reading are impaired; in other cases, only the rate of oral reading is impaired in dyslexia (Lovett, 1987). Oral reading of only pseudowords may be impaired or oral reading of both real words and pseudowords may be impaired. After the fourth-grade transition to silent reading, significant problems in silent word reading rate and written spelling are typically observed (Niedo, Lee, Breznitz, & Berninger, 2014). Consistent with the cascading levels of language impairment, some—but not all—individuals with dyslexia may show signs of co-occurring dysgraphia.

OWL LD is first observed during the preschool years, at which time affected individuals tend to be late talkers and struggle with understanding heard language, as well as combining words to express ideas and intentions in oral language. However, during the school years, both oral and written language disabilities can interfere with academic learning (Bishop & Adams, 1990; Catts, Fey, Zhang, & Tomblin, 1999, 2001; Catts, Hogan, & Adloff, 2005; Fey, Catts, Proctor-Williams, Tomblin, & Zhang, 2004; Scott, 2004; Scott & Winsor, 2000). Consistent with the cascading levels of language impairment, some (but not all) individuals with OWL LD may show signs of co-occurring dysgraphia and/or dyslexia.

Dyscalculia is also a word of Greek origin. Affected individuals are impaired in the condition of calculation (i.e., computational procedures for basic addition, subtraction, multiplication, and division operations). Thus, they may or may not be impaired in all quantitative skills or the visual-spatial skills involved in math learning.

TEACHING TIPS

TEACHING TIP 2-1: Specialized, differentiated instruction for SLDs in dysgraphia, dyslexia, and OWL LD should aim at multiple language systems with both multiple sensory and multiple motor systems in mind: language by ear, language by eye, language by mouth, and language by hand.

This tip is associated with Research Lesson 2-1. Instruction should also be provided for the impaired level(s) of language in a specific language system in the diagnosed SLD for an individual student: dysgraphia (subword handwriting), dyslexia (word decoding and spelling), and syntax of all four language systems (OWL LD). See Chapters 3–5.

TEACHING TIP 2-2: If a student struggles with math, instruction should be tailored to whether the student has disabilities in quantitative, visual-spatial, and/or language processes contributing to math learning.

This tip is associated with Research Lesson 2-2. If the student has co-occurring disabilities in language by ear, eye, mouth, or hand, that should also be considered in planning, implementing, and evaluating individually tailored math instruction. See Chapter 6.

TEACHING TIP 2-3: Differentiated instruction is needed in general education to provide specialized, appropriate instruction individually tailored to the nature of all the various SLDs students may have.

This tip is associated with Research Lesson 2-3. Instruction should be aimed both at the impairments associated with a particular diagnosis and at the coordination of all the multileveled language systems or math systems involved. That is, instruction for dysgraphia, dyslexia, and OWL LD should be designed to create connections across levels within and across all four language systems, as well as provide individually tailored instruction for those levels and language systems that are impaired (Berninger & Niedo, 2014). Likewise, if calculation skills are impaired, specialized instruction should focus on teaching underlying math concepts, procedures, and application to problem solving as separate and coordinated skills and not through drill on isolated skills.

Teaching single language skills in isolation should be avoided because multiple brain systems have to be coordinated so they work in concert for successful learning. See Chapters 3–6 and 9.

NATURE–NURTURE INTERACTIONS IN CAUSES AND TREATMENTS FOR SPECIFIC LEARNING DISABILITIES

On the one hand, SLDs have biological bases in both variant genes and brain structures and functions. On the other hand, SLDs are treatable with instruction and appropriate learning activities. Thus, nature and nurture contribute to learning for students with SLDs.

BIOLOGICAL BASES—GENES AND BRAINS
Research Lesson 2-4

Genetics and brain research have shown a biological basis for SLDs. Genetics research has made considerable progress in identifying the genetic bases of SLDs such as dyslexia and specific language impairment, as well as attention-deficit/hyperactivity disorder, which often co-occurs with dysgraphia and other SLDs. Research on twins that share 100% genetic inheritance (identical twins) compared to twins with approximately 50% common genetic inheritance (fraternal twins) has shown that both genetic and environmental influences contribute to SLDs. Even among twins who show response to instruction, the genetic influences are not eliminated (Samuelson et al., 2008). These genetic variations that influence later written language learning have been studied beginning in infancy and continuing through the school years and in many countries (e.g., Grigorenko et al., 2001; Lyytinen et al., 2004).

Chapter 1 provided an overview of segregation analyses of modes of genetic transmission, chromosome linkage studies, and candidate gene studies of variants (alleles) that may be associated with phenotypes (behavioral markers of SLDs) and endophenotypes (brain markers of SLDs). For example, Roeske et al. (2011) identified gene interactions associated with specific brain-related endophenotypes. Currently, there are at least 14 genetic candidates for dyslexia, which is thought to be a heterogeneous genetic disorder (for a review, see Raskind, Peters, Richards, Eckert, & Berninger, 2012). Numerous brain imaging studies have identified brain locations, distributed pathways, and patterns of structural and functional connectivity that differentiate the brains of students with and without the four SLDs that are the focus of this book: dysgraphia, dyslexia, OWL LD, and dyscalculia (for a review, see Berninger & Dunn, 2012).

Thus, there are individual differences in the biological bases of learning disabilities that interfere at the behavioral level with reading and writing skills. Not all students with the same profile of impaired reading and writing skills necessarily have the same genetic bases for those impairments or show impairments in all the phenotypes, which are the behavioral expression of genetic variants, associated with those skills. Nevertheless, the sets of learning skills and associated phenotypes that are likely impaired for dysgraphia, dyslexia, OWL LD, and dyscalculia can be predicted, and based on assessment of these, individually tailored instruction and progress monitoring can be provided (see Berninger & Richards, 2010).

Instruction and Epigenetics

Despite the biological bases, research has also shown that the SLDs are responsive to instruction tailored to the nature of an SLD. Evidence supports effectiveness of early intervention for students identified for low achievement in specific reading or writing skills (for an overview of programmatic research from Grades 1–4, see Berninger, 2008, 2009; Berninger & Richards, 2010). Because the severity of SLDs and many of the self-concept and emotional problems associated with chronic learning struggles can be prevented through early identification and intervention, Chapters 3–6 and associated appendices for each chapter focus on assessment–intervention links for students with SLDs.

However, a systems approach to treatment is needed because these SLDs exhibit patterns of impairments rather than single deficits (see Research Lessons 2-1, 2-2, and 2-3 and Teaching Tips 2-1, 2-2, and 2-3). Indeed, epigenetics research (Cassiday, 2009; *Science*, 2010) shows that behavioral expression may change based on environmental stimulation without changing the underlying gene sequencing. Thus, a student may respond to individually tailored instruction at one grade level, but then in later grades may re-experience struggles when the nature of the curriculum changes and requirements increase. Therefore, screening, progress monitoring, and specialized instruction may be needed in the upper grades as well as early grades.

TEACHING TIP 2-4: Although there are biological bases of SLDs, they are treatable through specialized, appropriate instruction; however, evidence-based diagnosis and instruction are needed throughout schooling for students with SLDs.

Behavioral expression of the underlying genetic bases may alter through appropriate instruction and epigenetic mechanisms, but underlying genetic vulnerability may remain. Nevertheless, with appropriate, evidence-based early intervention and ongoing appropriate and evidence-based progress-monitoring and explicit instruction, the learning and emotional outcomes may be substantially better than if such early and ongoing assessment and intervention were not in place. Thus, this book provides a developmental model of assessment–instruction links from K–12 for different language and math skills featured in different chapters.

CONTEMPORARY CHALLENGES IN TEACHING STUDENTS WITH SPECIFIC LEARNING DISABILITIES

Education, like the platforms for the technology tools we use, is ever changing. Contemporary educational practices have introduced additional challenges that the pioneers in the field of learning disabilities did not have to address.

Common Core or Other State Standards

Students with SLDs may not pass the high stakes tests that are required by most states related to the Common Core Standards or other state standards. If these students are pulled out of the general education program for special education services, they often miss instruction relevant to those standards. Failure to pass the tests may cause significant social and emotional problems for the affected students and their families. It is timely to figure out how Common Core Standards or other state standards can be adapted to the evidence-based individual and developmental differences in learning and using language and math (see Chapters 4–6 in Berninger, 2015). Although high expectations for all learners are important, they also have to be realistic and appropriate. Students are most likely to respond to instruction when taught in their zone of proximal development at their instructional level (e.g., Leslie & Caldwell, 2005; Woods & Moe, 2003)—an important concept neglected in the Common Core Standards.

Accommodations Plus Explicit Specialized Instruction

Although students with SLDs are often given accommodations under Section 504 of the Rehabilitation Act of 1973 (PL 93-112), the accommodations given may not be related to the nature of their SLDs. More emphasis should be placed on providing accommodations carefully linked to the identified impairments in a student's profile of learning and phenotype skills. In addition, students with SLDs benefit not only from accommodation, but also from ongoing explicit instruction geared to the nature of their SLD. They also benefit from explicit instruction in using the multiple modes of input and output of language with technology tools (see Chapter 11).

Monitoring Response to Instruction

Evidence supports the effectiveness of differentiated instruction models in general education (Slavin, 1987). However, in addition to grouping students by instructional levels within classrooms or across classrooms in a walk-about model during a common instructional block, students benefit from ongoing feedback about their learning on a more regular basis than the widely used response to intervention models provide—typically three times a year at the beginning, middle, and end of school year (see Chapter 7).

Translating Research
Lessons into Teaching Tips
for Developing Students K–12

Some people there are who, being grown, forget the horrible task of learning to read. It is perhaps the greatest single effort that the human undertakes, and he must do it as a child . . . [it is] the reduction of experience to a set of symbols. For a thousand thousand years these humans have existed and they have only learned this trick—this magic—in the final ten thousand of the thousand thousand. . . . I remember that words—written or printed—were devils, and books, because they gave me pain, were my enemies.

Steinbeck (1976, p. xi)

Not only reading, but also writing, oral language, and math may pose challenges for some children and youth. Research is showing, however, that screening annually to identify specific grade-appropriate skills with which individual students struggle and then teaching those skills helps most children reach grade-appropriate levels. In Section II, we first provide overviews of the research (numbered Research Lessons) for letter-level handwriting (Chapter 3), word reading and spelling (Chapter 4), multiword oral and written language (Chapter 5), and math (Chapter 6) and then present applications to instruction (numbered Teaching Tips). A developmental model of assessment–instruction links is provided in each chapter, with a focus on both prevention through early identification and intervention and ongoing progress monitoring and individually tailored instruction aimed at all the levels of the multiple language systems (by ear, mouth, eye, and hand) including math-specific vocabulary, as well as math concepts (quantitative and visual spatial) and math procedures.

Each chapter has three appendices closely linked to the text of the corresponding chapter. Appendix A lists widely available assessment tools for the relevant skills featured in the chapter. Appendix B lists widely available instructional tools for the same skills. For both Appendix A and B, the available tools are listed in alphabetical order by first author surname within specific skills. Both the assessment tools and instructional tools are meant to be representative and not exhaustive of what might be used. An asterisk indicates that the assessment tool requires individual administration; otherwise, the assessment can be group administered. Guidance is provided in the chapter for linking the assessments with instruction in developmentally appropriate, individually tailored ways, but the full citations or sources for locating the tools are in the appendices. Guidance for implementing the assessment–intervention links, which should involve classroom teachers with support from interdisciplinary teams, is provided in Chapters 8 and 9 in Section III. In addition, Appendix C provides teacher resources for reaching out to parents regarding the topic of the corresponding chapter to create positive home–school relationships through annual parent questionnaires, portfolios with students' work at school and at home, and parent conferences in person and over the phone and/or Internet.

Assessment–Instruction Links for Handwriting

Handwriting involves multiple motor, sensory, cognitive, language, and attention/executive function processes. Therefore, handwriting should be taught by engaging these multiple brain systems, and assessed in reference to these brain systems.

 ## Research Lessons

Note that Chapter 3 has five Research Lessons, each of which is followed by one or more related Teaching Tips.

HANDWRITING DRAWS ON MULTIPLE BRAIN SYSTEMS
Research Lesson 3-1

Handwriting draws on five brain systems. Key research findings are organized by each of the brain systems involved in handwriting.

Motor Systems
For a comprehensive review of the motor processes involved in handwriting, see Graham and Weintraub (1996). Fine motor skills involved in writing letters by hand are referred to as grapho-motor skills. Fine motor skills involved

in naming letters (or words composed of letters) by mouth are referred to as oro-motor skills. Grapho-motor skills are involved in gripping tools for producing letters stroke by stroke and for pressing keys with letter forms when typing on keyboards. These fine motor finger skills draw on planning, control, and production motor processes in different brain regions. Rutberg (see first study in Berninger, Rutberg, et al., 2006) studied students who already showed unusual difficulty in letter writing at the beginning of first grade. She compared the instructional approaches used by occupational or physical therapists with those used by educators. The results showed that the treatment used by the occupational and physical therapists that worked on muscle strength of hands and fingers, for example, by playing with clay, and fine motor control, for example, by doing mazes, prior to teaching letter formation resulted in more accurate letter formation. The treatment used by educators that only taught plans for letter formation and writing from memory resulted in more automatic letter writing.

Sensory Systems

The contribution of all the teaching methods, inspired by the work of Orton and colleagues (see Chapter 1), was the emphasis on multiple sensory systems: auditory through the ear (for listening to named letters), visual through the eye (for viewing letters to copy and inspecting written letters), and somatosensory, which refers to receiving incoming messages from multiple senses—touch, pressure, kinesthesia (perceiving movement in skin sensation), and vestibular. For example, writers have to learn the right touch for holding a pencil or pressing a keyboard. This touch needs to take into account the amount of pressure exerted. Some writers experience pain from the pressure exerted to hold a pen or pencil; others tire from exerting more pressure than needed. Kinesthetic sensation, which is the perception of movement, plays an important role in learning to form letters by sequential strokes or by sequential key presses on a keyboard. Finally, the vestibular sense contributes to the perception of where the hand is in space as the hand guides the writing tool. See Chapter 1 for the history of how practitioners discovered the important role of these senses in learning to produce letters through the grapho-motor system.

Language Systems

Despite the widespread beliefs that handwriting is purely a motor skill or that only multisensory methods are needed to teach handwriting, multiple language processes are also involved in handwriting. Handwriting draws on language by hand (letter production), language by ear (listening to letter names when writing dictated letters), language by mouth (saying letter names), and language by eye (viewing the letters to be copied or reviewing for accuracy the letters that are produced from memory). For example, Berninger and Fuller (1992) and Rutberg (see Berninger, Rutberg, et al., 2006) found that letter names play a role in accessing and retrieving letter forms from memory and producing letters on paper.

Cognitive Processes

Writing also involves multiple cognitive processes to which handwriting (letter production) contributes. These include transcription—spelling written words and using them to translate ideas and plans into written text—and reviewing handwriting legibility and revising it if necessary (Hayes & Flowers, 1980). Research shows that handwriting, spelling, and composing are separable processes; however, when all of these component cognitive processes are taught explicitly not only alone but also together, they work in concert in the functional writing system (see Berninger & Richards, 2002, Chapter 9; Wong & Berninger, 2004). Engaging students in authentic composing activities is necessary but not sufficient (see Graham & Harris, 1994; Graham & Perin, 2007a, 2007b). Without handwriting instruction explicitly linked to spelling and written composition (Berninger & Amtmann, 2003), developing writers, especially those with specific learning disabilities (SLDs), may experience difficulty in translating their ideas into written language.

Attention and Executive Systems

Effective handwriting instruction does not need to involve a large part of the instructional day or mindless copying of the same letters over and over. In fact, the brain may habituate or stop attending to and benefitting from repeated writing of the same letter(s) over and over without some novelty in the instructional activity (Berninger & Richards, 2002). This research finding—that less can be more—should be good news for teachers at a time in education when they are under pressure to help students meet Common Core Standards and pass annual standardized tests. At the same time, practice distributed over time is needed—daily in the early grades until letter formation is mastered. These brief but daily handwriting lessons have to include all of the essential instructional components for handwriting to become both legible and automatic. Automatic letter production reduces the attentional demands on letter production so that more mental resources can be devoted to using the letters to spell and compose.

Teachers should monitor students' attention during writing instruction and writing activities in the classroom. Aspects of attention to assess include students' ability to 1) focus on the relevant parts and ignore the irrelevant parts of a writing task, 2) sustain attention during a writing task, and 3) switch from one task to another task during writing instruction or independent work. Writing in the air in the Slingerland® beginning handwriting instruction, as discussed in Chapter 1, engages the frontal attention system in the brain via large motor movements of the arm, which are regulated by both the frontal areas in the central nervous system and the peripheral nervous system. Some students with dysgraphia (impaired handwriting) also have attention-deficit/hyperactivity disorder (ADHD) and do not respond to handwriting instruction or produce legible letter writing until they receive medication for ADHD. The improvement in handwriting following careful diagnosis of ADHD and beginning medication is often remarkable. With that said, medication is not the cure for all kinds of handwriting problems. Some students may have difficulty self-regulating their attention during writing for reasons other than ADHD. For example, students may have trouble with one or more supervisory attention/executive functions in working memory; such students may respond to instructional strategies aimed at these attention/executive function skills.

Accurate diagnosis of ADHD, which can co-occur with other SLDs, requires a multidisciplinary team (see Chapter 13). Many psychologists have training relevant to diagnosing ADHD; however, in most states, only physicians can prescribe medication for ADHD and need to be involved, along with the parents, in making the decision as to whether medication may be helpful for treating attention problems. If the decision is to pursue a trial of medication, teachers should continue to monitor attention and handwriting in the classroom and share their observations with the student's parents, physician, and other relevant professionals. Decisions to use any medication for learning problems should be made cautiously, based on careful diagnosis, and monitored closely. When more than one drug is prescribed for a student, the possibility of adverse drug interactions should be considered. Teachers can help by sharing with the parents, physicians, and psychologists the problems the student is having with focusing on task at hand, switching between tasks, and sustaining attention to stay on task or self-regulate behavior. Teachers can also provide helpful feedback about the response to intervention when students are placed on medications. For example, after medication begins, does the student's handwriting improve, does the student attend better to handwriting instruction, and does the student sustain engagement in writing for a longer period of time?

Social-Emotional Systems

Students who cannot produce legible letters are often emotionally devastated because others cannot read their handwriting. Students are keenly aware that the purpose of writing is to communicate with others. Some students have likened their illegible writing to having a speech articulation problem. Whether letter writing or speech is hard for others to understand, the students are likely to feel like failures. Students who cannot write letters automatically or sustain letter writing over time may not complete many of their written assignments within a reasonable time frame. Teachers often misattribute this failure to complete written assignments to a lack of motivation or effort. The real reason may be that these students cannot write legible letters automatically and have difficulty sustaining attention to task. Also, while pausing, these students may lose track of the writing goals at hand. Chronic struggles in writing due to handwriting may result in negative self-concepts and lack of hope for success as a writer. Teachers should work with the whole interdisciplinary team and parents to address these social-emotional issues in additional to teaching specific handwriting skills.

TEACHING TIP 3-1: Facilitate the connections between handwriting and various content areas of the curriculum.

Handwriting instruction should include multiple components, each aimed at one of the relevant brain systems. In addition, instruction and handwriting learning activities should be designed so that the different systems work together in a coordinated fashion. For example, teach to create connections among visual letters, auditory sounds or names of letters, kinesthetic touch (Cox, 1992; Slingerland, 1971), and for production through the various writing tools for letter production.

All language systems can provide cues—listening through ears to the teacher's writing instruction, naming letters or saying the steps of letter formation through the mouth, writing letters through the hand, and reading written letters for self-monitoring. Strengths in one or more of these modalities can be used to help a student with weaknesses in one or more of these modalities. Teaching the sequence of writing component strokes helps focus students' attention to letter forms. Teaching legible and automatic letter writing so that students can communicate with others helps avoid negative self-concepts and affect. Beginning in kindergarten, students can learn to express ideas in their written compositions if they can write letters (see the story of Jennifer Katahira in Berninger, 2015). In general, the initial focus for manuscript handwriting during first grade should be to form legible letters that others can recognize, in keeping with the social and emotional factors in learning handwriting.

Research Lesson 3-2

Handwriting should be taught in developmentally appropriate ways and during early childhood and middle childhood. Before the era of Common Core Standards, most public school districts taught manuscript in the first two grades and cursive in the next two grades. This approach allowed students to learn to write manuscript (unconnected) letters legibly in first grade and then automatically (effortlessly and quickly without sacrificing legibility) in second grade. Likewise, this approach then allowed students to move on to learn to write cursive (connected) letters legibly in third grade and then automatically in fourth grade. This approach is still sensible despite the fact that Common Core Standards drop cursive altogether and reduce manuscript to kindergarten and first grade. The use of manuscript printing in the first two grades allows beginning writers to see the same symbol forms used for reading most printed matter in English—in books used for instruction, read with parents and teachers, and read independently and on screens of technology tools that display one's own writing and the writing of others. The use of cursive in third and fourth grade can facilitate learning to spell (see Research Lesson 3-3). In general, during the first four grades, it is advisable to focus on a single style of writing during a given school year—manuscript or cursive. In the year the style is introduced, the focus is on legibility; in the following year, the focus is on legibility and automaticity. Beyond the first four grades, once students have learned to form lowercase and uppercase manuscript and cursive letters, periodic tune-ups should review both styles, just as car owners periodically get their car engines tuned up so that they work efficiently. However, after formal handwriting instruction, students typically choose their preferred handwriting—manuscript, cursive, or a mix of the two. Any choice is fine, as long as it is legible and automatic (see Berninger, 2015, Chapters 4 and 5).

A number of factors need to be considered in providing developmentally appropriate handwriting instruction tailored to individual needs. The instructional components relevant for handwriting depend on where a student is in his or her writing journey. Initially, it is necessary to work on fine motor control and strength and identify the dominant hand for handwriting. The teacher should observe and correct students' pencil grip, posture, and paper position for handwriting during lessons; in upper grades, these should also be monitored.

TEACHING TIP 3-2A: Develop fine motor control and strength.

Do mazes with pencils, pens, or markers to develop fine motor control by staying inside the lines. Play with clay to develop strength in hands and fingers.

TEACHING TIP 3-2B: Identify the dominant (preferred) hand for handwriting.

Before handwriting instruction begins, teachers should determine each student's hand preference. For most students, dominance is established by kindergarten age, but a few students may be insecure in knowing which hand to use for writing as late as age 8 or 9 years. The patterning for instruction and practice of handwriting requires consistent development of brain–muscle memory of the form of each letter—that is, the connection between the central and peripheral nervous systems underlying the sequential formation of each letter, stroke by stroke. The hand used for letter writing sends signals to the opposite side of the brain; continually switching hands may confuse the brain, especially when pathways communicating between the left and right sides are not yet fully matured in kindergarten through fourth grade. In most cases, the teachers can determine a student's hand preference with a few simple activities, such as the following:

1. While facing the student, the teacher offers a pencil, piece of chalk, marker, or other writing implement, depending on the writing surface being used. The teacher holds the object toward the student's chest and notes the hand with which the student takes the writing implement.

2. The teacher asks the student to write his or her name with the hand he or she used to accept the writing utensil. The teacher should note whether the student switches the implement to the other hand, the way the student

holds the writing implement, the facility with which it is used, and the consistency of script. The teacher should then ask the student to write his or her name again with the opposite hand.

3. The teacher repeats the activity by requesting that the student draw a house—first with one hand, then with the other. Again, the teacher should note rate, organization, and quality of the finished product. If the names and houses are completed side by side, it is easy to compare results. Some students know immediately which hand they prefer, and they say so. Most students can tell which hand is easier to use.

4. If a student's hand preference is still not clear, a timed pegboard activity based on the Jansky Kindergarten Index (Jansky & de Hirsch, 1966, p. 14) can be helpful. The teacher places a pegboard and pegs in front of the student and asks the student to place the pegs in the board using only one hand. The teacher allows 30 seconds and should note the number of pegs, their arrangement (in rows or haphazard), and the dexterity with which the student places the pegs in the pegboard. The student then repeats the task with the opposite hand. It is seldom necessary to proceed beyond this activity. If there is still uncertainty about which is the stronger hand, the student can be referred for neuropsychological or neurological assessment, which typically includes a hand preference test.

When a student's preferred hand is identified, discuss ways that he or she can be helped to remember which hand to use. Some parents provide a watch or bracelet to wear on the writing hand, or teachers can mark the correct hand with a sticker or a marker. It helps students to associate hand preference with the classroom environment. Teachers can mark the correct side of the desk or remind students that their writing hand is toward the windows or another classroom landmark when facing the front of the room.

TEACHING TIP 3-2C: Teach and monitor pencil grip.

Check students' pencil grip as they prepare to write. They should use a tripod grip in which the pencil rests on the first joint of the middle finger, with the thumb and index fingers holding the pencil in place and the pencil held at a 45-degree angle to the page. Students should hold the pencil firmly with a relaxed arm and hand. The pencil should point toward the shoulder of the writing arm for both left- and right-handed students. An awkward pencil grip is more tiring and may affect letter formation and slant.

As the demand for writing increases through elementary school, maladroit pencil grip can become an increased liability. Affected students may experience writer's cramp; they may not be able to keep up with the writing rate requirements and thus produce less writing on written assignments diminishing the quantity and quality of writing (Levine, 1987). An attentive teacher with consistency and patience can help a student change pencil grip.

When an incorrect grip is observed, the teacher can redirect the class with the following prompts:

1. "Stop, place your pencils on the desk with the point toward you."

2. "Pinch your pencil." With the index finger and thumb in a pinch position, teachers should ensure that students lightly grasp their pencils approximately 1 inch from the point or where the point begins.

3. "Lift your pencil." As the students lift their pencils, they will fall back into correct writing position and rest on the first joint of the middle finger.

After a few practice sessions, students will only need to hear, "Stop, pinch, lift," to adjust their pencil grips. Teacher perseverance will help students become accustomed to the feel of the new position and use it consistently. After a time, only those students who have continued difficulty will need reminders. Older students will have increasing difficulty with changing their pencil grips and will have greater need for teacher intervention.

The use of a plastic pencil grip or a metal writing frame can aid students in changing a fatiguing grip to a typical, less tiring one (Phelps & Stempel, 1987; Texas Scottish Rite Hospital for Children, 1990, 1996). Grips come in a variety of forms from plastic triangles and shaped grips to wire frames. Frames have the advantage of eliminating tension when students are learning to write because the hand simply rests on the frame without gripping the pencil. Students may need to experiment with a variety of pencil grips or frames to determine which one works best for them. Teachers should be aware, however, that many students who use grips and frames often become frustrated with them once the novelty has worn off.

While students write, they receive feedback in the form of pressure and the pull of the pencil against the paper. Pencils with soft lead require less pressure from the student, thus reducing fatigue. Students with impaired kinesthetic feedback will benefit from using softer leads that will not break as they press firmly in an attempt to receive that feedback when writing (Levine, 1987). A number 2 or softer pencil with no eraser is recommended so that students can trace letters with the unsharpened end without marking the paper. The absence of an eraser eliminates the temptation for students to spend time repeatedly erasing and avoiding the writing task at hand. Also, teachers can monitor progress in handwriting performance and use their observations to inform future lesson planning and handwriting instruction. To encourage self-monitoring and revising (high-level executive functions), teachers can encourage students to put brackets around or draw a single line through mistakes and rewrite the word correctly.

TEACHING TIP 3-2D: Teach students the correct paper position.

Many handwriting programs recommend that when using manuscript writing, right-handed students keep their papers parallel to the bottom of the desk to help them keep their manuscript letters straight. Left-handed writers should keep the edge of the paper parallel to the writing arm, which should be at approximately a 45-degree angle to the edge of the desk. When using cursive writing, right-handed students should keep the right corner higher than the left, whereas left-handed students should slant in the opposite direction, with the left corner higher than the right. This approach allows students to see what they are writing and avoids smudging as their arms move across the page. It also prevents "hooking," or a curled wrist, which is common among left-handed writers. Some teachers draw a line or place tape on students' desks at about a 45-degree angle to serve as a guide for paper alignment until students are able to judge and keep the slant for themselves. In all cases, students should anchor their papers at the top with their non-writing hands.

TEACHING TIP 3-2E: Teach gross and fine motor movement and paper positioning.

By starting with activities that involve gross motor movement, the writer is allowed to feel the movement necessary in the shoulder and arm to produce the letter and thus receives kinesthetic feedback for motor movements (Levine, 1987). Initial instruction can begin at the chalkboard or dry-erase board, where the teacher can make large patterns for the students to trace using full arm movements. Instruction can then move to smaller and smaller tracing areas—to folded unlined paper with large spaces 6–8 inches high, then to narrower 3- to 4-inch spaces, then to wide-lined (1-inch) paper, then to primary-grade lined paper, and finally to regular lined notebook paper. The size of the spaces between lines is adjusted downward as the students master the letter forms. As students write and practice, the teacher should circulate around the room, watching carefully to see that students maintain correct posture, full arm movement, and correct form. If a student's writing deteriorates, he or she may not be ready for reduced-sized paper. Remind students that large (gross) muscle movement helps establish stronger memory of the feel of the letter for writing. Remind students that if they continue to use good form, they may continue on narrower lined paper. See Figure 3.1 for suggested paper sizes for handwriting.

Equally important is using lined paper that has space and lines appropriate for grade level. For example, kindergarten, first-grade, and second-grade students learn handwriting most effectively with resting lines and top lines that are solid and divided lines midway between the solid lines. This spacing supports their learning of the relative positioning of letter strokes that often differentiate letters from each other. For example, *h* and *n* differ only on the height of the left vertical stroke; other letters have ascenders above or descenders below the resting line, such as *b* and *p* (see Figure 3.1).

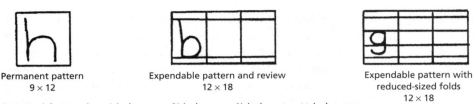

Permanent pattern
9 × 12

Expendable pattern and review
12 × 18

Expendable pattern with
reduced-sized folds
12 × 18

Commercial paper sizes: 1-inch spaces, ¾-inch spaces, ½-inch spaces, ⅜-inch spaces

Figure 3.1. Suggested paper sizes for handwriting. (Duplicating masters are also available from Slingerland® Institute for Literacy: http://www.slingerland.org)

TEACHING TIP 3-2F: Teach legible formation of manuscript letters.

Teachers should model the order of strokes for forming each letter. Students imitate by writing those strokes in the order modeled. Lowercase and uppercase letters should be taught separately. Capital letters are sometimes introduced first because they are often easier to learn, but lowercase manuscript letters should probably be taught first because they are encountered far more often in written material. Regardless of which is taught first, introduce the letters grouped by similar formation strokes. This approach allows students to master one type of movement before focusing on another. Figures 3.2 and 3.3 show examples of one way both manuscript and cursive letters can be grouped by strokes. Provide daily explicit instruction and guided practice in forming manuscript letters.

TEACHING TIP 3-2G: Teach naming of letters and orally stating steps, that is, ordered procedures for forming them.

Letter names are taught because names play an important role in finding, accessing, and retrieving letter forms from long-term memory, where they are stored in alphabetical order. The teacher should explain that letters have

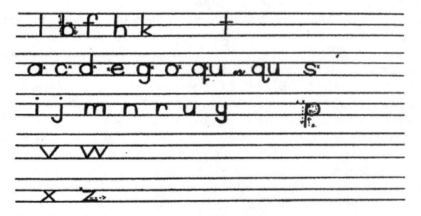

Figure 3.2. Manuscript letters grouped by strokes.

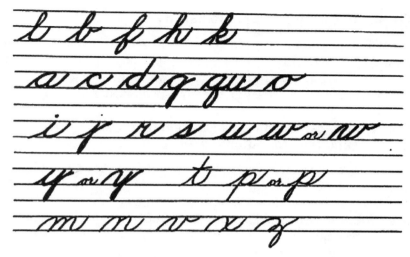

Figure 3.3. Cursive letters grouped by strokes.

names just like people. Then, the teacher can present one letter at a time and later in a different order than alphabetic order. Students are asked to name them—first as a group in unison and then by two teams, who alternate their turn at bat for letter ball. The teacher keeps score for each team until they have practiced naming all the letters two or three times and displays the score for all to see.

In the initial learning of letter formation, verbalization of consistent, precise directions for forming each letter is helpful. These descriptions often accompany teacher manuals for handwriting programs. For example, when writing the letter *d*, students might say, "Around like an *a* and tall stem up and down to the writing line." When writing the letter *b*, they might say, "Tall stem down and away from my body" (if right handed) or "Tall stem down and across my body" (if left handed) (Slingerland, 1971, p. 62).

TEACHING TIP 3-2H: Practice writing named letters from dictation.

Because letter names play such an important role in letter retrieval from memory, students should also be asked to write letters from dictated names on appropriately lined paper.

TEACHING TIP 3-2I: Teach for transfer of handwriting to other writing skills.

In the early grades, it is important to practice letter writing daily, especially at the beginning of lessons on spelling and composing. Provide feedback about letters that are not legible in spelling or compositions (e.g., circle them and ask the student to fix so the letters are legible).

TEACHING TIP 3-2J: Teach for automaticity.

Once manuscript letter formation is legible, provide learning activities to promote automatic production (see Appendix 3B). Learning activities that require students to hold a letter in the "mind's eye" without looking at it on paper, and then open their eyes and write the letter from memory, help develop automaticity.

TEACHING TIP 3-2K: Teach cursive writing first for legibility and then for automaticity.

In third grade, cursive writing should be introduced. As with manuscript writing, group the letters with common strokes together when introducing them and teach the lowercase letters first. One advantage of cursive is that the continuous strokes, once learned, reduce the number of times the pencil has to be lifted from the page. In addition, the connecting strokes may help the student link the sequence of adjacent letters into a word unit, which facilitates learning to read and spell words (see Research Lesson 3-3). In general, it is advisable to teach both manuscript and cursive writing. In the upper elementary grades, let students choose their preferred format—manuscript or cursive—but keep in mind that many students will use a combination of both.

Research Lesson 3-3

Handwriting instruction should be linked to assessment. Effective handwriting instruction should be linked to developmentally appropriate assessment of students' strengths and weaknesses in handwriting and related processes and other modes of letter production including keyboarding. That is, differentiated instruction is needed to teach developing writers to be hybrid writers (Berninger, 2012, 2013) who can write in manuscript (transfers to word reading, James & Atwood, 2009), cursive (transfers to spelling and composition, Alstad et al., 2015), and keyboarding (helps with producing multiple drafts and revisions especially after students progress beyond hunting and pecking to touch typing, MacArthur, 2008, 2009).

The goal of Chapter 3 is therefore to provide evidence-based models of which handwriting or related processes to assess at which grade level and then which evidence-based model of which instructional approaches to use teach these handwriting skills if assessment shows there is a weakness at a specific grade level. That is, the goal is to present a developmental model of assessment–instruction links for handwriting that provides both assessment tips and related teaching tips.

TEACHING TIP 3-3: Use Chapter 3, Appendix 3A, and Appendix 3B to link assessment to instruction for handwriting.

In the text, examples of assessment tools for specific kinds of handwriting or handwriting-related skills are described, organized by grade levels to provide a developmental framework, and referred to by their abbreviated titles by which they are known in the schools. In Appendix 3A specific assessment tools for assessing each kind of skill are provided along with their full names spelled out and citations for locating the assessment tools. For linking handwriting assessment to handwriting instruction, see Research Lesson 3-4, Teaching Tip 3-4, and Appendix 3B. Likewise, in Appendix 3B, specific instructional tools are provided along with citations for locating them. Thus, the text and Appendices are designed to use in conjunction with each other for a developmental model of assessment–instruction links for handwriting.

Also see Chapter 13 for a discussion of how a multidisciplinary team can support the general education teacher in 1) conducting the assessments to identify students needing individually tailored instruction for specific handwriting or handwriting-related skills, and 2) implement that instruction. Tools for assessment in Appendix 3A indicate whether the test requires individual administration or could be adapted to give in a group. Tools for instruction in Appendix 3B are linked to research on writing development (Berninger, 2009; Berninger et al., 2015). The instructional tools can be used in large-group instruction or small-group instruction formed for students with similar instructional needs. The following guidelines can be used in linking instruction to assessment (see Research Lesson 3-3).

EVIDENCE-BASED ASSESSMENT

To use Chapter 3 and Appendix 3A for evidence-based handwriting assessment, at each grade level, choose and administer at least one measure of each of the *skills* from Appendix 3A at the beginning of the school year. Repeat it at the end of the school year to monitor progress during that school year.

Kindergarten

Assess pencil-and-paper mazes (fine motor control). Use the ABC 2 Mazes subtest to assess.

Assess copying geometric forms with lines and shapes used in writing letters and numerals. Use Beery Test of Visual-Motor Integration to assess.

Assess visual perception memory. Use Slingerland® Prereading Screening. Ask the student to view a drawing or numeral on a card and then when the card is removed to draw it.

Assess copying lowercase manuscript letters. Use teacher-prepared index cards with one lowercase manuscript letter and one uppercase manuscript letter on each card. Scramble the cards. Ask the student to copy each letter, displayed one at a time, on lined paper with appropriate spacing for kindergarten.

Assess naming manuscript letters. Use the same index cards with one lowercase and one uppercase manuscript letter on each. Scramble the cards. Ask the student to name each letter. On a teacher-prepared, duplicated form, record which letters are named correctly and which ones are missed.

Assess writing named manuscript letters. Use lined paper with appropriate spacing for kindergarten. Dictate named letters in scrambled order. First, ask students to write each dictated letter in lowercase manuscript. Second, ask students to write each dictated letter in uppercase manuscript.

Assess near point and far point copying. Use the Slingerland® Prereading Screening.

First Grade

Assess visual perception memory and near point and far point copying. Use Slingerland® Prereading Screening as in kindergarten.

Assess writing the alphabet from memory in lowercase manuscript. Give the PAL-II RW Alphabet Task. Score for the number correct (legible and in correct alphabetical order) in the first 15 seconds and total legibility. The number correct in the first 15 seconds is an index of the orthographic loop in working memory supporting automatic writing of legible letters in alphabetic order. Legibility is an index of accurate letter formation.

Assess copying a sentence with all letters of the alphabet (best and fast manuscript writing). Give DASH-2 Copy Best and Copy Fast. Copy Best assesses ability to self-regulate handwriting to write it as good as possible. Copy Fast assesses writing fluency for producing letters in written words.

Assess copying a paragraph at near point in manuscript letters. Give PAL-II RW Copy Paragraph at 30, 60, and 90 seconds. This test assesses sustaining writing over time at different time intervals.

Assess rapid automatic naming (RAN) letters. Give the Wolf and Denckla RAN or KTEA-3 Letter Naming Facility. RAN is a measure of the phonological loop of working memory, that is, fast integration of name codes with letter or other visual codes.

Assess compositional fluency. Give DASH-2 Free Writing, KTEA-3 Writing Fluency, PAL-II RW Compositional Fluency (score for handwriting legibility and number of words), or WJ III Writing Fluency. These tests assess speed of composing sentences or short texts.

Second Grade

Assess near point and far point copying. Use the Slingerland® Screening Form A.

Assess writing the alphabet from memory in lowercase manuscript. Give the PAL-II RW Alphabet Task. Score for the number correct (legible and in correct alphabetical order) in the first 15 seconds and total legibility. See first grade for skills assessed.

Assess copying manuscript letters from a model sentence in best and fast writing. Give DASH-2 Copy Best and Copy Fast. See first grade for skills assessed.

Assess sustained copying of a paragraph over time. Give PAL-II RW Copy Paragraph at 30, 60, and 90 seconds. See first grade for skills assessed.

Assess phonological loop of working memory (RAN letters). Give Wolf and Denckla RAN or KTEA-3 Letter Naming Facility. See first grade for skill assessed.

Assess compositional fluency. Give DASH-2 Free Writing, KTEA-3 Writing Fluency, PAL-II RW Compositional Fluency (score for handwriting legibility and total number of words), or WJ III Writing Fluency. Score for text or sentences, respectively, produced within a time limit. See first grade for skills assessed.

Third Grade

Assess writing the alphabet from memory in lowercase manuscript. Give the PAL-II RW Alphabet Task. Score for the total number correct (legible and in correct alphabetical order) in the first 15 seconds. See first grade for skill assessed. Compute the scaled score based on norms but also use the raw score to compare with the same task in cursive.

Assess writing the alphabet from memory in lowercase cursive. Give the same alphabet task in cursive and compare raw scores for the total number correct in cursive and manuscript.

Assess copying a sentence with all letters of the alphabet. Give DASH-2 Copy Best and Copy Fast. See first grade for skills assessed.

Assess sustained copying of a paragraph over time. Give PAL-II RW Copy Paragraph at 30, 60, and 90 seconds. See first grade for skill assessed.

Assess RAN letters. Give Wolf and Denckla RAN and KTEA-3 Letter Naming Facility subtest. See first grade for skill assessed.

Assess compositional fluency. Give DASH-2 Free Writing, KTEA-3 Writing Fluency, PAL Compositional Fluency (score for handwriting legibility and total number of words), or WJ III Writing Fluency. Score for handwriting legibility. PAL-II RW alternative prompts can also be given—one in manuscript and one in cursive—to compare for relative strengths across modalities. See first grade for skill assessed.

Fourth and Fifth Grades

Assess writing the alphabet from memory in lowercase manuscript. Give the PAL-II RW Alphabet Task. Score for the total number correct (legible and in correct alphabetical order) in the first 15 seconds. Compute the scaled score based on norms but also use the raw score to compare with the same task in cursive and touch typing (with blindfold on student so keys cannot be viewed).

Assess writing the alphabet from memory in lowercase cursive. Give the same alphabet task in cursive and compare raw scores for the total number correct in cursive and manuscript.

Assess copying a sentence with all letters of the alphabet. Give DASH-2 Copy Best and Copy Fast. Note whether the usual handwriting chosen, per the instructions, is manuscript, cursive, or a mix.

Assess compositional fluency. Give DASH-2 Free Writing, KTEA-3 Writing Fluency, PAL-II RW Compositional Fluency (score for handwriting legibility and total number of words), or WJ III Writing Fluency. Score for handwriting legibility. PAL-II RW alternative prompts can also be given—one in manuscript and one in cursive—to compare for relative strengths across modalities. See first grade for skills assessed.

Compare texts written in class and for homework by pen and keyboard. Keep these in a writing portfolio and reflect with students about their progress in both handwriting and keyboarding, as well as how they might set goals for using each mode in future writing.

Transfer the preferred mode of letter writing to spelling and sentence writing. Determine from review and reflection of compositions in the writing portfolio what goals the student might set to improve each mode of handwriting for composing.

Sixth to Eighth Grades

Assess writing the alphabet from memory—lowercase manuscript. Instruct students to write the whole alphabet in alphabetical order from memory and draw a line when time is called at 15 seconds. See first grade for skill assessed.

Assess writing the alphabet from memory—lowercase cursive. Instruct students to write the whole alphabet in alphabetical order from memory and draw a line when time is called at 15 seconds.

Assess the alphabet from memory—lowercase touch typing. Instruct students to produce the whole alphabet in alphabetical order from memory without looking at keys (ask the student to wear a blindfold).

Complete cross-mode comparisons. Compare raw scores on alphabet tasks across modes to identify relative strengths and weaknesses.

Assess composition by manuscript, cursive, and touch typing. Ask the student to compose in manuscript for 5 minutes, in cursive for 5 minutes, and by keyboard for 5 minutes on comparable but not identical teacher-designed prompts. Compare the legibility of handwriting letters and the quality of composing across the three letter production modes.

Ninth to Twelfth Grades

Assess alphabet from memory—by manuscript, cursive, and touch typing. See sixth to eighth grades.

Assess composing by manuscript, cursive, and touch typing. See sixth to eighth grades.

EVIDENCE-BASED METHODS OF HANDWRITING INSTRUCTION
Research Lesson 3-4

Effective handwriting instruction should be developmentally appropriate, continue across early and middle childhood, and include multiple modes of letter production including keyboarding. That is, differentiated instruction, which is developmentally appropriate and individually tailored, is needed to teach developing writers to be hybrid writers (Berninger, 2012, 2013). Writing in manuscript transfers to word reading (James & Atwood, 2009), writing in cursive transfers to spelling and composition (Alstad et al., 2015), and keyboarding helps with producing multiple drafts and revisions, especially after students progress beyond hunting and pecking to touch typing, MacArthur (2008, 2009).

TEACHING TIP 3-4: Draw on many handwriting instructional resources to provide differentiated handwriting and letter production instruction linked to assessment.

Many effective ways for teaching handwriting have been developed. General education classrooms may draw on all of them across the school year within a grade and across grades to teach grade-appropriate handwriting and related skills that all students benefit from with specialized, differentiated instruction individually tailored to weaknesses in handwriting, which assessment identifies for individual students. In the text we explain these methods in a developmental model from the early grades to the intermediate grades to the upper grades.

The longest standing handwriting program designed for use in the general education classroom from kindergarten throughout the elementary grades is published by Zaner-Bloser. Classroom kits provide teacher manuals and teaching aids. Both manuscript and cursive handwriting are covered in a structured, systematic, way and developmentally (initially manuscript and then cursive).

In the Slingerland® method of handwriting instruction, as introduced in Chapter 1, beginning writers move from tracing a letter pattern and then forming it in the air before writing with rhythm and fluency to develop automaticity. The class writes, names, and traces each letter repeatedly (about three times) until the next letter is given. Each time the students write the letter, they name it and, if necessary, remind themselves verbally of the correct formation. That is, they engage their hands, mouth, ears, and eyes. (See Teaching

Tip 3-1.) Teacher judgment will determine the amount of structure required during review. In this way, students are developing their self-monitoring and self-regulating skills.

Occupational therapists specializing in early childhood development have also developed handwriting instruction methods. For example, *Big Strokes for Little Folks* (Rubel, 1995) teaches component strokes in letter formation by groups of letters that share common strokes and includes supplementary activities for developing small motor and muscle skills related to writing. Designed to introduce students to manuscript handwriting, this program includes 1) letter mazes for grapho-motor control, 2) personalized letters that call attention to letter names and associated sounds (e.g., *K* is kicker), 3) observing and imitating the teacher modeling the sequence of strokes in letters with the eraser end and writing end of the pencil, and 4) copying letter forms. Some of these instructional design elements were incorporated in Rutberg's research on beginning handwriting (e.g., Berninger, Rutberg et al., 2006).

In programmatic research in schools with first-graders, the most effective treatment for teaching manuscript letters compared to alternative treatments (only numbered arrow cues, only writing from memory, or only motor modeling and imitation or a contact control treatment—phonological awareness) was the method that included each of the following instructional components (Berninger et al., 1997):

- Students study the numbered arrow visual cues in a model letter named by the teacher to learn a plan for forming a letter stroke by stroke. Names help find letter forms in memory.

- Students cover the named letter, close their eyes, and hold the letter in their mind's eye for a few seconds.

- Students open their eyes when the teacher names the letter and then write it from memory and compare the letter they wrote with the model letter.

In all 24 lessons, each of the 26 letters was practiced once to help students learn to write all the letters they might need to spell or recognize in words they read. This treatment also reduced reversals in letter writing when compared with a control treatment (Brooks, 2003; Brooks, Berninger, Abbott, & Richards, 2011). The most effective treatment also improved both automatic legible letter writing in alphabetic order from memory and compositional fluency (length of text within time limits). Graham, Harris, and Fink (2000) also showed that explicit handwriting strategies benefited beginning writers with handwriting problems and handwriting instruction transferred to improved written composition.

Beyond writing letters legibly and automatically, students must also learn how to retrieve letter forms automatically from long-term memory while reading and spelling words. This automatic retrieval depends on searching and accessing a specific letter form within the ordered 26 letters. Storing them in alphabetical order has an advantage for automatic letter retrieval. The before-and-after alphabet letter game was developed in research to help students become automatic in letter retrieval (Berninger, Abbott, Whitaker, Sylvester, & Nolen, 1995). In this game, students are asked to tell or write the letter that comes before or after another letter in alphabetical order. In a writing tutorial in the summer between third and fourth grades for students at risk for writing problems in fourth grade, the students who played these before-and-after games wrote longer compositions than those who did not play the games, suggesting transfer to the written expression of ideas (Berninger, et al., 1995). See Berninger (1998a) for lessons with before-and-after letter-writing activities. Also, see the activities under Teaching Tips in this chapter for teaching first-graders (and even older students) alphabetic order for a variety of literacy goals. For example, students may be asked to write the letter that comes in between two named letters.

Relatively less research has been devoted to cursive than manuscript handwriting. However, many teachers and researchers have observed individual differences in skill with and preference for cursive versus manuscript. Some students have difficulty with manuscript but not cursive and others with cursive and not manuscript. Therefore, there are individual differences related to handwriting style. Students with SLDs may also vary in their ability and preferences for cursive versus manuscript. In addition to the Slingerland® and Zaner-Bloser programs, another one that has been developed for teaching cursive is *Loops and Groups: A Kinesthetic Writing System* (Benbow, 1990).

Multiple approaches can be used for teaching and reviewing handwriting and keyboarding skills at different grade levels. (See Appendix 3B for instructional resources for handwriting and citations for locating them.) These can be linked to the assessment of the taught skills as discussed earlier in Chapter 3.

If a student is below the average range or the most average score for the age or grade on handwriting measures used for assessment (see Appendix 3A), select a grade-appropriate handwriting program (manuscript in Grades 1 and 2 and cursive in Grades 3 and 4) from the resources in Appendix 3B. Also use information gathered in Teacher Resources (Appendix 3C) and Teaching Tips discussed in Chapter 3 in designing and implementing handwriting program(s). At the end of the school year, administer the handwriting measures given at the beginning of the year again to assess handwriting progress across the school year.

Periodic handwriting tune-ups that review handwriting skills and include strategies for self-monitoring handwriting legibility are also recommended for Grades 5 and above. See text and Appendix 3B for ways to do so. Touch typing (see Appendix 3B) should also be introduced in the upper elementary grades. At all grade levels, integrate handwriting instruction with teaching other written language skills, such as word spelling and composing, using resources in Appendix 3B or teacher-designed ones.

ROLE OF HANDWRITING IN LEARNING TO WRITE, READ, AND CALCULATE

Research Lesson 3-5

There are handwriting paths to word reading and spelling (see Chapter 4), written composing (see Chapter 5), and math (see Chapter 6). Although handwriting is considered a low-level skill in the writing process, both legible letter writing and automatic letter writing contribute uniquely to the amount and quality of written composition in Grades 1–6 (Graham, Berninger, Abbott, Abbott, & Whitaker, 1997) across content areas of the curriculum, whereas numeral writing contributes to math (Busse, Berninger, Smith, & Hildebrand, 2001). In fact, explicit instruction in handwriting and numeral writing in the first and second grades may prevent more significant written composition and math calculation problems, respectively, in the later grades.

Moreover, there may be special benefits for each of the handwriting styles. Research has shown that teaching manuscript handwriting transfers to learning to read words (Berninger et al., 1997; James & Atwood, 2009; also see Chapter 6) and that cursive contributes to learning to spell in middle childhood to early adolescence, probably through connecting strokes that link letters into word units (Alstad et al., 2015; Wolf, submitted). The concept that technology tools may benefit various writing tasks, especially in middle childhood and adolescence, was introduced in Chapter 3 for assessment and related instruction, but will be considered in more depth in Chapter 11.

TEACHING TIP 3-5A: To facilitate the connections between handwriting and various content areas of the curriculum, handwriting instruction should call attention to links with its use in the various content domains.

Always follow handwriting instruction with spelling and composing instruction.

TEACHING TIP 3-5B: Teach and re-teach in varied ways, then review repeatedly.

There are many ways to teach handwriting, just as there are many ways to write the same letter, although each way shares a common name, such as m, *m*, **m**. Teachers should draw on a variety of approaches to engage student interest in letters. Different fonts for printing manuscript letters are also taught, such as ball and stick or slanted D'Nealian letters. Although many students learn to write letters regardless of the specific fonts or styles taught, all students should be given guided practice in reading (recognizing letters) in the various fonts they are likely to encounter in written material. Whichever style of letter writing that is being taught, it is advisable within a few weeks to introduce all the lowercase forms in a particular style so that the student knows all 26 needed to read and spell English words in that style. Then capital letters, which are used in only approximately 2% of writing, can be introduced as signals for marking the beginning of a sentence (an idea unit) and names of people and other items.

Once all letters in a given format are introduced, the following guidelines are helpful for selecting letters for review in particular lessons:

1. Review letters when students show difficulty forming or executing connections between them.

2. Review groups of letters that share common formation components. In manuscript writing, these groups may include those beginning with a down stroke (e.g., *l, h, b, m, n, r, p, k*) or those beginning with the formation of *a* starting at the "2-o'clock" position (e.g., *c, d, g, qu, s*). In cursive writing, letters would also be grouped by similar strokes (see Figures 3.2 and 3.3).

3. Practice spelling dictated single target words and sentences containing those target words.

4. For cursive writing, teachers should teach and practice cursive connections, with special attention to the difficult ones. All but four cursive letters end with a connecting stroke near the writing line. The exceptions are those that connect at the midline—*b, o, v,* and *w.* The connections to these letters require specific instruction and consistent review. When teaching difficult connections, the teacher can provide prepared patterns to be traced, copied, and written from memory. Extra practice should be provided for frequent combinations, such as *br, oa, vi,* and *wh* (see Figure 3.4 for the example of *or*). Henry (2003) pointed out that third-graders often need practice in these linkages when they are using cursive writing for spelling more complex words.

An important skill in reviewing alphabet letters is alphabetical order. Learning alphabet order helps students find and retrieve letters in long-term memory during reading, handwriting, spelling, and composing. Also, learning alphabet order helps with finding words in the dictionary and other literacy activities. Alphabetical order should be taught beginning in first grade and continuing as needed. A Japanese proverb states that if you wish to know the highest truth, you must begin with the alphabet. Learning the alphabet is a student's first introduction to literacy and later to abstract scientific and logical thinking in Western culture (Logan, 1986). In addition to the alphabet's use in automatic recognition of letters and their names and in communicating language, it is used to classify information through alphabetization; it also relates to functional dictionary use and organizational systems, including understanding telephone books, encyclopedias, and filing systems. Students with SLDs may have difficulty recalling the alphabet in sequential order. Having the alphabet at

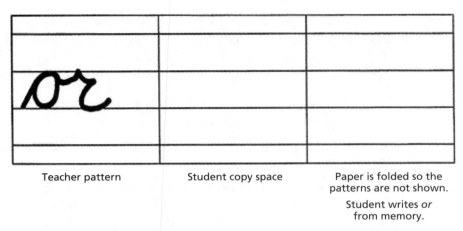

Teacher pattern   Student copy space   Paper is folded so the
                                                       patterns are not shown.

                                                       Student writes *or*
                                                       from memory.

Figure 3.4.   Practicing letter connections in cursive writing with letter connections for *or*.

each student's desk provides students with a constant point of reference to aid uncertain recall. Other activities that can be used, depending on the students' developmental levels and instructional needs, include the following:

1. Start each day by having students recite the alphabet orally or sing the alphabet song.

2. Put the alphabet to use as students put things away by letter or are called to line up for dismissal in alphabetical order. Begin with a different letter each time so that students can practice picking up the alphabet from a particular letter rather than always starting with *a*.

3. Ask students to name the letter that comes after or before another letter. Ask them to name the letter that comes between two other letters.

4. Have the students copy the words in alphabetical order and illustrate each word—not only in language arts but also science and social studies.

5. Practice alphabetizing. Call three students to the front of the room. They should have clearly printed name tags. Ask class members to arrange the three students in alphabetical order. As the class becomes proficient, increase the numbers of students to be alphabetized. Delay using two or more students whose names begin with the same letter until the performance with different letters is automatic. Then, bring everyone whose names begin with the same letter to the front. Show how the second letter, or even the third, becomes part of the alphabetizing process.

TEACHING TIP 3-5C: Teach for transfer of handwriting to content areas in the curriculum at all grade levels.

At all grade levels, teachers should provide opportunities to practice letter writing in words, word combinations, and sentences. In this way, students will learn to apply letter writing to writing larger units of written language and developing compositional fluency. In Orton-Gillingham based approaches, as introduced in Chapter 1, handwriting practice and review are integrated into the written language lesson to provide success with spelling and other written language tasks. For example, if students will be expected to write the word *work*, they will practice the letter forms and connections necessary to successfully write the word (e.g., *wo, or, wor, rk*).

Letter writing is also relevant to learning to read. In the alphabetic phonics approach (see Chapters 1 and 4 and Appendix 4C), students can practice handwriting during the decoding activities of the reading lesson. Rhythmic movement from one letter to another as the teacher names them helps students to link serially ordered letters into word units. In the Slingerland® Approach, each day starts with a writing lesson when students are the most rested and freshest to prepare them for the daily written work of the day. Examples of skills in daily practice include 1) moving from one letter to the next smoothly to develop a rhythmic tempo and 2) forming one dictated letter, then tracing, and then writing and tracing the next one as it is named. If students are unable to write a letter satisfactorily, the teacher returns to the tracing step at the board or on large paper patterns or to forming letters with large muscle groups in the air. Students should also practice rhythm, fluency, and the spacing between letters.

Finally, writing numerals is necessary to write number facts and perform written computations for basic addition, subtraction, multiplication, and division operations needed to solve math problems. Therefore, the various strategies for teaching alphabetic order should be applied to writing numerals in order and transfer of this skill to math learning. This topic is explored in further detail in Chapters 6 and 8.

Assessment of
Handwriting and Related Skills

Assessment tools are organized by skill and within skill appear in alphabetical order by first author surname. Note that an asterisk (*) means individual assessment is required; otherwise the assessment tool is designed to be used in a group or can be adapted for group administration.

MOTOR AND VISUAL-MOTOR SKILLS

These resources can be used if responses on a parent questionnaire indicate history of motor problems.

*Beery, K. (1982). *Administration, scoring, and teaching manual for the Developmental Test of Visual-Motor Integration* (Rev. ed.). Cleveland, OH: Modern Curriculum Press.

*Henderson, S., Sugden, D., & Barnett, A. (2007). *Movement assessment battery for children* (2nd ed.). London: Pearson.
Mazes.

HANDWRITING (COPYING)

Both handwriting measures below are typically given individually but could be adapted for group administration if each student had a test booklet and teacher adapted instructions for giving copying tasks to the group.

Barnett, A., Henderson, S., Scheib, B., & Schulz, J. (2007). *Detailed Assessment of Speed Handwriting, Second Edition (DASH-2)*. London: Pearson.
Copy Best and Copy Fast.

Berninger, V. (2007b). *Process Assessment of the Learner: Diagnostic for Reading and Writing (PAL-II RW)*. San Antonio, TX: Pearson.

Copy Paragraph (30, 60, 90 seconds). Ask students to draw a vertical line where they are when time is called at 30 seconds, then at 60 seconds, and finally at 90 seconds. Practice drawing vertical lines when time called before beginning.

HANDWRITING: WRITING THE ALPHABET FROM MEMORY

PAL-II RW

Alphabet Task. Score for number of legible letters in correct alphabetical order at 15 seconds and total legibility (number correct regardless of time taken to write alphabet). Adapt for group administration by having student draw a vertical line when time is called at 15 seconds on alphabet task.

SLINGERLAND® HANDWRITING ASSESSMENT MEASURES

Slingerland, B. (1997). *Prereading screening procedures to identify first grade academic needs*. Cambridge, MA: Educators Publishing Service.

The writing subtests of the Prereading Screening Procedures consist of tests of *near point copying*, in which the student copies geometric figures and some letters of the alphabet from samples on the test page; *far point copying*, in which the student copies geometric figures and some letters of the alphabet from samples on a chart; and *visual perception memory*, in which the child is shown a card with a letter, numeral, or shape, and after the card is taken away, the child is asked to write or draw what they have seen. An additional alphabet test is compared with an alphabet test that requires identification of letters, but no writing. Evaluation includes comparison of performance on the various subtests of near point copying, far point copying, visual perception memory, and an additional alphabet test that is compared with an alphabet test that requires no writing. Evaluation includes comparison of performance on the various subtests with performance on tests that require no writing.

Slingerland, B. (2005). *Slingerland® screening tests for identifying children with specific language disability*. Cambridge, MA: Educators Publishing Service.

The writing subtests of Slingerland® screening forms A, B, C, and D vary only in the difficulty of the geometric forms and the words selected for copying or recall. They consist of tests of *near point copying*, in which the student copies a list of words printed in the test booklet; *far point copying*, in which the student copies a paragraph that has been read by the teacher and is posted in the front of the room. The *visual perception memory test* consists of age-appropriate geometric forms, letter sequences, words, and phrases in which the child is shown a card with a letter, numeral, or shape, and after the card is taken away, the child is asked to write or draw what they have seen. Evaluation includes comparison of performance on the various subtests of *near point copying, far point copying*, and *visual perception memory.* Evaluation includes comparison of performance on the various subtests with performance on tests that require no writing.

COMPOSITIONAL FLUENCY

Compositional fluency is dependent on handwriting automaticity and rate. These are typically given individually but can be adapted for group administration.

DASH-2
  Free Writing.

PAL-II RW
  Compositional Fluency (two prompts).

Kaufman, A., & Kaufman, N. (2012). *Kaufman Test of Educational Achievement, Third Edition (KTEA-3)*. San Antonio, TX: Pearson.
  Writing Fluency.

Woodcock, R.W., Mather, N., & McGrew, K. (2008). *Woodcock-Johnson III Tests of Achievement (WJ III ACH)*. Rolling Meadows, IL: Riverside.
  Writing Fluency.

RAPID AUTOMATIC NAMING: LETTERS

Rapid automatic naming (RAN) letters is a handwriting-related skill.

*KTEA-3
  Letter Naming Facility.

*Wolf, M., & Denckla, M. (2005). *RAN/RAS Rapid Automatized Naming and Rapid Alternating Stimulus Tests*. Austin, TX: Pro-Ed.
  RAN Letters.

PLANNING INSTRUCTION BASED ON ASSESSMENT RESULTS AND PROGRESS MONITORING

- Identify individual students who fall below the lower limit of the average range (-^{2}/$_3$ standard deviation or 25th percentile or standard score of 90 on a test with a most average/mean score of 100 or a scaled score of 8 on a test with a most average/mean score of 10 or a z-score of -.66z on a research measure with a most average/mean score of 0). In some schools, the interdisciplinary team may decide to also identify any students who fall below the most average/mean score (50th percentile).

- Go to Appendix 3B and choose an instructional tool for each skill that meets the first or second criterion above.

- For progress monitoring, re-administer the assessment tool after the instructional program is completed.

Instructional Resources for Handwriting and Related Skills

MANUSCRIPT HANDWRITING

Berninger, V. (1998b). *Process Assessment of the Learner: Handwriting lessons*. San Antonio, TX: Pearson.
Ball and stick and D'Nealian formats, desk cards with numbered arrow cues, study named letter forms with numbered arrow cues, hold them in the mind's eye, open eyes and write them from memory, and compare to model letter form; practice each of 26 letters once in a lesson.

Rubel, B. (1995). *Big strokes for little folks*. Tucson, AZ: Therapy Skill Builders.
Tracing, imitating, copying, associating sounds with letters.

Slingerland, B. (2014). *Manuscript writing instructional packet*. Bellevue, WA: The Slingerland® Institute for Literacy.
Systematic handwriting instruction program incorporating many of the pioneering insights of Slingerland as explained in Chapter 1 and Chapter 3. Embeds handwriting instruction in structured language instruction at other levels of language.

Wolf, B.J. (2011). Teaching handwriting. In J. Birsh (Ed.), *Multisensory teaching of basic language skills: Theory and practice* (3rd ed., pp. 179–206). Baltimore, MD: Paul H. Brookes Publishing Co.
Teaching strategies based on both research and teaching experience that can be used with other programs.

Zaner-Bloser (Columbus, OH; http://www.zanerbloser.com/fresh/hand-writing-overview.html)
Publishes manuscript handwriting instructional programs that can be implemented in the general education classroom for all students by grade, pre-K to Grade 6.

CURSIVE HANDWRITING

Benbow, M. (1990). *Loops and groups: A kinesthetic writing system*. San Antonio, TX: Therapy Skill Builders.
Instructional activities for cursive organized by letter groups sharing common formation strokes and connecting strokes.

Slingerland, B. (2014). *Cursive writing instructional packet*. Bellevue, WA: The Slingerland® Institute for Literacy.
A contemporary approach drawing on the pioneering insights of Slingerland; see Chapter 1 in this book.

Wolf, B.J. (2011). Teaching handwriting. In J. Birsh (Ed.), *Multisensory teaching of basic language skills: Theory and practice* (3rd ed., pp. 179–206). Baltimore, MD: Paul H. Brookes Publishing Co.
Teaching strategies based on research and teaching experience that can be used with other programs.

Zaner-Bloser (Columbus, OH; http://www.zanerbloser.com/fresh/handwriting-overview.html)
Publishes cursive handwriting instructional programs that can be implemented in general education classes for all students by grade, pre-K to Grade 6.

TOUCH TYPING

Fry, E. (1999). *Dr. Fry's computer keyboarding for beginners*. Westminster, CA: Teacher Created Resources.
Lesson plans for teachers to use in the classroom.

KEYTIME (http://www.keytime.com)
Provides consultation to schools as well as private lessons. Use of standard keyboard is recommended.

King, D. (2005). *Keyboarding skills* (Rev. ed.). Cambridge, MA: Educators Publishing Service.
This program was developed specifically for students with dyslexia.

Ten Thumbs Typing Tutor (http://tenthumbstypingtutor.com)
Available online to use at school or home.

HANDWRITING TUNE-UPS AND REVIEWS

Berninger, V. (1998a). *Process Assessment of the Learner (PAL): Guides for intervention—Reading and writing.* San Antonio, TX: Pearson.
See page 193 for 24 before-and-after alphabet retrieval games, which have benefits for finding letters in memory during word reading and spelling.

Berninger, V., & Wolf, B. (2009b). *Helping students with dyslexia and dysgraphia make connections: Differentiated instruction lesson plans in reading and writing.* Baltimore, MD: Paul H. Brookes Publishing Co.
Spiral book with teaching plans from the University of Washington Research Program. See Units I, II, III, and IV for ways to do handwriting warm-ups for review of handwriting with older students in Grades 4 to 9 during reading-writing or writing workshops.

INTEGRATING HANDWRITING WITH OTHER LANGUAGE SKILLS

Berninger, V., & Abbott, S. (2003). *PAL research-supported reading and writing lessons and reproducibles.* San Antonio, TX: Pearson.
See Lesson Set 3 for early grades and Lesson Sets 7, 8, and 10 for upper-elementary grades for teaching handwriting with transfer to word spelling and text composing in mind.

Teacher Resources for Reaching Out to Parents About Handwriting and Related Skills

At the beginning of the school year teachers can send home questionnaires that include questions about handwriting and related skills that will help them identify those students who may need extra help and ongoing monitoring with their handwriting skills. The first set of questions can be asked of parents whose child is in kindergarten or first grade. The remaining questions can be asked at all grade levels. Each student should keep a writing portfolio to collect samples of their writing at school across the school year. In addition, students can keep a homework folder in which they organize the assignments they do at home but bring to school for the teacher to review with them. Finally, parent conferences in person and over phone and e-mail are helpful ways to reach out to parents to help their child in developing the necessary handwriting and technology supported skills for letter production.

PARENT QUESTIONNAIRE

1. Before kindergarten, did your child have difficulty with fine motor skills? For example, did it take longer than usual to do any of the following: Begin finger feeding? Manipulate objects during play? Play with pegboards? Control a crayon or marker to connect dots or stay in the lines within a maze? Learn to tie shoelaces?

2. Since starting school, has your child had difficulty with handwriting? If so, please explain what kinds of problems your child has had with handwriting.

3. Does your child use a laptop at home? If so, for what kinds of school-related activities? Does your child have a mobile phone? Does your child text?

WRITING PORTFOLIOS

Keep a folder for each student. Ask the student to place all written activities at school in the folder. From time to time, review the writing with the student. On a monthly basis, select written work that is representative of the work for the month. Ask students to explain how they think their writing has improved since the beginning of the year. Ask them to set goals for writing skills to work on.

HOMEWORK

Have each student keep a folder with all their homework assignments. Periodically, discuss with the student whether he or she is keeping up with assignments and the quality of his or her writing using either handwriting or keyboarding. Ask the student how much help he or she gets at home during homework.

PARENT CONFERENCES

1. *In person*: Review selective, representative work from the writing portfolio and homework folder with the parent(s). Collaboratively evaluate where the student is making progress and what skills need further attention and work.

2. *Over the telephone*: If a student is falling behind in completing written assignments in class or at home, call the parent(s) to try to gather information and problem-solve.

3. *Over e-mail or web site*: Use school-approved, web-supported tools for informing parents of assignments and writing activities at school. Be careful not to communicate information that identifies a student personally, which violates confidentiality.

Assessment–Instruction Links for Word Reading/Spelling and Related Language Processes

Word level reading (translating written words into spoken words) and spelling (translating spoken words into written words) share many common language processes, but how those common language processes become interrelated may differ in some unique ways. Nevertheless, there are benefits to assessing how both word reading and word spelling and each of the related common language processes are developing at specific grade levels. These language processes include phonological awareness, orthographic awareness, and morphological awareness.

According to Torgesen (1996) phonological awareness is the ability to notice, think about, or manipulate the individual sounds of words. Adams (1990) explained that phonological awareness is neither the ability to hear the difference between two sounds nor the ability to pronounce individual sounds. Rather, a beginning reader must understand that heard words can be segmented into small sounds and then learn to relate this sound awareness to the awareness of their representation in single letters or letter groups in written words (orthographic awareness). By convention, sounds are denoted by slashes (e.g., /k/), but letters are denoted by italics (e.g., *c*). Research shows that phonological awareness of syllables, phonemes, and onset rimes within syllables enables oral decoding during reading (translating spelling units into speech), and decoding also enables development of phonological awareness (reciprocal relationships). Learning to decode (translating written spellings into sounds) and encode (translating sounds into written spellings) also requires orthographic awareness—of the letter identities, positions, and sequences in written words—and enables development of reciprocal relationships of orthographic-phonological awareness. Students also need to recognize the affixes (prefixes at beginning of words and suffixes at the end of words) in written words and understand the morphology of language—how base words, prefixes, and suffixes can be used to decode and spell the longer, complex words that they will encounter more often in reading material in Grades 4 and above (Henry, 2003) and use in their own writing.

 # Research Lessons

Four Research Lessons are presented, each followed by one Teaching Tip, except for Research Lesson 2, which supports three Teaching Tips.

INSTRUCTION SHOULD BE LINKED TO SYSTEMATIC, DEVELOPMENTALLY APPROPRIATE ASSESSMENT OF BOTH WORD SPELLING AND READING

Research Lesson 4-1

Beginning in kindergarten and continuing through the school years, assessment should be informed by research showing which word reading and word spelling skills and processes related to learning to read and spell words should be assessed because research shows they can be taught effectively if identified at appropriate times in literacy development. Such an approach can prevent and even overcome severe SLDs. For example, dyslexia is not just a reading disorder—it is also a spelling disorder that can interfere with the development of written composition (Berninger, Nielsen, Abbott, Wijsman, & Raskind, 2008). Spelling problems may be more difficult to remediate than the reading problems in dyslexia (Lefly & Pennington, 1991; Schulte-Korne et al., 1998), especially if not treated early and throughout the school years. Thus, even in the computer age (see Chapter 11), both word spelling and word reading should be assessed to make sure they are developing normally and if not provide relevant, evidence-based instruction to facilitate their development.

TEACHING TIP 4-1: Link instructional planning to assessment at the beginning of each school year and response to instruction to reassessment at the end of each school year.

Assess developmentally appropriate word reading and spelling and related processes at the beginning of each school year and use the results to plan and implement individually tailored instruction during the school year so that students respond to instruction that year. Give the measures again at the end of the school year to assess progress. More assessment measures should be given during the K–5 grades because if student language learning is carefully monitored during those foundational years and linked to instruction, the SLDs affecting language learning are more likely to be prevented.

The goal of Chapter 4 is therefore to provide evidence-based models of which word reading or spelling skills or related processes to assess at which grade level; assessment results that identify one or more weaknesses in individual students can inform individually tailored instruction at a specific grade level.

In the text, examples of specific kinds of word reading or spelling or related skills to assess are described, organized by grade levels and referred to by their abbreviated titles by which they are known in the schools. In Appendix 4A specific assessment tools for assessing relevant skills are provided along with full names of assessment tools spelled out and citations for locating the assessment tools. Likewise, teacher resources in Appendix 4D also can be used to obtain relevant assessment information for planning and implementing instruction during the school year. Appendices 4B and 4C contain instructional tools that can be linked with assessment findings in planning or evaluating response to instruction. Thus, the text and appendices are designed to use in conjunction with each other for a developmental model for assessing word reading and spelling and related processes. Also see Chapter 13 for a discussion of how a multidisciplinary team can support the general education teacher in 1) conducting the assessments to identify students needing individually tailored instruction for specific word reading or spelling or related skills, and 2) implementing that instruction. Appendix 4A also indicates whether the test can be given in a group or requires individual administration.

EVIDENCE-BASED ASSESSMENT

At each grade level, choose and administer at least one measure of each of the *skills* from Appendix 4A at the beginning of the school year. Repeat it at the end of the school year to monitor progress during that school year.

Kindergarten

Naming alphabet letters. This skill requires cross code integration of spoken names and orthographic letter forms used in word reading and spelling. Use the same assessment as for handwriting in kindergarten as described in Chapter 3. Use index cards with one lowercase and one uppercase manuscript letter on each. Scramble the cards. Ask the student to name each letter. Record on a teacher-prepared, duplicated form which letters are named correctly and which ones are missed.

Copying alphabet letters. This skill assesses ability to produce letter forms by hand from a model. Research has shown that writing letters facilitates perception of letters in learning to read. Use the same index cards as for naming alphabet letters and ask the student to copy the letter on lined paper with appropriate spacing for kindergarteners. Again record on a teacher-prepared, duplicated form which letters are copied correctly and which are missed.

Phonological awareness. Ability to hold spoken words in memory and analyze component sounds in them is needed to respond to early reading and writing instruction. Give PAL-II RW Rhymes, Syllables, Phonemes items at the kindergarten level.

Orthographic awareness. Ability to hold viewed words in memory and analyze component letters in them is needed to respond to early reading and writing instruction. Give PAL-II W Receptive Coding (whole words, single letters, letter groups) items at the kindergarten level.

First Grade

Phonological awareness. For the same reason as in kindergarten, give PAL-II RW—Syllable and Phoneme items at the first grade level.

Orthographic awareness. For the same reason as in kindergarten, give PAL-II RW—Receptive coding (whole word, single letters, letter groups) items at the kindergarten level.

Rapid automatic naming (RAN) letters. By first grade, the speed of cross-code integration of spoken name codes and written letter codes is important in enabling students to respond to word reading and spelling instruction. Give Wolf and Denckla RAN Letters.

Accuracy of oral real word reading in isolation. At the beginning of first grade, students will differ as to whether they can or cannot pronounce real words on a list; and if they can, at what grade level, which is relevant for grouping them at their instructional levels for reading. Give WJ III Letter and Word Identification or other measure listed under real word reading.

Accuracy of oral pseudoword decoding, an index of decoding—pronouncing nonwords without meaning. At the beginning of first grade, it is important to assess whether students are able to apply the alphabetic principle to decode unknown words or are only able to read familiar words from multiple exposures. Give WJ III Word Attack or other measure listed under Pseudoword Reading (pronounceable nonwords).

Accuracy of word-specific spelling identification. Ability to integrate spelling, pronunciation, base words with affixes, and semantic meanings underlies accurate word reading and spelling. Give PAL-II Word Choice (choose the correctly spelled word among choices that when pronounced sound like real words) at first grade level. Score for accuracy and rate.

Second Grade

Phonological awareness. For the same reasons as in first grade, give PAL-II RW Syllables and Phonemes.

Orthographic awareness. For the same reasons as in first grade, give PAL-II RW Receptive Coding (whole words, single letters, letter groups).

RAN letters. For the same reasons as in first grade, give Wolf and Denckla RAN.

Accuracy and rate of oral real word reading in isolation. Beginning in second grade assess both the accuracy (give WJ III Letter and Word Identification) and rate (TOWRE Sight Word Reading Efficiency) of pronouncing real words on a list.

Accuracy and rate of oral pseudoword reading. In the early grades it is important to monitor whether students are really learning to decode unfamiliar words. Beginning in second grade, assess both accuracy (give WJ III Word Attack) and rate (give TOWRE Phonemic Reading Efficiency) of decoding pronounceable nonwords without meaning.

Word-specific spelling identification. For the same reasons as for first grade, give PAL-II RW Word Choice. Score for accuracy and rate.

Accuracy of dictated spelling. Beginning in second grade, it is important to monitor if students are learning to spell in handwriting from dictation real words (give WIAT III Spelling) and pseudowords (give WJ III Spell Sounds).

Third Grade

Phonological awareness. For the same reasons as in first grade, assesses phonological awareness but give grade-appropriate deletion tasks. Give PAL-II RW Phoneme, and Rime Deletion. Rimes are the part of the syllable with the onset phoneme deleted.

Orthographic awareness. For the same reasons as in first grade, assess orthographic coding. Give PAL-II RW Receptive Coding (whole words, single letters, letter groups).

RAN letters. For the same reasons as in first grade, give Wolf and Denckla RAN.

Rapid Automatic Switching letters and numerals. In third grade, also give Wolf and Denckla RAS because decoding polysyllabic words requires frequent switching of attention across graphemes within and across syllables.

Accuracy and rate of oral real word reading in isolation. For the same reasons, give the same measures as in second grade.

Accuracy and rate of oral pseudoword reading. For the same reasons, give the same measures as in second grade.

Accuracy and rate of word-specific spelling identification. For the same reasons, give the same measures as in second grade.

Accuracy of dictated spelling—real words and pseudowords. For the same reasons, give the same measures as in second grade.

Fourth and Fifth Grades

Phonological awareness. Increasingly students have to hold longer and longer heard words in working memory to analyze component sounds and accurately reproduce them. Give CTOPP Nonword Repetition. For those who continue to struggle with analyzing sounds, also give PAL-II RW Phonemes and Rimes.

Orthographic awareness. After the transition from the primary to the intermediate grades, students not only need to hold and analyze spelling units in the mind's eye but also reproduce them in handwriting. Give PAL-II RW Expressive Coding (whole words, single letters, and letter groups).

Morphological awareness. After the transition from the primary to the intermediate grades, students need to analyze the morphology of increasingly longer and more complex words. Give PAL-II RW Is It A Real Fix? (deciding if common spelling pattern is a true prefix or suffix), Does It Come From? (deciding if one word in a pair is derived from the other word in the pair), Does It Fit? (deciding if an affixed pseudoword could fit the blank in the sentence syntax).

RAN letters. For the same reasons as in the earlier grades, give Wolf and Denckla RAN.

Rapid automatic switching (RAS) attention—letters and numbers. For the same reason as in third grade, give Wolf and Denckla RAS.

Rate of oral real word reading in isolation. For the same reasons, give the same measure as in third grade.

Rate of oral pseudoword reading. For the same reasons, give the same measure as in third grade.

Accuracy and rate of oral morphological decoding. After the transition to reading increasingly longer and more complex words, it is necessary to assess decoding when the affixes on the base words changes. These changes affect the phonology and orthography of the base words. Give PAL-II RW Morphological Decoding.

Accuracy and rate of word-specific spelling identification. For the same reasons as in the earlier grades, give PAL-II Word Choice. Score for accuracy and rate.

Accuracy and rate of silent sentence comprehension. As children transition to mainly silent reading at school, it is important to assess that they are integrating their word identification with their sentence-level syntax comprehension). Give PAL-II RW Sentence Sense. Score for accuracy and rate.

Accuracy of dictated spelling—real words and pseudowords. For the same reasons, give the same measures as in third grade.

Sixth to Eighth Grades

Dictated spelling. It is important to continue to monitor spelling skills. Give WIAT III Spelling.

Word-specific spelling. It is important to continue to monitor word-specific spelling skills (with PAL-II RW up to Grade 6) and TOC Word Choice (throughout the middle school grades) as well as abstraction of orthotactic patterns (give TOC Word Scrambles).

Follow-up with diagnostic individual assessment of skills assessed in earlier years depending on review of possible difficulties reported by last year's teacher or parents.

Ninth to Twelfth Grades

Same as Grades 6 to 8.

- If a student is below the average range for the age or grade on word reading or spelling measures used for assessment (see Appendix 4A), select a grade appropriate word reading or spelling program from the resources in Appendix 4B and Appendix 4C, which contain full citations and sources for locating them. These are meant to be representative but not exhaustive. Use the remaining Teaching Tips in Chapter 4, and also relevant information gleaned from teacher resources in Appendix 4C, in implementing chosen word-reading and spelling program(s). Again, Chapter 4 and its appendices are designed to be used in conjunction.

- At the end of the school year, administer the word reading and spelling measures given at the beginning of the year again to assess word reading and spelling progress across the school year. At all grade levels, integrate word reading and spelling instruction with teaching other written language skills, such as passage reading and composing, respectively, using resources in Chapter 4 appendices or teacher-designed ones.

ENGLISH IS A MORPHOPHONEMIC ORTHOGRAPHY
Research Lesson 4-2

Because English is a morphophonemic orthography, phonological, orthographic, and morphological skills need to be taught to read and spell English. Phonics (i.e., alphabetic principle) is necessary (Balmuth, 2009) but not sufficient. English is a morphophonemic orthography (see Nagy & Anderson, 1999; Venezky, 1970, 1999), meaning that instruction should explicitly direct students' attention to the phonology, orthography, and morphology involved in reading and spelling words (see Henry, 1988, 1989, 1990, 1993; Nunes & Bryant, 2006). Effective instruction therefore includes learning activities for developing phonological, orthographic, and morphological awareness. Because both those with and without dyslexia or other SLDs may show individual differences in their development of phonological, orthographic, and morphological skills needed for both word reading and spelling, instruction should be tailored to developing stepping stones for each of the three kinds of linguistic awareness and individual differences in reaching these developmental milestones (for a review, see Garcia, Abbott, & Berninger, 2010). Explicit strategies for teaching the interrelationships among the three kinds of linguistic awareness should also be taught for both word reading and word spelling (see Berninger & Wolf, 2009a; Henry, 1988, 1989, 1990, 1993; Nunes & Bryant, 2006).

Although some evidence points to strategic stages in spelling development from phonological to orthographic to morphological (e.g., Templeton & Bear, 1992), other evidence suggests that all three processes—phonological, orthographic, and morphological—contribute jointly to spelling throughout writing development beginning in the elementary school years (Garcia et al., 2010). However, how the three word forms and their parts are related to each other may change with writing development (e.g., Berninger, Raskind, et al., 2008). For example, when first learning to spell a new word, one may rely on conscious strategies for transforming subword phonological units into orthographic and morphological units (e.g., Treiman, 1993). Once the word is familiar and practiced until the spelling is recalled automatically (e.g., Steffler, Varnhagen, Friesen, & Treiman, 1998), spelling then relies on accessing or retrieving a word-specific, precise spelling in the autonomous orthographic lexicon. As students learn to spell longer and morphologically more complex words, they rely on morphological spelling rules that specify spelling at the end of a base word and beginning of suffixes that are affixed to the base word (e.g., Dixon & Engelmann, 2001).

When all the language processes are working together in concert, the autonomous orthographic lexicon supports automatic direct retrieval of word-specific spellings from implicit memory. Spelling may appear deceptively on the surface to be a mechanical skill because it does not require conscious attention to integrate it with composing processes in a fluent manner. However, the research evidence shows that spelling is a complex skill drawing on many language processes, including vocabulary meaning, acquired over time (Stahl & Nagy, 2005).

TEACHING TIP 4-2A: Teach each of the three kinds of linguistic awareness.

Teaching Phonological Awareness Teaching phonological awareness requires more than teaching phoneme awareness. Students benefit from learning the six types of syllables (Moats, 2000):

1. Closed syllables have one vowel that has a short sound and end with a consonant (e.g., *flip, cast, drop, tub, them*).

2. Open syllables end in a vowel, and the vowel is long (e.g., *go, me*). Two-syllable words such as *secret* contain both open (initial long vowel) and closed (final short vowel) syllables.

3. Vowel–consonant–e syllables have a vowel followed by a consonant and a silent *e*, which indicates that the vowel before the consonant is long (e.g., *safe, bike, hope, these*).

4. Vowel team syllables have two letters together that stand for one phoneme. In vowel digraphs, the phoneme is one of the possible options for a letter in the pair, such as *ai* (e.g., *m-ai-n*). In a vowel diphthong, the letter-pair stands for a new sound that does not correspond to either single letter, such as *oi* (e.g., *j-oi-n*). Point out to students that *w* and *y* are usually consonants but may be vowels in vowel diphthongs (e.g., *t-ow-n* or *b-oy*).

5. R-controlled syllables are letter pairs containing a vowel followed by *r*, which together represent a new vowel sound not corresponding to either the vowel letter or *r* alone (e.g., *arm, term, bird, for, hurt*).

6. Consonant–le syllables are spelling units in which the sounds are pronounced in a different sequence (/schwa/ → /l/) than they are spelled (*le*). Syllable boundaries between this syllable and the preceding syllable depend on speed of pronouncing the word (e.g., *puddle, giggle*), which might be segmented so that the consonant preceding the *le* syllable is heard at the end of the preceding syllable or beginning of the *le* syllable.

Simply teaching phonics may not be sufficient. The most impressive gains in reading achievement may occur when students receive both phonological awareness and phonics instruction. Kaufman (1995) proposed six phonological awareness activities, which have been incorporated in various ways in many research studies and found to be effective:

1. *Rhyming tasks:* Students must learn to attend to the sounds of the words, not just the meaning. Teachers should begin by explaining what a rhyme

is and providing examples. Many students think that words rhyme if they begin with the same sounds, so the teacher should make it clear that only words that share ending sounds rhyme. As students develop proficiency, the teacher can use the cloze procedure in which the students supply the rhyming word (e.g., "Little Jack Horner sat in the _____.").

2. *Categorization tasks:* To promote further development of phonological awareness, the teacher can introduce activities in which students categorize spoken words on the basis of shared sound units. For example, they might indicate the one that does not go with the others on the basis of rhyme endings (e.g., *book, look, like, took*) or beginning phonemes (e.g., *boy, toy, bat, buy*).

3. *Syllable identification tasks:* These tasks are the next developmentally appropriate phonological task (Brady, Fowler, Stone, & Winebury, 1994). In these tasks, students are asked to find word parts in various positions throughout the word. For example, the teacher can identify a word part (e.g., /all/), and the students must tell whether that syllable appears in the words the teacher names (e.g., *fall, tall, ran, land, always, recall, baker, farmer*).

4. *Segmenting and blending tasks:* Blending is introduced once the student can segment by words. Next, students are asked to segment spoken words by breaking off the first phoneme and then subsequent phonemes of a word or syllable. This analytical activity requires insight that sounds can be isolated. Next, students are asked to synthesize—that is, blend. If necessary, the student might repeat /c/ /a/ /t/, then blend *cat*. This synthesizing activity is generally thought to be easier than analytic tasks that break whole words apart. However, it has a memory component that requires students to recall sounds in sequence while resynthesizing before repeating the word.

5. *Phoneme manipulation tasks:* In these tasks, students are asked to manipulate the phonemes in a word and then a nonword (Liberman, Shankweiler, Fischer, & Carter, 1974). The initial or ending consonants may be changed, or the vowel may be changed or reordered in a word (e.g., *split, spilt*). Alternatively, the student may be asked to add or delete phonemes (e.g., *cap, casp, clasp*). Kaufman (1995) recommended using words that are only partially decodable with older students so that they have to think about the sounds rather than specify spelling-sound correspondences.

6. *Word segmentation tasks in sentences:* Word segmentation tasks (Brady et al., 1994) require the insight that words can be isolated throughout a spoken sentence, which has a musical melody holding the spoken words together. Teachers may also request that students say a part of the phrase and decide what to omit. Appropriately leveled readers or storybooks can supply sentences, or teachers can make up their own.

The lesson sets in Berninger and Wolf (2009a) include research-supported approaches to incorporate phonological awareness activities into reading and writing instruction for students in Grades 4–9 who struggle with written language learning.

Teaching Orthographic Awareness

Appendix 4B provides orthographic awareness activities that are based on research and can be used for teaching handwriting, word reading/decoding, and spelling. In addition, orthographic awareness learning activities can be used in conjunction with phonological awareness learning activities for students in Grades 4–9, as shown in Berninger and Wolf (2009b). For high-frequency word families for teaching spoken and written rimes in onset-rimes, see the companion reproducibles in Berninger and Abbott (2003, p. 47).

Teaching Morphological Awareness

Sometimes, base words are referred to as *roots* when they have been modified by an affix; the transformed base word is the root of the newly formed word. Prefixes give shades of meaning to base words, which may or may not already have one or more suffixes affixed to them; for example, *premeeting* has one prefix (*pre-*) and one suffix (*-ing*) and *reconnections* has one prefix (*re-*) and two suffixes (*-ion* and *-s*). However, suffixes do more than modify shades of meaning—they transform grammatical functions of base words. Inflectional suffixes mark tense (e.g., past versus present), number (e.g., singular versus plural), and comparison (e.g., of two items or more than two items). Derivational suffixes transform part of speech (e.g., the verb *build* becomes a noun by adding the suffix *-er* to form *builder*).

Begin to teach inflectional suffixes in second grade, prefixes in third grade, and derivational suffixes in fourth grade; however, it will probably take a number of years until the affix system is fully mastered (see Nagy, Osborn, Winsor, & O'Flahavan, 1994). For example, teach that *lock* is what you do, *locking* is what you are doing, *locked* is what you did, *locks* means you have more than one lock or tells what someone does, and *locker* means something or one that locks. Prefixes change the meaning of a base word. *Unlock,* for example, is the opposite of *lock.* Some approaches to decoding recommend that students identify the affixes first and then decode the base word and synthesize it with the affixes. Other approaches encourage students to look for the base word first to find meaning, then deal with affixes. In a word such as *reconstruction,* for example, students would look for a word part that they recognize, such as *construct,* and then identify the prefix *re-* and the suffix *-ion.* Students can benefit from the explicit teaching of both approaches. Nunes and Bryant (2006) showed that pronunciation is typically predictably constant across suffix spellings, even when alphabetic principle cannot be applied to spell all the suffixes. By identifying affixes first, the student is breaking the word into smaller, recognizable, and manageable pieces and is more able to recognize each unit.

TEACHING TIP 4-2B: Explicitly teach phonological, orthographic, and morphological awareness in reference to the order of their developmental stepping stones, which follow.

For phonological awareness: syllable awareness → phoneme awareness → onset-rime awareness → accent patterns in polysyllabic words

For orthographic awareness: receptive coding (letter sequence in whole word, single letter in word position, letter group in word position decision), followed by expressive orthographic coding (letter sequence of whole word, single letter, letter group written output)

For morphological awareness: *-ing* and the inflectional suffixes for tense, number, and comparison (e.g., *-s, -es, -d, -ed, -er, -est*) → prefixes → derivational suffixes for marking part of speech (e.g., transforming verbs like *run* into nouns like *runner* or nouns like *nation* into adjectives like *national*)

In addition, beginning in the preschool years, developing language learners abstract patterns from spoken and written words. For spoken words, they abstract phonotactic patterns for identity of component sounds, permissible positions of specific sounds words, and permissible sequencing of sounds in spoken/heard words. For written words, they abstract orthotactic patterns for identity of component letters, permissible positions of specific letters, and permissible sequencing of letters in read/written words. For both heard/spoken and read/written words, they abstract morphotactic patterns for base words and affixes at the beginning of base word (prefix) and end of base word (suffix).

TEACHING TIP 4-2C: Explicitly teach multiple strategies for interrelating phonology, orthography, and morphology in word reading in developmentally appropriate ways.

Students need to develop not only awareness of phonology, orthography, and morphology but also strategies for interrelating these different aspects of language to decoding and spelling. Slingerland and Murray's (2008) teacher's word lists can be used as a source of words in teaching the many strategies of decoding, including, but not restricted to, phonics.

Students also have to be taught to apply their phonological, orthographic, and morphological awareness to decoding written words so that they can pronounce them during oral reading or identify them during silent reading. The goal is to provide structured, guided practice in applying the three kinds of linguistic awareness to the word decoding/identification process.

It is usually advisable to begin with the sequential application of the alphabetic principle across the written word from left to right because the grapheme–phoneme correspondences in written English are typically more predictable than syllable boundaries, as is explained later in this section. Decoding instruction should move from simple unambiguous words with short vowels in closed syllables (ending in a consonant) to long vowels in open syllables (ending in a vowel), diphthongs (two vowel letters, one new sound; e.g., *oi*), vowel digraphs (two vowel letters corresponding to one vowel in the letter combination [e.g., *ay*]; or two consonant letters, with one sounding different from either alone [e.g., *ch*]), and *r*- and *l*-controlled vowels that are pronounced differently than if the vowel was not followed by an *l* in a different context (e.g., *salt* versus *sat*) or an *r* in a different context (e.g., *short* versus *shot*). Because many of the graphemes in the English alphabetic principle involve two letters rather than one letter, it is important to weave this into teaching the decoding process in a left-to-right direction across sequential, adjacent graphemes. One way is to print out the words for decoding in the daily lesson in alternating black and red graphemes so that attention is drawn to the letter or letter group in the grapheme.

Students also need specific structured teaching in decoding contractions and possessives. For example, students can be asked to convert two words (e.g., *can, not*) into a contraction (e.g., *can't*) and dissect a contraction (e.g., *don't*) into its word parts (e.g., *do, not*). They can also be asked to use words that are pronounced the same but spelled differently depending on whether the word signals possession (e.g., *The boys' toys were lost*) or does not signal possession (e.g., *The boys lost their toys*).

Syllables may also be described by patterns of consonants (C), vowels (V), and consonant blends (two or three letters that are pronounced in sequence very fast to avoid a vowel intrusion (e.g., /b/-/short u or schwa/-/l/ for /bl/). The following sequence, organized by level of difficulty, is often used in teaching decoding:

CVC	*hat*
CVCC	*hand*
CCVC	*clap*
CCVCC	*craft*
CCCVC	*splat*

When teaching students to decode multisyllabic words, it is important to keep in mind that the timing of spoken syllables is not uniform in the English language (Venezky, 1970, 1999). Consider the oral pronunciations of *basket*, in which syllable boundaries may be between the two consonants (*s* and *k*) or after the consonant blend *sk*. Therefore, it is important for teachers to not teach rigid rules about syllabication based only on written syllable patterns. It is often helpful to have students say the word syllable by syllable, write the word syllable by syllable, and also clap the relative stress patterns of each syllable in a multisyllabic word both in and out of a sentence context (the musical melody or prosody of words read orally). Also, when teaching polysyllabic words, it is important to introduce the schwa—an unaccented vowel that may or may not form its own syllable but can be spelled with any of the vowel letters, rather than a predictable phoneme–grapheme correspondence in alphabetic principle.

Teachers should provide guidance in helping students decode, but other students may provide input and reinforcement while one student is practicing the decoding process. This prosocial, cooperative learning approach teaches important social skills along with reading.

Students develop independence by applying decoding skills in many situations, moving from words in isolation to words in text—from guidance to independence. Decoding practice may be provided in many ways. A very helpful approach is to select a set of 5–10 target words that will be in the text used for the daily guided reading lesson and have the group practice decoding them at beginning of the reading lesson before students read the text independently. However, many students learn to decode words in isolation but do not automatically apply their skills when reading. Independent seat activities following the guided reading lessons should offer students practice in transferring their decoding skills to a variety of words and reading activities.

When each decoding concept is mastered, teachers can play games such as Tic-Tac-Toe with the whole class. To begin the game, the teacher calls on one student, who at end of his or her turn calls on the next student, until all words are decoded. If the student decodes correctly, he or she may place an X or an O in the Tic-Tac-Toe box on the board. Because the students do not know which team they are on, every student cheers for everyone. The goal of the game is not only to read the word correctly but also to practice the decoding process.

For students who struggle in learning to decode, the teacher should keep in mind that some students struggle as a result of difficulty in directing their attention from left to right across sequential spelling units (one- and two-letter units that correspond to phonemes) embedded in written words. Others have difficulty remembering the sounds that go with spelling units—they may forget the beginning sounds or omit sounds elsewhere in the word and need to start over. Still other students can produce the correct sounds in order but cannot synthesize them to construct a whole spoken word. Vowels often pose the biggest challenge in the decoding process because their position in the word (whether the neighboring letters are another vowel, *r*, *l*, or a final *e*) determines the sound the spelling unit will make and the number of syllables.

Not all students may be in the same place at the same time in their journey for learning the multiple ways to interconnect phonology, orthography, and morphology to read and spell a morphophonemic orthography. Students can learn to make multiple connections between written and spoken words for oral decoding of written words and written encoding/spelling of spoken words in the following evidence-based ways organized as developmental stepping stones:

- Connections between one- or two-letter graphemes and phonemes in reading direction for oral reading (Berninger et al., 1999) and between phonemes and one- or two-letter graphemes in spelling direction for written spelling (Berninger et al., 1998) in the early grades

- Connections between written onsets (initial one- or two-letter grapheme) and rimes (remaining letters in a written syllable, often referred to as a *word family*) and oral onsets (initial one or two blended phonemes) and rimes (remaining sound unit in spoken syllable), as well as connections between oral onsets and rimes and written onsets and rimes in syllables (Berninger et al., 2000) in the early grades

- Connections between written bases and suffixes and oral bases and suffixes (with or without phonological shifts in pronounced base words for added suffix) in reading direction (Carlisle, 2000a) or between spoken bases and suffixes (with or without orthographic shifts in the written word in the spelling direction; Carlisle, 1994) in the middle grades

- Connections among phonotactic (Apel, Oster, & Masterson, 2006; Treiman, Kessler, Knewasser, Tincoff, & Bowman, 2000), orthotactic (Apel et al., 2006; Pacton, Fayol, & Perruchet, 2005; Pacton, Perruchet, Fayol, & Cleeremans, 2001), and morphotactic (Pacton et al., 2005) patterns in the middle grades

The first three—grapheme–phoneme correspondences, onset rimes, and bases and affixes—involve conscious, strategic *slow mapping* across spoken and written or written and spoken words. However, some students can rely on fast mapping outside conscious awareness of abstracted phonotactic, orthotactic, and morphotactic patterns in spoken and/or written words (Bahr et al., 2009). Both slow and fast mapping contribute at all grade levels.

EXPLICIT, SYSTEMATIC SPELLING INSTRUCTION IS STILL NEEDED DESPITE COMPUTER SPELL CHECKS
Research Lesson 4-3

Just because a student is learning to read words, it does not follow that the student can spell all those words; thus, both must be taught. Effective instruction may differ for word reading and spelling. For word reading, the most effective instruction for learning taught and transfer words (the same graphemes or phonemes but in different word contexts) included the alphabetic principle and naming all the letters in the whole word (Berninger, Abbott, et al., 1998). For word spelling, combined naming of all letters in the whole word *and* training in onset rimes transferred best to taught and transfer word spelling, but the alphabetic principle (in the phoneme-to-grapheme direction) transferred best to spelling during independent composing (Berninger, Vaughn et al., 1998).

Like decoding and word identification, spelling requires applying the alphabetic principle (but in the spelling direction, which is not completely the same as the reading direction in English), as well as the phonological, orthographic, and morphological cues for encoding a word (i.e., transforming a dictated spoken word or internal pronunciation linked to meaning, letter patterns, and morphology) into a written spelling. Spelling problems can interfere with the written composition of students (Berninger, Nielsen, et al., 2008) and adults (Connelly, Campbell, MacLean, & Barnes, 2006) with dyslexia; and spelling is also related to development of composing in typically developing writers (Abbott, Berninger, & Fayol, 2010.

TEACHING TIP 4-3: Teach spelling (encoding from spoken to written language) explicitly and systematically in English, a morphophonemic orthography.

Spelling is a complex process. It is not rote memorization that relies totally on visual recall. The sound sequences, letter patterns, and morphemes depend to a large extent on word origin—whether a word is of Anglo-Saxon, Latinate, French, or Greek origin (Henry, 2003). Words connected by meaning are also connected by spelling. The silent *b* at the end of the word *bomb* is articulated in the words *bombard* and *bombardment*. Morphology often preserves the spelling of the meaningful parts of words, although pronunciation may vary, as in *define* and *definition* or *doubt* and *dubious.*

Multimodal methods for spelling instruction teach students to repeat the word, listen to the sounds in sequence, think of each vowel sound in the word, associate it with the letter or letters that spell the vowel sound, repeat the word, recall the sounds of words in sequence, and spell the whole word. Repeating the word helps students to hear sounds in sequence and feel the speech production in sequence. Listening for the vowel sounds allows students to address difficult and ambiguous parts of the word first. Repeating the word again allows students to once more hear and feel the sounds in sequence and associate them with their letter counterparts, which is necessary for spelling the word in writing.

Teachers should consider the order in which phonics elements are introduced for spelling in writing dictated spoken words. After teachers introduce students to five or six consonants, they can then introduce the letter *a*, which stands for the short vowel sound for /a/ as in *cat*. Presenting too many phonic elements at once can overload some beginning students and does not allow sufficient practice to build the functional use of spelling. Once the highly predictable correspondences are taught, options are taught for spelling the same sound (e.g., *ee* as in *feet* and *ea* as in *bead*); Venezky (1970, 1999) called these "alternations." Other students benefit from learning all the high frequency sound-spelling correspondences in a relatively short time period so they can rely on them while spelling during their own composing.

Students should practice recalling the correct option for a particular word with a specific meaning. Teach students to use the most common alternatives first. They should learn that when they hear the long /a/ at the end of a word, they will have several choices of spelling, but some (e.g., *ai, ei*) will not occur at the end of the word. Thus, the position of a sound or letter in a word is also informative, in addition to spelling–phoneme correspondences and syllables. When the correct choice is made, the student spells the word.

Teachers can check the dictionary for correct spellings while the class observes. Depending on the age and reading ability of the students, the teacher or a student may read the definition. If the word does not appear in the dictionary, try an alternative spelling. Eventually, students may check the dictionary independently. Students learn words that sound the same, are spelled differently, and have different meanings. Students can also create their own dictionaries with words they use frequently in their writing (see companion reproducibles, pp. 14–40, in Berninger & Abbott, 2003).

Students need to understand the factors that govern spelling word origin, syllabication, and generalizations. Many words in reading texts and students' written productions in the first three grades are one- or two-syllable high-frequency words of Anglo-Saxon origin. Many of the words in textbooks and students' written production in the upper grades, however, are of Latinate origin (often three to five syllables with unaccented schwas) or Greek origin, with some different spelling–sound correspondences and morpheme patterns than words of Anglo-Saxon origin (Balmuth, 2009; Henry, 2003). In addition, vowel sounds and spellings are often governed by their placement in the word. Here are a few examples for words of Anglo-Saxon origin:

1. If the syllable is closed (consonant–vowel–consonant), the vowel sound will be short.

2. Vowels at the end of accented syllables are usually long, as in *baby, secret, tiger, pony,* and *music.*

3. The vowel at the end of an unaccented syllable may have a schwa (reduced vowel sound), as in *away* or *afraid.*

4. These multiletter consonant groups—*ck, dge, tch*—occur immediately after a short vowel.

5. The letters *f, l, s,* and *z* are doubled at the end of a one-syllable short-vowel word.

Morphology is also relevant to spelling. Words that share the same root may have similar but not identical spellings (e.g., *sign, signal*). Understanding the past tense suffix *-ed* is important in beginning spelling. It may be pronounced /d/, /t/, or /ed/, but spelling errors are less likely to occur if students understand that the past tense suffix is spelled *-ed* for all three sounds (except for a few exceptions that remain from Old Anglo-Saxon English, such as *knelt, slept,* and *crept*).

There are three consistent spelling rules for adding suffixes to one-syllable words:

1. The *doubling* or *one-one-one rule* refers to words of one syllable ending in one consonant after one vowel. The final consonant is doubled if the suffix being added begins with a vowel (e.g., *running*).

2. The *silent e rule* refers to the silent *e* being dropped if the suffix being added begins with a vowel (e.g., *hiked*). If it does not begin with a vowel, simply add the suffix (e.g., *wisely*).

3. The *y rule* refers to changing the *y* to an *i* if the suffix being added begins with a vowel (e.g., *candied*), except when the suffix begins with an *i* (e.g., *carrying*).

Spelling is related to word reading, but it is not the mirror image of word reading. For example, if one applies the alphabetic principle to spelling words, the number of correspondences between a phoneme and a grapheme (one- or two-letter spelling unit) is greater in the direction of translating spoken words into written words than in the direction of translating written words into spoken words. For example, the single letter *a* is typically associated with a long /a/ sound (in an open or silent *e* syllable), a short /a/ sound (in a closed syllable), or a schwa (reduced vowel). However, the long /a/ phoneme could be spelled with the letter *a* in an open or silent *e* syllable, or the letters *ai* as in *gain*, *ay* as in *say*, *ey* as in *they*, *eigh* as in *weigh*, or *ea* as in *great*. That is, in the sound-to-spelling direction, English has more alternations or options than in the spelling-to-sound direction. These options can be called *substitutes* in the spelling direction and *nicknames* in the reading direction to draw explicit awareness to the alphabet principle in both directions, with its alternations (see companion reproducibles, pp. 41–46, in Berninger & Abbott, 2003) for charts students can keep at their desk to help them access the optional correspondences. A good analogy that teachers can tell students is that, just like a coach substitutes players so that one player does not get too tired, English substitutes different spelling units for the same sound so that no one spelling unit is overworked or gets too tired.

The spelling bee—once a mainstream instructional activity in the little red schoolhouse in rural America—is regaining popularity. Local, state, regional, and national competitions are being held, and both television and movies are featuring stories about spelling bees. Many spelling bees allow students to ask before spelling a word if they are uncertain about a particular word. The types of questions students ask are revealing about the processes that contribute to word spelling. Some ask for the meaning—a definition. Some ask for the word to be used in a sentence. Some ask for it to be pronounced again. Others ask for word origin. Students who participate in spelling bees typically use meaning cues, the associated sounds, and the sound and morpheme cues specific to word origin to help them remember or construct the most probable word spelling. Spelling is a meaning-driven skill that draws on phonological, ortho-graphic, and morphological aspects of words and is fundamentally important for transcribing thoughts in creating written text.

In addition to words of Anglo-Saxon, Latinate and French, and Greek ori-gins, other words are making their way into American English from computer technology and the large waves of families moving to the United States from all over the world. For example, in the Seattle area, a recent count by one of the large school systems in the region showed that 161 languages were spoken by families of students in the school system. Words are dynamic, flexible linguis-tic units that are continually being added to the spoken and written language. General education teachers can include in spelling instruction some of these words from the languages spoken by students in their classrooms.

Good spellers may be able to rely on fast mapping (one or a few expo-sures) to initially learn how to spell words (Apel et al., 2006), as well as how to read them. Because good spellers are sensitive to the phonotactic and orthotactic structures (i.e., the probable identity, sequencing, and positioning of sounds within spoken words and letters in written words, respectively) within their implicit, unconscious memory, fast mapping results in accurate spelling; therefore, these students may seem like natural spellers. In contrast, students with dyslexia or dysgraphia impairing spelling do not have typical phonotactic and/or orthotactic sensitivity and cannot rely on fast mapping to the same extent as good spellers when learning to spell. Rather, these students need to rely on slow mapping in which they apply phonological-orthographic strategies, such as the alphabetic principle (phoneme-to-grapheme direction), onset and rime, lexical naming of spoken words and all the letters in a word, and morphological strategies in conscious working memory to learn to spell words.

General education teachers can accommodate students who do and do not learn to spell easily because all students benefit from explicit instruc-tion and instructional activities focused on mapping of phonological, orthographic, and morphological word forms and their parts. Such explicit instruction does not have to be confined to direct transmission of informa-tion. It can also include activities to promote enjoyment of words, includ-ing word play for humor, as in riddles and puns; multiple meanings for the same sound patterns, as in homonyms; and word hunts to find words that have certain morphological or other characteristics. For examples of this kind of instruction, see Berninger and Abbott (2003). One tutor in the after-school clubs designed to help students score better on the state's high-stakes test shared her surprise when play with words was combined with direct instruction strategies. Four reluctant fourth-grade writers started consulting a dictionary spontaneously and were engaged in a meaningful discussion about word spelling and word meaning related to an independent writing assignment. The transfer of spelling to written composition is most likely if spelling lessons are followed immediately by composition activities in which students write freely on grade-appropriate topics (Berninger et al., 1998) or are asked to use grade-appropriate, high-frequency spelling words in their compositions (Berninger, Vaughan, et al., 2000).

Research supports the following guidelines for teaching spelling:

1. *Less is more.* In what might be the first scientific research on instructional practices, Rice (1897) studied spelling instruction in classrooms throughout the country. The results showed that students who received just 15 minutes of daily spelling instruction achieved higher spelling scores than those who received 1 hour a day of spelling instruction. What may matter more than absolute amount of time spent on spelling is the nature of the spelling instruction received. More time should be spent teaching spelling strategies and less time relying solely on assessing spelling once a week by giving dictation tests.

2. *Learning occurs over time.* Teaching and practicing spelling should occur in brief sessions daily that are distributed over time and occur frequently. The programmatic spelling research of Dreyer, Luke, and Melican (1995) showed that what differentiated good and poor spellers was memory for word spelling in the long run, not the short run. Thus, instructional programs for spelling should distribute spelling practice for particular words across time intervals that span several months, not just sequential days within the school week.

3. *Teach high-frequency words.* Fry (1996) incorporated the 1,000 most frequently used words into his spelling lessons for Grades 1–6; these were developed and validated over the years for students who received services in his Rutgers University clinic for learning problems. Each spelling lesson begins with teaching and practicing explicit strategies for learning to spell single high-frequency words, which are called "instant words." This strategy instruction and practice is followed by sentence dictation activities in which students practice spelling the same words in sentence context, which clarifies the meaning of each word. Sentence dictation requires that students hold multiple words in sentence syntax in conscious working memory as they spell, much as they must do when composing. Both the alphabetic principle and morphology are taught to support spelling learning. Many spelling lessons in Berninger and Abbott (2003) draw on Fry's lessons. Graham, Harris, and Loynachan (1994) created another list of grade-appropriate, high-frequency words to use in spelling instruction at different instructional levels. This list is based on the high-frequency words students use in their own compositions at various grade levels. See Lesson Set 5 in Berninger and Abbott (2003) for examples of how these high-frequency words for writing can be used in written composition activities to encourage students to learn to spell them correctly in their own writing and not just on a dictated spelling test.

4. *Teach multiple spelling strategies.* These strategies should focus on phoneme–grapheme correspondence, onset rimes, and whole words (naming each letter in the whole word; Berninger & Abbott, 2003; Berninger
et al., 1998). Students should also be taught selective reminding (Hart,
Berninger, & Abbott, 1997), in which they practice spelling a small set of
high-frequency words in each lesson, but on subsequent trials only practice those missed in the prior trials (Berninger, 1998a). Most of the phonemes in content words (nouns, verbs, adjectives, and adverbs) tend to
correspond predictably to graphemes, whereas function words (conjunctions, prepositions, pronouns, helping verbs, articles) tend to be only partially decodable compared with content words (i.e., have fewer phonemes
that correspond to conventional graphemes). However, training automatic
phoneme–grapheme correspondences, sorting phonemes into categories
for alternative possible graphemes on a substitution card (e.g., /z/ can be
spelled with *s* or *z*), and playing spelling bingo for the high-frequency,
partially decodable function words improved students' spelling of function as well as content words (Berninger, Vaughan, et al., 2002; Berninger
& Abbott, 2003).

5. *Play with language.* Word sorts (Bear, Invernizzi, Templeton, & Johnston,
2000) and riddles, puns, and jokes can be effective instructional components for spelling (e.g., Berninger, Abbott, Abbott, Graham, & Richards,
2002). Students at risk for spelling (and reading) problems may develop
an understanding of how language is used to create humor at a slower
rate than typically developing readers and spellers. For example, a sixth-
grader who had participated in several of the earlier treatment studies
finally "got" the jokes and riddles used at the beginning of each session of
the new study, while younger students in that treatment study still struggled with perceiving the humor in the word play. In a before-school club
that always began with about 10 minutes of students choosing their favorite riddle, pun, or joke of the day from paperbacks and other collections
the researchers provided, one second-grader asked her teacher—in all
seriousness—if jokes always had to be funny. Until students reach a certain level of linguistic awareness, the humor in language may not be readily apparent. Word hunts for words with specific syllable or morpheme
patterns were part of the effective writing instruction that improved writing on state high-stakes tests as well as individually administered standardized tests of composition (Berninger, Rutberg, et al., 2006).

6. *Teach orthographic strategies.* Teaching multiple orthographic strategies
resulted in improved spelling (see Mark Twain Lesson Set [Unit II] in
Berninger & Wolf, 2009b). These strategies included Photographic Lep-
rechaun (naming all the letters in a word, closing eyes and seeing the
word in the mind's eye, opening eyes and spelling word), Proofreaders
Trick (spelling the word in the mind's eye from end to beginning), Visual

Search (finding correctly spelled words in the horizontal, vertical, or diagonal rows of otherwise random letters), and Anagrams (unscrambling letters to find correctly spelled words; Dixon & Engelmann, 2001).

7. *Teach morphological strategies.* Dixon and Englemann (2001) provided strategies for building words from roots and affixes; decomposing words with affixes into their roots, prefixes, and suffixes; and morphological spelling rules. Henry (1990, 2003) and Henry and Redding (1996) described the phonological, orthographic, and morphological units in words of Anglo-Saxon, Latinate, and Greek origins. Fry (1996) included morpheme variants as applied to spelling. Berninger and Abbott (2003) provided companion reproducibles for high-frequency prefixes (pp. 54–58), inflectional suffixes (p. 49), and derivational suffixes (pp. 50–53). Students can keep these in their Personal Dictionaries and use these in both spelling and decoding instruction.

TEACH BOTH WORD READING AND SPELLING ACROSS THE CONTENT AREAS
Research Lesson 4-4

Both word reading and spelling should be taught beginning in kindergarten and throughout K–12. Initially, the focus is on decoding new words never before encountered, identifying familiar ones in reading material, and spelling new and familiar words used in learning to compose. Subsequently, the focus should be both on these same skills within the language arts curriculum and also specific to the words used in other content areas of the curriculum—math, science, and social studies.

TEACHING TIP 4-4: For students who have experienced chronic struggles in learning to read and spell, always remember the importance of teaching there is *hope*—they can learn to read and spell well across areas of the curriculum.

For students who learn to read easily, reading is magic. It is a means of delivering the thoughts and language of one person into the language and mind of another. Students who are resistant or appear to be unmotivated to read typically have been defeated in their efforts to learn the magic of reading. These students, however, usually want desperately to learn to read. In Beverly Wolf's classroom, 7-year-old Travis said, "The Christmas presents don't matter. I just need to know how to read." Third-grader Raizel said, "My dream is to be a reader."

According to Masland (1979), the magic of reading stems from the complexity of processes that must be mastered so that words can be decoded (if not familiar) or identified (if familiar) so that reading can proceed without effort. These processes include applying the alphabetic principle of grapheme-phoneme correspondences, as well as the phonological, orthographic, and morphological cues in the written words.

Many students also may have difficulty learning to spell. As one student expressed it, "If I could just write my ideas instead of having to choose only those words I can spell without embarrassment." Another sixth-grader was thrilled when the spellcheck on his computer could finally recognize his spelling well enough to provide a menu of word choices. Previously, the student's spelling was so unconventional that even spell check could not recognize it. Most important, never forget that English is a morphophonemic orthography.

Assessment of Word Reading, Spelling, and Related Skills

Assessment tools are organized by skills and within skills in alphabetical order by first author surname. Note that an asterisk (*) means individual assessment is required; otherwise the assessment tool is designed to be used in a group or can be adapted for group administration.

ORAL READING OF SINGLE REAL WORDS ON LIST WITHOUT CONTEXT CLUES: ACCURACY

*Kaufman, A., & Kaufman, N. (2012). *Kaufman Test of Educational Achievement, Third Edition (KTEA-3)*. San Antonio, TX: Pearson.
Letter and Word Recognition.

*Wechsler, D. (1991). *Wechsler Individual Achievement Test, Third Edition (WIAT III)*. San Antonio, TX: Harcourt Assessment.
Word Reading.

*Woodcock, R.W., Mather, N., & McGrew, K. (2008). *Woodcock-Johnson III Tests of Achievement (WJ III ACH)*. Rolling Meadows, IL: Riverside.
Letter and Word Identification.

ORAL READING OF SINGLE REAL WORDS WITHOUT CONTEXT CLUES AUTOMATICITY: RATE

*KTEA-3
  Timed Word Recognition.

*Torgesen, J., Wagner, R., & Rashotte, C. (1999). *Test of Word Reading Efficiency, Second Edition (TOWRE 2)*. Austin, TX: Pro-Ed.
  Sight Word Reading Efficiency.

ORAL READING OF PSEUDOWORDS: ACCURACY

*Berninger, V.W. (2007b). *Process Assessment of the Learner, Second Edition (PAL-II): Diagnostic for Reading and Writing (PAL-II RW)*. San Antonio, TX: Pearson.
  Pseudoword Reading.

*KTEA-3
  Nonword Reading.

*WIAT III
  Pseudoword Reading.

*WJ III
  Word Attack.

ORAL READING PSEUDOWORDS AUTOMATICITY: RATE

*PAL II R-W
  Pseudoword Reading.

*KTEA-3
  Nonword Reading Rate.

*TOWRE 2
  Phonemic Reading Efficiency.

SILENT WORD READING WITH AND WITHOUT CONTEXT: RATE

Hammill, D., Widerholt, J., & Allen, E. (2006). *Test of Silent Contextual Reading Fluency (TOSCRF)*. Austin, TX: Pro-Ed.

Mather, N., Hammill, D., Allen, E., & Roberts, R. (2004). *Test of Silent Word Reading Fluency (TOSWRF)*. Austin, TX: Pro-Ed.

SPELLING

PAL-II RW
  Word Choice—accuracy and rate.

Mather, N., Roberts, R., Hammill, D., & Allen, E. (2008). *Test of Orthographic Competence (TOC).* Austin, TX: Pro-Ed.
Sight Spelling.

WIAT III
Spelling.

WJ III
Supplementary Battery—Spelling Sounds.

CRITERION-REFERENCED INFORMAL READING INVENTORIES FOR IDENTIFYING INSTRUCTIONAL LEVELS: WORD READING IN AND OUT OF CONTEXT (PASSAGES)

*Leslie, L., & Caldwell, J.S. (2011). *Qualitative Reading Inventory-5 (QRI-5).* Boston, MA: Pearson.

*Woods, M.L., & Moe, A. (2003). *Analytical reading inventory* (7th ed.). Upper Saddle River, NJ: Merrill.
This inventory can be used with students in Grades 1–9 and includes three narrative forms, one social studies form, and one science form.

RELATED SKILLS
Phonological Awareness

*PAL-II RW
Rhymes, Syllables, Phonemes, Rimes.

*Wagner, R.K., Torgesen, J.K., & Rashotte, C.A. (1999). *The Comprehensive Test of Phonological Processing (CTOPP).* Austin, TX: Pro-Ed.
Nonword Repetition.

Orthographic Awareness

*PAL-II RW
Receptive Coding and Orthographic Coding.

Morphological Awareness

*PAL-II RW
Is It a True Fix? Does It Come From? Does It Fit?

*Wolf, M., & Denckla, M. (2005). *RAN/RAS Rapid Automatized Naming and Rapid Alternating Stimulus Tests.* Austin, TX: Pro-Ed.
Rapid Automatic Naming and Rapid Automatic Switching.

PLANNING INSTRUCTION BASED ON
ASSESSMENT RESULTS AND PROGRESS MONITORING

- Identify individual students who fall below the lower limit of the average range ($-\frac{2}{3}$ standard deviation or 25th percentile or standard score of 90 on a test with a most average/mean score of 100 or a scaled score of 8 on a test with a most average/mean score of 10 or a z-score of -.66z on a research measure with a most average/mean score of 0). In some schools, the interdisciplinary team may decide to also identify any students who fall below the most average/mean score (50th percentile).

- Go to Appendix 4B and choose an instructional tool for each skill that meets the first or second criterion above.

- For progress monitoring, readminister the assessment tool after the instructional program is completed.

Instructional Resources for Word Reading, Spelling, and Related Skills

Note: These resources have been used in research and teaching for students with and without specific learning disabilities (SLDs). Also see Appendix 4C for programs specially designed for students with SLDs.

SOUND GAMES (PHONOLOGICAL AWARENESS)

Adams, M., Foorman, B., Lundberg, I., & Beeler, T. (1998). *Phonemic awareness in young children: A classroom curriculum*. Baltimore, MD: Paul H. Brookes Publishing Co.

Berninger, V.W. (1998a). *Process Assessment of the Learner (PAL): Guides for intervention—Reading and writing*. San Antonio, TX: Pearson.
Sound games for phonological awareness syllables and phonemes organized by four learning activities (pp. 195–219).

LOOKING GAMES (ORTHOGRAPHIC AWARENESS) AND LEARNING ACTIVITIES FOR BASES, PREFIXES, AND SUFFIXES (MORPHOLOGICAL AWARENESS)

Berninger, V., & Abbott, S. (2003). *PAL research-supported reading and writing lessons and reproducibles*. San Antonio, TX: Pearson.
See Lesson Set 15.

Nunes, T., & Bryant, P. (2006). *Improving literacy instruction through teaching morphemes (Improving Learning Series)*. New York, NY: Routledge.
Teaches morphological awareness for words of different word origin.

PHONOLOGICAL, ORTHOGRAPHIC, AND MORPHOLOGICAL AWARENESS AND THEIR INTERCONNECTIONS

Berninger, V., & Abbott, S. (2003). *PAL research-supported reading and writing lessons and reproducibles*. San Antonio, TX: Pearson.
See Lesson Sets 11, 12, and 15 for instructional activities for teaching students in Grades 2 to 6 phonological, orthographic, and morphological awareness for words of different word origin.

Berninger, V., & Wolf, B. (2009b). *Helping students with dyslexia and dysgraphia make connections: Differentiated instruction lesson plans in reading and writing*. Baltimore, MD: Paul H. Brookes Publishing Co.
Spiral-bound book with teaching plans from the University of Washington Research Program that explain how to teach phonological, orthographic, and morphological awareness and their interrelationships to students in Grades 4 to 9.

TEACHING TO ALL LEVELS OF LANGUAGE AND LANGUAGE SYSTEMS

Berninger, V., & Abbott, S. (2003). *PAL research-supported reading and writing lessons*. San Antonio, TX: Pearson.
See Lesson Sets 11, 12, and 15 for reading lessons aimed at all levels of language and multiple language systems.

Slingerland, B. (2013). *The Slingerland® multisensory approach: A practical guide for reading, writing, and spelling* (2nd ed.). Bellevue, WA: The Slingerland® Institute.

LINKING VOCABULARY, READING, AND SPELLING

Bear, D. Ivernezzi, M., Templeton, S., & Johnston, F. (2000). *Words their way: Word study for phonics, vocabulary, and spelling instruction* (2nd ed.). Upper Saddle River, NJ: Prentice Hall.

ORAL DECODING

Balmuth, M. (2009). *The roots of phonics: A historical introduction* (Rev. ed.). Baltimore, MD: Paul H. Brookes Publishing Co.

Berninger, V., & Abbott, S. (2003). *PAL reading and writing lessons*. San Antonio, TX: The Psychological Corporation.
See Lesson Sets 1, 2, 6, 9, 11, 12, and 15.

Blachman, B., & Tangleman, D. (2008). *Road to reading: A program for preventing and remediating reading difficulties*. Baltimore, MD: Paul H. Brookes Publishing Co.

Starfall (http://www.starfall.com)
This is an interactive web site to promote early decoding skills.

SPELLING INSTRUCTION

Berninger, V., & Abbott, S. (2003). *PAL research-supported reading and writing lessons and reproducibles*. San Antonio, TX: Pearson.
See Lesson Sets 4, 5, 7, 8, 10, and 14.

Dixon, R., & Englemann, S. (2001). *Spelling through morphographs*. Columbus, OH: SRA/McGraw-Hill.
This provides a program for the next developmental stepping stone in spelling once students have completed the Dr. Fry Spelling program.

Fry, E. (1996). *Spelling book: Grades 1–6: Words most needed plus phonics*. Westminster, CA: Teacher Created Materials.
Contains lessons with words and strategies for teaching children to spell high-frequency words alone and in dictated sentences and apply phonics knowledge to spelling. Provides a placement test for placing children at their instructional levels.

Henry, M. (2010). *Unlocking literacy: Effective decoding and spelling instruction* (2nd ed.). Baltimore, MD: Paul H. Brookes Publishing Co.
Explains how to teach the decoding of words of Anglo Saxon, Latinate, and Greek origin based on the phonological, orthographic, and morphological units in words.

Masterson, J., Apel, K., & Wasowicz, J. (2006). *Spelling Performance Evaluation for Language and Literacy (SPELL 2)*. Evanston, IL: Learning by Design.
Spelling assessment software for Grade 2 through adult, with assessment linked to instruction.

Slingerland, B. (2013). *The Slingerland® Multisensory Approach: A practical guide for teaching reading, writing, and spelling* (2nd ed.). Bellevue, WA: The Slingerland® Institute.
Teaches spelling in a multimodal way integrated with other language skills.

Wasowicz, J., Apel, K., Masterson, J., & Whitney, A. (2004). *SPELL-links to reading and writing: A word study curriculum and supplemental program for K–adult*. Evanston, IL: Learning by Design.

Zaner-Bloser Spelling Connections (https://www.zaner-bloser.com/spelling-connections?qt-view__product_specific_menu__block=0)
Spelling program provides classroom instructional materials by grade, from pre-K to Grade 6.

Instructional Programs
Developed for Students with Word
Reading and Spelling Disabilities

Program	Use	Levels	Size	Time	Multisensory	Handwriting
Alphabetic phonics (http://www.altaread.org): a diagnostic O-G adaptation for remedial use with materials, and criterion-referenced benchmark measure	Remedial	Ungraded, elementary	Individual, group	45–60 minutes, 4–5 times per week	Yes	Cursive
Association method (http://www.usm.edu/dubard): a method using a slower speech rate, precise articulation of phonemes, extensive auditory training, and delay of teaching rules. Color differentiation rules are taught in upper levels.	Remedial	N/A	Individual, group, class	2–35 hours per week	Yes	Cursive
Language! (http://www.teachlanguage.com): a comprehensive literacy curriculum that provides an integrated approach to instruction and includes an ESL component	Preventive, remedial, general	Grades 3–12, ESL, ELL	1–20 per group	1–2 hours daily	Yes	Manuscript and cursive
Lindamood-Bell (http://www.lindamoodbell.com): a method developed to teach auditory conceptualization skills and designed to complement any reading program; includes an emphasis on speech processes	Preventive, remedial, general	All	Individual, group, class	20 minutes to 6 hours daily	No	Manuscript and cursive
Orton-Gillingham Approach (http://www.ortonacademy.org): the basis for most structured, sequential, multisensory language programs	Preventive, remedial	Kindergarten to adult	Individual, group	2 hours, 2–5 times per week	Yes	Cursive
Project Read (http://www.projectread.com): a program developed for the public school classroom that includes detailed guides providing a systematic sequence of skills	Preventive, remedial, general	Kindergarten to adult	1–10 per group	Variable session length	Yes	Manuscript and cursive
Slingerland® Approach (http://www.slingerland.org): O-G based, systematic, structured, interactive approach that includes special techniques for developing reading comprehension and fluency; can be used with any text materials	Preventive, remedial, general	Kindergarten to adult, ELL	Individual, group, class	1–2 hours daily during reading, language arts	Yes	Manuscript and cursive
Sonday System (http://www.sondaysystem.com): originally used with older students, emphasizes the structure of the English language as well as phonology and morphology; includes prepared lesson plans	Preventive, remedial, general	Kindergarten to adult, ELL	Individual, group, class	Variable session length, 2–5 times per week	Yes	Manuscript and cursive
Spalding method (http://www.spalding.org): a method in which all sounds are taught before reading begins; heavy emphasis on phonics, rules, and generalizations	Preventive, remedial, general	Primary	Individual, group, class	2 hours, 5 times per week	Yes	Manuscript and cursive
Wilson Reading (http://www.wilsonlanguage.com): systematic, interactive, thorough instruction with emphasis on encoding and decoding; can be used with Grades 3 and above or with Grades 1 and 2	Preventive, remedial, general	Kindergarten to adult	1–15 per class	30–90 minutes, 5 times per week	Yes	Manuscript and cursive

Key: ELL, English language learner; ESL, English as a Second Language; O-G, Orton-Gillingham.

Teacher Resources for
Word Reading and Spelling

At the beginning of the school year teachers can send home questionnaires that include questions about word reading and spelling and related skills that will help them identify those students who may need extra help and ongoing monitoring with these skills. Each student should keep a reading and spelling portfolio to collect samples of their oral reading, depending on grade level, and writing at school across the school year. In addition, students can keep a homework folder in which they organize the assignments they do at home but bring to school for the teacher to review with them. Finally, parent conferences in person and over phone and e-mail are helpful ways to reach out to parents to help their child in developing word reading and spelling skills.

PARENT QUESTIONNAIRE FOR STUDENTS IN K–2

1. When you read books orally to your child, does your child look at the words on the page?

2.   Does your child read independently for pleasure?

3.   Can your child name letters of the alphabet?

4.   Can your child write letters of the alphabet?

5.   Does your child know some sounds that go with letters?

6.   Can your child write her or her first name?

7.   Can your child write her or his last name?

8. Does your child ever try to express ideas in writing using invented spellings?

PARENT QUESTIONNAIRE FOR STUDENTS IN GRADES 1–12

1. Do you have any concerns about your child's reading or spelling development last year in school?

2. Is there a history of reading or spelling problems in your family?

3. Is there anything you would like to share with the school so that the teachers can help your child this year?

4. Are there any stressors in your child's life that you think the school should know about?

READING AND WRITING PORTFOLIOS

Grades 1–3

1. Record an oral reading of a passage used in classroom instruction each month.

2. Keep samples of dictated spelling of single words and sentences each month.

Grades 4–12

Keep the results of screening assessments at the beginning of the year and any measures of response to instruction. Include growth graphs during lessons and readministration of screening tests later in the school year.

HOMEWORK

1. Does your child have anyone in the home to help with homework?

2. Does your child have a computer to use for homework?

3. Does your child have special software to help with reading and writing activities?

PARENT CONFERENCES

What is the best way for the teacher/s to communicate with you about your child during the school year? Please indicate if each option below works and, if so, provide contact information. Because the teacher is busy working with many students during school hours, it is not possible to respond to texted messages during the school day.

In person:

Over the telephone:

By e-mail or web site:

Assessment–Instruction Links for Listening and Reading Comprehension and Oral and Written Language Expression

 Research Lessons

Two Research Lessons are presented in Chapter 5. The first has one associated Teaching Tip and the second has 25 Teaching Tips.

SOME SPECIFIC LEARNING DISABILITIES ARE RELATED TO IMPAIRMENTS IN BOTH ORAL AND WRITTEN LANGUAGE

Research Lesson 5-1

Some reading and writing disabilities are related to oral language problems first observed during the preschool years (see Chapter 2). Researchers in English-speaking countries have conducted large-scale longitudinal studies in which a student's oral language is first studied in the preschool years and then reassessed, along with written language, during the school years (Aram, Ekelman, & Nation, 1984; Bishop & Adams, 1990; Catts, Fey, Zhang, & Tomblin, 1999; Catts, Hogan, & Adloff, 2005; Fey, Catts, Proctor-Williams, Tomblin, & Zhang, 2004; Scarborough, 2005). These longitudinal studies showed that preschoolers with oral language problems may not only continue to have oral language learning problems during the school years, but also written language learning problems. These language learning problems may include listening and reading comprehension skills (Cain & Oakhill, 2007; Carlisle & Rice, 2002), but also oral and written expression problems at the syntax or discourse levels (Scott & Winsor, 2000; Silliman & Scott, 2009). Thus, dyslexia, diagnosed on basis of word-level reading and spelling impairment, is not the only reading disability (see Chapter 2 and Chapter 4).

The findings from longitudinal studies are consistent with current research showing that oral and written language difficulties are explained better by a model of multiple, multileveled language systems rather than by a receptive/expressive language model (Bishop & Snowling, 2004; Catts & Kamhi, 2005; Snowling & Hayiou-Thomas, 2006; Tomblin, Zhang, Weiss, Catts, & Ellis Weismer, 2004). The model of language level by modality predicts four diagnostic groupings, each with different implications for intervention: oral and written language impairment (low skills in all components), specific comprehension impairment (high sound/word-level skills and low sentence/discourse level skills across modalities), dyslexia (low sound/word-level skills but high sentence/discourse; listening comprehension better than reading comprehension), and normal language (at least average skills in all components) (Nelson, Plante, Helm-Estabrooks, & Hotz, 2016). Similar profiles have been described elsewhere in the literature (Nation & Snowling, 2004; Scarborough, 2005; Silliman & Berninger, 2011).

Teachers should teach both oral language skills and written language skills and link oral language skills to learning reading and writing. Indeed, oral discussion is an evidence-based pedagogical tool for reading, writing, and math instruction (e.g., Nussbaum, 2002; Reznitskaya et al., 2001). Students' relative strengths and weaknesses in listening comprehension and oral expression may influence their ability to participate in such discussions and thus influence their resulting academic achievement. Programmatic research has demonstrated the benefits for engaging students in oral text talk about written texts (e.g., Beck & McKeown, 2001, 2007). However, without a clear understanding of how oral language skills complement written language skills in academic learning, educators may not have the necessary knowledge for optimizing all students' reading and writing.

Spoken language is a complex process. It begins with a thought in prelinguistic form. It is assumed the thought is generated in the brain at an unconscious level until it is transformed into language that allows conscious access to thought. To translate thought into oral language, an individual must select the appropriate words, arrange them in the correct syntactic order to convey the desired meaning, recall the phonology (phonetic structure) of words or phrases, and activate the speech mechanism (mouth, tongue, breath) to speak the words that convey the thought. Individuals pass through these processes so quickly and with such seeming ease that we are not aware of the breakdowns that can occur in the thought-to-language translation process. In contrast, as pointed out by Oliphant (1976), when a person is listening to oral language produced by another speaker, the heard speech must be deciphered before the thought behind the language can be inferred. Thus, many levels of language are involved, including syntax or multiword constructions, and not just single words.

Systematically teaching aural (through the ear) and oral (through the mouth) sentence structures enhances a student's ability to comprehend and compose written sentences (Haynes & Jennings, 2006; Johnson, 1991). In turn, reading contributes to oral vocabulary growth and syntactic development (Johnson, 1991). Thus, oral language and written language reciprocally influence each other. Also, both aural and oral language difficulties can interfere with social interactions with teachers and other students (Dickinson & McCabe, 1991).

Students may struggle with aural and/or oral language for many reasons. Some have difficulty perceiving the sounds in the words they hear. Some have difficulty understanding the meaning of words they hear. Some are distracted or are confused by background noises and have difficulty distinguishing aural language and aural nonlanguage stimuli in the background. Others have difficulty understanding multiword constructions such as phrases or syntax (independent with or without dependent clause). Some students have difficulty in constructing oral messages through the mouth due to language rather than speech difficulties. Some struggle with finding words in long-term memory. Other students have difficulty in putting words together in clauses to create syntax that is grammatical and complete. Creating syntax depends on both word order and combining function words (prepositions, conjunctions, pronouns, and articles) that "glue" content words (nouns, verbs, adjectives, adverbs) together.

Some students have difficulty with only one of these aural/oral language skills, but others have more than one difficulty. As a result, these students may not appear to pay attention to teacher talk, say very little, produce immature or very simple oral productions, or have difficulty in self-regulating their attention during language processing. For example, a student may raise his or her hand to answer a question but, when called on, lose his or her thought and appear "wordless." For other students, who speak a great deal, the excessive wordiness may mask underlying language problems. For example, they may start at the beginning of a story and try to tell every detail because they do not sort relevant and irrelevant information or arrange ideas hierarchically with a main idea and supporting details. Other students may struggle with the speech mechanisms—mouth, tongue, teeth, breath. Students may have difficulty with oral language construction only, speech only, or both.

Given these individual differences in students, an interdisciplinary team approach is recommended for aural and oral language and speech difficulties. On the one hand, assessment and problem-solving consultation by a speech-language pathologist or communication disorders specialist is often helpful. On the other hand, there is much that the classroom teacher can do to facilitate oral language development in the general education classroom, as explained next.

TEACHING TIP 5-1: Identify an individual student's profile of strengths and weaknesses in oral and written language early in the school year to plan and implement differentiated instruction as needed.

DEVELOPMENTALLY APPROPRIATE, INDIVIDUALLY TAILORED ORAL AND WRITTEN LANGUAGE INSTRUCTION

Teachers should think about whether individual students may have strengths or weaknesses in specific language systems (language by ear, language by mouth, language by eye, and/or language by hand). They should also think about whether individual students may have strengths or weaknesses in specific levels of language within each of these systems—subword, word, syntax, discourse/text levels. They can base this assessment of relative strengths and weaknesses on assessment tools in Appendix 5A and classroom observation of behaviors, response to instruction, and portfolio assessment of work samples; then, they should consider what the instructional implications may be for an individual student's unique profile. See Appendix 5C for use of portfolio assessment and parent questionnaires in conjunction with formal test assessment and observation of students in the classroom. Also, it is advisable to consult with the interdisciplinary team to request assessment targeted to the observations of where the weaknesses may be and discuss any information in the parent questionnaire, portfolio, or otherwise shared by parents that may be relevant to differentiating instruction for an individual student (see Chapter 13). Assess developmentally appropriate multileveled oral and written language skills at the beginning of each school year and use the results to plan and implement individually tailored instruction during the school year to increase likelihood that students respond to instruction that year. Give the measures again at the end of the school year to assess progress. More assessment measures should be given during K–5 to optimize language learning and prevent more severe struggles with oral and written language learning in the upper grades.

The goal of Chapter 5 is therefore to provide an evidence-based model of which oral and written language skills to assess at which grade level. In the text, examples of assessment tools for specific kinds of oral and written language skills, organized by grade levels are provided and referred to by their abbreviated titles by which they are known in the schools. In Appendix 5A full names of assessment tools are spelled out and citations are provided for locating the assessment tools. Likewise, Appendix 5C can be used to obtain relevant assessment information for planning and implementing instruction during the school year. Thus, the text and appendices are designed for use in conjunction for a developmental model for assessing oral and written language. Also see Chapter 13 for a discussion of how a multidisciplinary team can support the general education teacher in 1) conducting the assessments to identify students needing individually tailored instruction for specific oral and written language skills (using instructional resources in Appendix 5B and Teaching Tips in Chapter 5), and 2) implementing that instruction. Appendix 5A also indicates whether the test can be given in a group or requires individual administration.

EVIDENCE-BASED ASSESSMENT

At each grade level, choose and administer at least one measure of each of the skills from Appendix 5A at the beginning of the school year. Repeat it at the end of the school year to monitor progress during that school year.

Kindergarten

Vocabulary meaning. Ability to explain orally what words mean is an index of a student's ability to translate thought into oral language about word meaning. For students who are age 6 or older, give WISC-4 Vocabulary at the beginning of the year or later in the year when they turn age 6.

Listening comprehension. Because ability to learn from teacher talk is an important way students learn at school, give the WJ III Oral Comprehension and Following Directions subtests.

Oral syntax construction. Because students with oral language problems that emerged in the preschool years often have difficulty with expressing their ideas in oral language involving multi-word syntax, give CELF-5 Formulated Sentences.

First Grade

In first grade, give all *Test of Integrated Language and Literacy Skills™ (TILLS™)* (Nelson, Plante, Helm-Estabrooks, & Hotz, 2016) subtests that are relevant to these levels of aural and oral language. For any student with identified oral language weaknesses also give the TOPL-2 to assess pragmatics, social use of language.

Vocabulary meaning. For the same reasons as in kindergarten, give WISC-4 Vocabulary.

Listening comprehension. For the same reasons as in kindergarten, give the WJ III Oral Comprehension and Following Directions subtests.

Oral syntax construction. For the same reasons as in kindergarten, give CELF-5 Formulated Sentences.

Reading comprehension. Because students are learning to integrate word identification and sentence syntax comprehension, give PAL-II RW Sentence Sense.

Timed written sentence construction. Because students are expected to order words in syntactic structures that are acceptable English in timed written work, give WJ III Writing Fluency.

Second Grade

Vocabulary meaning. For same reasons as in first grade, give WISC-4 Vocabulary.

Listening comprehension. For the same reasons as in kindergarten, give WJ III Oral Comprehension and Following Directions.

Oral syntax construction. For the same reasons as in kindergarten, give CELF-5 Formulated Sentences.

Oral word finding. Because some students with oral expression difficulties struggle with finding words in memory, give D-KEFS Verbal Fluency.

Reading comprehension. To compare reading comprehension to oral comprehension for unfolding texts, give WJ III Passage Comprehension. Also give PAL-II RW to assess sentence level comprehension.

Timed sentence construction. For the same reasons as in first grade, give WJ III Writing Fluency.

Third Grade

Vocabulary. For the same reasons as in first grade, give WISC-4 Vocabulary.

Oral word finding. For the same reasons as in second grade, give D-KEFS Verbal Fluency.

Listening comprehension. For the same reasons as in second grade, give WJ III Oral Comprehension and Following Directions.

Oral syntax construction. For the same reasons as in earlier grades, give CELF-5 Formulated Sentences.

Oral word finding. For the same reasons as in second grade, give D-KEFS Verbal Fluency.

Reading comprehension. For the same reason as in second grade, give WJ III Passage Comprehension and PAL-II RW Sentence Sense.

Timed sentence construction. For the same reason as in the earlier grades, give WJ III Writing Fluency.

Written expression. Because multiple levels of language are involved in written expression, give WIAT III Written Expression that assesses word finding, sentence combining, and text composing.

Fourth and Fifth Grades

Same as third grade but add a measure of silent reading comprehension rate from Appendix 5A.

Sixth to Eighth Grades

Same as third to fifth grades but if listening and reading comprehension or oral and written expression problems are persisting, then do a thorough diagnostic work up involving the interdisciplinary team.

Ninth to Twelfth Grades

Same as third to fifth grades but if listening and reading comprehension or oral and written expression problems are persisting, then do a thorough diagnostic work up involving the interdisciplinary team.

USING ASSESSMENT RESULTS TO PLAN AND IMPLEMENT DIFFERENTIATED INSTRUCTION

If a student is below the average range or the most average score for the age or grade on measures used for assessment (see Appendix 5A), select a grade-appropriate instructional program from the resources in Appendix 5B. Use the Teaching Tips discussed in Chapter 5 in implementing chosen oral and written language program(s). At the end of the school year, administer the measures given at the beginning of the year again to assess progress across the school year. At all grade levels, integrate the selected instructional resources with the teaching tips for oral and written language skills discussed in Chapter 5 and teacher-designed ones. Also at all grade levels use information from Teacher Resources in Appendix 5C in linking assessment to instructional planning and implementation for individual students.

TEACH AURAL AND ORAL LANGUAGE ALONE PLUS THEIR RELATIONSHIPS TO READING AND WRITING ACROSS THE CURRICULUM
Research Lesson 5-2

Oral language is the key to learning at school. Listening comprehension, oral expression, reading comprehension, and written expression, which are all language skills, should be taught alone and in relationship to each other. Students have to process teachers' instructional talk, which is delivered via oral language, as well as their peers' oral language used in class and on the playground. They also have to communicate with their teacher and peers through oral language. The observant teacher does more than listen for correct answers. The quality of the student's language, organization, vocabulary, sentence length, and structure are noted and taken into account in teacher instruction. Slingerland's (1971) classic textbook was not just directed to reading disabilities but also to teaching students with specific language disabilities (SLDs) that include but are not restricted to dyslexia. Teachers should be prepared to take advantage of any teachable moments during the school day to develop oral vocabulary, listening skills, and other language concepts related to oral language comprehension and expression. The following teaching strategies (Teaching Tips 5-2A to 5-2Y) can be implemented by classroom teachers for teaching oral language.

TEACHING TIP 5-2A: Encourage conversation.

Social interaction provides language practice. Some students may need the teacher to guide them in engaging in conversational language. The teacher can ask questions, rephrase answers, and encourage oral expression.

TEACHING TIP 5-2B: Expect complete syntactic structure.

Although students may not use complete oral syntax in informal speech, doing so in the classroom provides practice in a skill necessary for learning written language. When students use fragmented syntax, the teacher should model complete syntax.

TEACHING TIP 5-2C: Maintain eye contact with the various members of the class or instructional group.

Encourage students to maintain eye contact. Doing so helps them gauge the audience's attention and adjust language, volume, or organization to be better understood, communicate more clearly, and receive nonverbal cues about their clarity.

TEACHING TIP 5-2D: Remind students to speak loudly and articulate clearly.

Encourage students to feel the muscles used for speech while they are talking. They also need to hear their own speech distinctly as they begin to learn written language. It is not easy to sound out a word for reading or spelling when it is not articulated clearly. In the classroom, speakers provide output that becomes aural input for themselves and for their listening classmates. Mumbled or misarticulated speaking will not hold the attention of the group and will not fully benefit the speaker or listeners.

TEACHING TIP 5-2E: Explain how tone of voice can change the meaning of what a speaker says.

Tone may be related to pitch, volume, speed, and rhythm. Many playground disagreements come about because of misunderstandings when students are using playground voices. It is not the words they use, but the volume and pitch, which can lead to misunderstanding of motives and attitudes. Conversely, when messages are too soft, they can be ignored or hard to understand.

TEACHING TIP 5-2F: Attend to listening skills.

Teachers need to ensure that students are listening by using consistent cues to get their attention. One school, for example, adopted the phrase, "It's listening time" for all classrooms. Students often are more effectively cued to attention if all school personnel use the same language for reminders. Some students might also benefit from posted written reminders, such as these.

- Good listeners give feedback to the speaker through eye contact, body language, and nods. They avoid interruption and distraction.

- Active listeners need strategies for recall. These strategies may include visualizing, rehearsing, or repeating the items to be remembered; finger counting; using mnemonic clues; or taking notes.

TEACHING TIP 5-2G: Summarize and learn from heard information.

Having students verbally summarize or otherwise discuss the information they hear should begin in kindergarten and continue with increasingly difficult questions as students grow older. Teachers should encourage students to ask for clarification when they do not understand something—students can ask the teacher directly or fellow students.

TEACHING TIP 5-2H: Ensure that instructional language is clear.

Young students may not understand words or concepts such as *top, center, indent, blanks,* or *missing.* Teachers must be certain that all students understand what is expected of them. For example, if a teacher says, "Let's check with Dick" every time a spelling question arises, the teacher should explain to new students that "Dick" is the nickname for the dictionary (rather than a classmate named Dick) and this means they should look for the proper spelling in the dictionary.

TEACHING TIP 5-2I: Teach recognizing, organizing, and expressing thoughts clearly.

Students are expected to understand the need for capitalizing the beginning of a sentence and placing a period or other punctuation at the end. This expectation assumes that students always recognize sentences, even though we do not always speak in complete sentences. By Grade 4, students should reliably write in complete sentences. Common Core Standards expect this to be mastered in second and third grade, but research shows that students are still mastering clausal construction during those grades (see Berninger, Nagy, & Beers, 2011). Being able to organize and express answers clearly first in oral language is a foundation for later writing of organized, clear sentences.

TEACHING TIP 5-2J: Model and guide sentence construction.

Some students have difficulty getting started with the wording of a sentence. Saying the beginning word or phrase for the student can help the student structure his or her response. Give students time for thinking and formulating an oral or written response. Students' explicit experience in both producing their own oral language and processing others' aural language with fully developed noun phrases and without ambiguous pronouns facilitates comprehension of reading material.

TEACHING TIP 5-2K: Incorporate a "question of the day" during instruction.

A question can be a part of each day's opening exercises, such as before or after taking roll. The exercise will only take 5 or 10 minutes if just 7–10 students are asked to respond each day. As students practice, this exercise will take less time. Teachers can even write the question on the board so that the students can read it and prepare their answers when they first come into the room. A suggested list of one-part, two-part, three-part, and process questions is provided in Box 5.1. If a student does not answer in complete sentences, the teacher should restructure the answer by modeling and asking the student to repeat the model. In a very short time, students often will become conscious of the *idea* of a sentence and will require little reminding.

Start with one-part questions that require only a simple declarative sentence:

Teacher: "What is your favorite animal?"

Student: "My favorite animal is _____."

When students are successfully answering one-part questions in complete sentences, move to two-part questions. When they are successful with two-part questions, move to three-part questions, which may be answered in two sentences:

Teacher: "What is your favorite animal? Why?"

Student: "My favorite animal is _____ because _____."

Teacher: "What is your favorite animal? Why? Tell me one thing about that animal."

Student: "My favorite animal is _____ because _____. It lives in _____."

Vary the activity by asking students to change the tense or to make compound and complex sentences.

Process questions are asked to solicit explanations from students:

Teacher: "What is the process for getting on a bus?"

Student: "First you walk up the steps. Then you pay the driver. Then you look for a seat."

Box 5.1. Questions of the Day

SAMPLE ONE-PART QUESTIONS

- What school did you attend last year?
- What is your job or responsibility at home?
- What is your favorite food?
- How many students are in your family?
- What pets do you have?
- What would you like to change about yourself?
- What do you do best?
- What do you like best about yourself?
- Where is your favorite place to go?
- What is your favorite after-school activity?
- What is something that bugs you?

SAMPLE TWO-PART QUESTIONS

- What sport do you play best? Why are you good at it?
- What sport would you like to learn or is hardest for you? Why?
- What school subject is easiest for you? Why do you think it is easy?
- What subject is hardest for you? Why?
- How do you remember a telephone number? What is yours?
- What is one good health habit? Explain why or how you carry it out.
- What three words describe you best? Why?
- Why do people like you? What do others like best about you?

SAMPLE THREE-PART QUESTIONS

- If you could buy a gift for someone, who would you buy it for, what would you buy, and why?
- If you could go anywhere, where would you go, why would you go there, and how would you get there?
- If your bicycle has a flat tire, what might you need to fix it, where would you go for help, and who could help you change it?
- What is your favorite sport, how did you learn to play (or when do you watch it), and why do you like it?
- What is your favorite wild animal, where does it live, and what does it do?

SAMPLE PROCESS QUESTIONS

A process is the exact order of steps that people or machines follow to get something done. The steps are explained in their exact order. No step is left out. Anyone who follows the same process can do the same thing.

- What is the process for washing your hands?
- What is the process for cleaning up your lunch space?
- What is the process for baking a cake?
- How do you make a peanut butter and jelly sandwich?
- What is the process for tying your shoes?

Each day, help the listeners summarize what they heard by asking questions such as, "What animal was mentioned most often?" "What reasons did people give for choosing a particular animal?" "What kinds of food did people need for their animals?" Answers should also be in complete sentences.

TEACHING TIP 5-2L: Ensure students understand the different parts of speech.

Parts of speech provide the building blocks for teaching students how to write sentences (Carreker, 2006). Throughout the year, read and discuss children's books, such as those listed in Appendix 5B, which are written in a lively, engaging way for developing language learners. Some are explicitly written toward the goal of teaching different parts of speech that students can identify with in their own oral and written language use.

Teaching parts of speech builds vocabulary and makes what is often taught as a separate subject a meaningful part of reading and writing. Teaching parts of speech introduces students to concepts such as the following that will allow the class to understand and answer the comprehension questions they encounter as they read text:

1. *Noun markers* (determiners) are articles and sometimes number words. They are markers for noun phrases. When students encounter a determiner such as *the,* their eyes should move along the page until they find a noun or naming word. The determiner along with the noun or naming word creates a noun phrase, telling "who" or "what."

2. *Nouns* mark the end of a phrase started by a determiner.

3. *Prepositions* mark phrases that usually tell "where" or "when." Prepositions and nouns together create prepositional phrases.

4. *Adverbs* tell "how," "when," or "where." Alert students to the suffix *-ly,* which tells "how."

5. *Conjunctions* join words, phrases, and sentences (see Table 5.2).

6. *Verbs* are action words. They tell what we do, will do, are doing, or did.

7. *Adjectives* describe size, shape, kind, and how many.

8. *Pronouns* take the place of a noun for subject, object, or possessive cases. Pronouns often cause problems for students with imprecise language. They need practice in determining the referents when pronouns are used: "Who is 'he'?" or "What is 'it'?"

9. *Punctuation* signals the rising intonation associated with questions or the falling intonation associated with statements or commands.

10. *Words can function both as nouns and verbs.* Some words function as more than one part of speech (e.g., *circle, train, coach*).

11. *Accent* affects some words. As accent changes, words may change from nouns to verbs (e.g., *rec' ord* versus *re cord'*).

An example of instructional activities that can develop awareness of parts of speech is the following activity (Slingerland, 1967) that builds awareness of prepositions. The whole class can be involved and the teacher can monitor with little difficulty:

1. Provide each student with three objects, such as a book, a pencil, and a piece of paper. Make sure the objects enable the whole class to be involved and allow the teacher to quickly see whether all students are following directions.

2. Give a direction and model the appropriate response. For example, "Put the pencil beside the book. Now, where is the pencil? *Beside the book* is a prepositional phrase. It tells where to put the pencil. So, the pencil is beside the book." By using the correct terminology from the beginning, students acquire vocabulary pertaining to parts of speech.

3. After giving several examples, ask students to respond independently in complete sentences:

    Teacher: "Put the paper under the book. Where is the paper?"

    Student: "The paper is under the book. *Under the book* is a prepositional phrase; it tells *where*."

    Teacher: "Where is the book?"

    Student: "The book is on the paper. *On the paper* is a prepositional phrase. It tells *where.*

As students learn to understand prepositions, they will place objects *between, inside,* and *beside* other objects, and they will excitedly point them out in text and conversations. Students who develop these concepts early have better reading comprehension because they understand phrases and have an awareness of "the words that go together" to tell "where."

Once possessives have been taught, students may create possessive noun phrases. This difficult task requires them to add *'s* or *s'* as required by the spelling of the word. Begin by presenting only words that require *'s* (shown in Table 5.1).

With experience, students may choose from lists of words to create their own phrases. When they are confident with this skill, the teacher will present a similar lesson with words of ownership that require *s* followed by an apostrophe with both singular (*bus'*) and plural (*boys'*) words. Finally, they will practice with a mixed list in which they must discriminate between the need for *'s* or *s'*.

Older students may identify the part of speech to be added, leading to better understanding of the use of affixes and their relationships within the phrase and sentence.

An important skill related to learning parts of speech is how some words help glue other words together. See Table 5.2 for strategies for teaching "glue words" such as conjunctions and prepositions.

Table 5.1.   Example of an activity for teaching possessives

Owner	Adjective	Noun	Phrase (written by child)
Bob	big	bike	Bob's big bike
The cat	long	whiskers	The cat's long whiskers

Table 5.2.   Small, important words that "glue other words together" in syntax

Word	Various meanings/usages
and	Connects words or phrases More of the same Lists words and phrases in a series Also, too, in addition
as	In the same way At the same time, while, during Because Just as or same as Like While
but	An exception, something different Connects two contrasting ideas Only
if	Condition Reason
only	Singly—only in its class Simply Merely
or	This or that Instead of Different Opposite
since	Because From a certain time until now
so	As a result of This came about
sometimes	Not always, periodically Now and then Once Past, erstwhile
than	Comparing/inequality More than
then	When After that At that time Following next
to	Tells where Attachment A direction Opposite ends
what	Shows stress Asks a question
when	At a certain time
while	Although During that time As
yet	A time word meaning "up to now" Even so However Excepting Nevertheless Still At the same time It is also the case

TEACHING TIP 5-2M: Use questions to guide sentence construction.

Sentence building is popular at all grade levels. The following adaptation from Slingerland (1971) allows students to answer editorial questions—who, what, where, when, and why—that lead to better reading comprehension and more effective written language.

1. Choose a subject. The teacher may choose one related to content material or the students may choose a subject. Then ask the students to add more information.

   Teacher: "What lives on both land and in the water?"

   Student: "A frog."

   Teacher: "Add two words, adjectives, to describe the frog."

   Student: "A *big, green* frog."

   Teacher: "Think of one word—did what?"

   Student: "Hopped."

   Teacher: "Put it all together to make a sentence."

   Student: "A big, green frog *hopped*."

2. Once an initial sentence is established, ask further questions so that the students can add more information and further build on the sentence. Each added phrase can be completed by a different student—involve as many students as possible. As a phrase is added, the student should repeat the entire sentence with the added phrase. Use as many phrases as the students can handle.

   Teacher: "Where did the big, green frog hop?"

   Student: "Through the grass. A big, green frog hopped *through the grass*."

   Teacher: "How did the big, green frog hop through the grass?"

   Student: "Quickly. A big, green frog hopped through the grass *quickly*."

   Teacher: "When did the big, green frog hop through the grass quickly?"

   Student: "This morning. A big, green frog hopped through the grass quickly *this morning*."

   Teacher: "Why did the big, green frog hop through the grass quickly this morning?"

   Student: "Because he saw a slug. A big, green frog hopped through the grass quickly this morning *because he saw a slug*.

TEACHING TIP 5-2N: Teach the role of word order in creating sentences.

Building on the activity described in Teaching Tip 5-2M, have participating students stand in a row in the front of the room in the order in which they added their phrases, and ask each one to repeat his or her phrase (e.g., "A big, green frog hopped quickly through the grass this morning because he saw a slug"). Then, instruct the students to rearrange themselves and repeat their phrases again. When they do so, new forms of the sentence emerge (e.g., "Because he saw a slug, a big, green frog hopped quickly through the grass this morning," "This morning, a big, green frog hopped quickly through the grass because he saw a slug"). With every new arrangement, the class should determine whether the order makes sense and add suggestions for the order in which the phrases should be arranged. As students are ready, they can make more complex or compound sentences by introducing connecting words such as *and, but, except,* and *then*. Ask students to change the tense to something that is happening now or something that will happen in the future. Introduce a written component: As each phrase is suggested by a student, the teacher can quickly write it on tag board strips. The student can then hold the strips so that the class can see the phrases in the correct order as each sentence is composed and again as phrases are rearranged.

TEACHING TIP 5-2O: Have students build phrases independently.

Independent work is a transitional step toward functional use. Students may create their own phrases by combining words from lists provided by the teacher. The words may be from the students' decoding lists or from reading or content texts. The difficulty of the activity may be varied by the words provided. Number words or plural noun markers such as *these, those,* or *some* may be used if the class knows how to form plurals.

1. Place a list of adjectives, a list of nouns, and a list of noun markers on the board. Have students choose one adjective and one noun from each list to create their own lists of noun phrases. The students can also illustrate their noun phrases. Students' lists will vary.

2. After students are successful with one adjective, have them choose two adjectives for each noun.

3. Have the students perform the same activity with prepositional phrases using a list of prepositions, noun markers, adjectives, and nouns.

TEACHING TIP 5-2P: Compile a class booklet of students' phrases.

Students can create a class booklet by writing a prepositional phrase to complete a sentence (e.g., "When my dog got lost I looked..."). Each student can write and illustrate a phrase to complete the sentence (e.g., *at the grocery store, in the park, under the bed*). When the pages are assembled into a booklet, students can practice reading the very long sentence. They can also write a conclusion to the story.

TEACHING TIP 5-2Q: Teach concept words.

Students with language problems often have difficulty with abstract temporal language concepts such as *before, after,* or *following,* and with sequences such as days of the week or months of the year. They also may have difficulty estimating the amount of time needed for an activity or project. This has a tremendous impact on students in the upper grades as they need to organize their time for longer assignments and juggle the requirements of multiple classes. Students may have an understanding that seasons—spring, summer, fall (autumn), and winter—are cyclical just as are days of the week and months of the year, but they may have difficulty in recalling them in sequence and associating them with the correct periods of time. For telling time and understanding the calendar, students need to recognize that the cycle of holidays, months of the year, days of the week, time of day, life cycles, and plant growth cycles repeat again and again and that they are related to science, math, and social studies. Regular practice and review will help to make this recall automatic. See Box 5.2 for others that can be taught to improve comprehension.

Students with language problems may need to see or hear concepts many times and review them frequently in many settings to learn and retain them thoroughly. These skills will be reinforced when the teacher regularly develops, discusses, reviews, and uses activities to strengthen awareness.

Box 5.2. Concept Words that Reinforce Comprehension

top	through	next to	away from	inside
some	not many	middle	few	farthest
around	over	widest	most	between
whole	nearest	second	corner	several
behind	in a row	different	after	almost
half	center	as many	beginning	side
other	alike	not first	last	every
below	matches	always	medium sized	equal
right	forward	zero	above	
separated	left	pair	skip	
in order	third	least	never	

A formal group language lesson may not be necessary if the teacher regularly and consciously includes these concepts in daily work (e.g., as part of the morning opening exercises, at story time, during "sponge" activities to fill those few minutes in line or before dismissal) and at every natural opportunity. The following activities can provide practice for such concepts. However, do not stop practicing them when a student can recite the days of the week or the months of the year. Review these concepts regularly until they are automatic for every student in every kind of oral or written performance. Serial organization or putting items in order is fundamental to learning oral and written language.

1. *Practice time of day:* When teaching students to tell time, include practice with an analog clock. The circle of the dial lends emphasis to the cyclical nature of times of day. Experience with an analog clock helps students understand the reason we say, "Ten *after* four" or "Quarter *to* ten." Include questions about time as questions of the day: "At what time of the day do you ... have your favorite meal? Wake up? Go to bed? Feed the dog?"

2. *Practice days of the week:* Students should be able to name the days of the week in order, starting with any day, and be able to identify what day is before or what day is after any named day. By Grade 3, students should be able to correctly spell the days of the week. As part of the daily calendar work, help students identify various days: "Today is...," "Yesterday was...," "Tomorrow will be...," "A week ago today was..."

3. *Practice months of the year:* Use oral activities with all grades and written activities when appropriate. Ask students to name the months in order, starting with any month. Naming in order takes practice, but it is an excellent introduction to any new month. "This is April. Let's name all of the months of the year starting with this month." Students can move (e.g., march, tiptoe, hop) in rhythm while reciting the months of the year. When the month in which their birthday occurs is named, they can put their hands above their heads. Ask students to identify which holiday comes in each month and then review holidays for other months in sequence: "Groundhog Day is in February. What holiday is in March? In April?" Ask students to identify the month before or after a given month. "May is before June and after April." "May is between April and June."

Have students practice writing the months of the year. If students copy the complete name of the month each time they head their papers, they will have many opportunities to practice the correct spelling. After spelling of months is firmly established, abbreviations may be taught, and students can learn to write the date in various acceptable formats: February 1, 2016; Feb. 1, 2016; 2/1/2016. Incorporate questions about months in the questions of the day: "What is the next holiday? When does it occur?" "In what season is [name a month]? What holidays occur in that month?" "What month comes after your birthday?"

TEACHING TIP 5-2R: Link oral language to preparation for reading passages.

All readers benefit from prereading structured activities to prepare them for reading a passage, but students with SLDs may need more than do classmates. Preparatory instruction is designed to activate background knowledge prior to reading a text that will contribute to understanding the text once read, builds confidence in succeeding on language tasks, and stimulates curiosity. Preparation and follow-up activities such as the following provide awareness of the language of the text and have beneficial effects on reading comprehension when students read written texts. New information may be processed more accurately and efficiently if students are optimally engaged because of the preparation activities. Beginning readers focus on single words. With preparatory activities and reading experience, they become aware of the structures linking multiple words, such as phrases beginning with prepositions; then phrases with noun markers; and then subject, action, and descriptive phrases. Eventually they become aware of syntax structures underlying sentence organization. With preparatory activities, students learn that endings of written words may mark number (singular or plural, as in *cow* or *cows*) or tense (present or past, as in *walk* or *walked*). They also learn how pronouns signal gender (e.g., *him* and *her*) and person (first, second, and third, as in *I, you,* and *they*). With preparatory activities, students learn how capital letters mark the beginning of a new sentence; how punctuation ends a sentence; and how the whole sentence unit is linked to the intonation (musical melody of spoken language) and systematically varies for statements, questions, and commands.

Also, because it is well established that students with language learning disabilities often have difficulty self-regulating their attention to words in left to right order, remind the students to read words in a sentence in order even if they decide at the end of a sentence to look back at an earlier word. Some students benefit from touching each word as they read it; others find it helpful to use a index card with a window cut out of the top left corner that is used to focus on one word or one phrase at a time as reader proceeds across the sentence and sometimes to the next row of print before completing it.

The preparation steps (Slingerland, 2013) discussed next can be used to improve both word recognition and comprehension. Low-achieving readers, particularly beginning readers who have not yet mastered decoding skills, need much prereading instruction and practice with both decoding *and* vocabulary at the word level. However, they also need prereading instruction and practice with skills involving units larger than the single word that influence comprehension of text when it is read. The goal is to develop rhythm for the musical melody of intonation. The teacher can select a list of 8–10 words or 6–8 phrases to be read from the material and print the list in clear manuscript on the board or a chart. See the examples in Tables 5.3 and 5.4 for decoding practice and phrases. A pointer can be used to underline each word or phrase as it is read. Phrase work begins after decoding practice.

Table 5.3.   Words for decoding practice

fermented	consumption	protection	remaining
complicated	cleaned	affordable	flavor
process	popularity	making	kilograms

The reading group or class repeats each phrase as it is read correctly by the teacher or another student. These same steps, followed with words and/or phrases, should also be used at the beginning of each reading lesson before students open their books.

1. The teacher reads each word or phrase from the list and offers clarification as needed. This is a teaching time for noun markers and prepositions, which give clues to meaning. This step provides practice with building awareness of unfamiliar words, punctuation, and linguistic cues. The class repeats the word or phrase.

2. The teacher says a word or phrase from the list and asks a student to point to the correct word or phrase from the list and read it. If the student is correct, the entire class repeats the word or phrase. Several students should have an opportunity to perform until all are confident with the vocabulary and are reading the phrases fluently. This step for guided practice builds security for when students are reading in a book, and it should not be skipped.

3. The teacher provides a concept clue such as, "Find a phrase that tells *where* the story takes place" (e.g., "in the garden") or "Find a phrase that describes the building in the story" ("the little white house"). Note that both phrases are about places, but only "in the garden" begins with a preposition and tells "where." The student then finds a word or phrase that answers the question. Again, the class repeats if the answer is right. The teacher allows as many students to perform as possible.

4. Finally, the teacher asks various students to read all of the words or phrases. If they have difficulty, the teacher will need to return to Steps 1 or 2.

Table 5.4.   Phrases for reading preparation

begin to smell like chocolate
any remaining pulp or pieces of the pods
from the fermented dried beans
a very long and complicated process
in order to bring out the chocolate flavor
from around the world
the cleaned and blended beans
in the cacao (kah-kow) pod

A part of each day's lesson should be devoted to teacher-guided reading to help students develop chunking skills to understand the word units that convey meaning. The teacher should begin by structuring the number of words that go together, forming a phrase (Slingerland, 2013). The teacher can help students break the sentences in the text into phrases (e.g., "The first three words tell 'who'"), continuing the phrase work begun during preparation and explicitly teaching the words that go together. Students should not start reading a phrase until they know all of the words in the phrase. The teacher continues to guide reading, helping students to project thought and anticipate the next phrases.

When students have read and studied the sentence silently, rereading it aloud gives students the opportunity for successful performance and to develop fluency. This strategy moves from small-phrase units to longer sentence units. In the course of time, less structuring is required, but it should not be dropped; only the amount should be modified. If a sentence is not rhythmically phrased, the rhythm should be tapped on the wall, table, or student's shoulder to help her or him feel the cadence of the language. Sweeping the arm from left to right is also a reinforcement of the feeling of the rhythm. Students should reread the whole sentence after they have phrased it to build comprehension of the way the chunks build a cohesive sentence.

TEACHING TIP 5-2S: Ask questions to prepare for reading comprehension and after silent reading.

Questioning for comprehension helps students think about what they are reading and focus on what they are to learn from a given passage. They can predict what they think they may learn from reading the passage. In addition, the following prereading comprehension activities facilitate reading comprehension:

1. Ask students to read the introduction before reading to answer purpose-setting questions (e.g., "Where does the story begin? "What kind of story or article is this? Why do you think so?").

2. Ask students to predict outcomes (e.g., "What will happen? How do you know?").

3. Read to find out whether your predictions were correct and "Where does the ending or conclusion begin?"

After reading the passage, ask students to summarize the passage (e.g., "Who were the characters?" "What was the plot?" "What was the outcome?" "What was the main idea?" "What were the supporting details?"). In addition, the teacher should use questioning strategies to guide the students in developing a greater understanding of the language used in the passage. For example, teachers should encourage students to find the specific words that provide the answer when answering questions about the text. The terminology used will vary according to student age or experience, but questioning strategies should include the following:

1. Asking students "who?" or "what?" Nouns or noun phrases marked by articles or determiners identify the individual. Noun phrases that include adjectives such as *the little brown dog* describe. Noun phrases may also give details about number of something (e.g., *The seven towering hills*)

2. Asking students "where?" or "when?" A prepositional phrase gives information, such as where something is located (e.g., *under the umbrella*) or when something occurs (e.g., *after lunch*)

3. Asking students to find adjectives and adjective phrases that describe (e.g., *smooth and slippery*)

4. Asking students to identify verb or action phrases (e.g., *was sliding, had eaten*)

5. Asking students to find what did happen or what will happen to aid understanding of how suffixes change or shade meanings by past, present, future time, possessive, number, gender, and so forth (*-ly* tells "how," *-ing* tells what someone or something is doing, and *-ed* tells what has happened).

6. Asking students to clarify use and meaning of pronouns (e.g., "To whom does *it* refer?" "Who is *she*?")

7. Asking students to demonstrate their understanding of punctuation and the ways it gives meaning in a sentence—including dashes, the many uses of commas, quotations, and others (e.g., "Why does this sentence end with an exclamation mark?" "What mark shows that this is additional information?")

8. Asking students to locate precise vocabulary that gives inferential information (e.g., "What word in the sentence tells how the character feels?" "Which words tell exactly where the gold was hidden?")

Reading comprehension is dependent on a student's own understanding of the structure of language. For example, a second-grade girl in Beverly Wolf's school was reading a book and came across the following sentence: "How quiet it was." A simple sentence, but the girl could not read it. Each time she tried, she would say, "How is," and then stop. Then the teacher said, "It's not a question." The student immediately read the sentence correctly. Her anticipation of what would follow the word *how* had made her say *is*. She expected a question and tried to make the sentence fit her expectation.

Each day, after students have some review and practice with seeing and reading phrases, they should move on to reading without teacher guidance. Students must be taught not to skip words or guess their identity from context. The interpretation of text depends on context but word recognition should not. However, it is not enough for students to correctly call the words. Students must read the sentence with good phrasing with attention to punctuation and prosody if they are to develop fluency and good comprehension skills. The teacher should intervene and restructure or model if a student has difficulty, asking the student to read *the one phrase* that needs improvement. The teacher should remind students of the articles and prepositions in a sentence before which the eyes should pause. Do students know all of the words in the phrase or sentence before they start to read? Do they keep all the describing words together until these words lead to the named word? Teachers should remind students to reread a phrase or sentence when the meaning is unclear. By rereading after studying aloud, students have the opportunity for successful performance. Teachers point out the relationships between the language students read and the language students speak. It is often helpful to remind students to reread as if they are talking.

TEACHING TIP 5-2T: Teach for oral reading fluency.

Teachers should listen to each student read aloud each day in order to check decoding and comprehension skills (Johnson, 2006). During silent reading, students put words together in phrases and sentences to convey thoughts. *Word callers,* who pronounce the words but do not put them together, miss rhythm and meaning for text cues. Fluency should be assessed. Oral reading fluency is how rapidly, smoothly, effortlessly, and automatically connected text is read. When students are fluent readers, they read with little conscious attention to decoding (Meyer & Felton, 1999). There is a direct relationship between fluency and comprehension because fluent readers attend to the meaning of the text rather than the mechanics of decoding (Adams, 1990). Fluency, however, does not mean speed reading. It means reading with ease, at a decent rate, and with good comprehension (Hall & Moats, 2001). Two skills are especially important for reading fluency (Wood, Flowers, & Grigorenko, 2001): 1) anticipatory processing of stimuli to be read—letters, written words, and written phrases; and 2) automatic, fast recognition time for processing the letters, words, or phrases. Thus, whereas phonological awareness affects the oral reading of words, orthographic awareness of letters in written words may affect reading fluency (Bowers & Wolf, 1993). Fluent readers' phrasing and intonation mirror their oral speech. They activate their vocabulary and use their prior knowledge of the structure of sentences to project thought for successful performance. Nonfluent readers decode slowly and haltingly. Their speed is inconsistent, with poor phrasing and poor recognition of prosodic features of the melody of spoken language. They may have inadequate sight word recognition and poor recognition of morpheme patterns. They may omit and substitute letters and/or words and ignore punctuation.

The most commonly used method to increase reading fluency is the repeated reading technique (Meyer & Felton, 1999). Beginning readers should practice naming letters, letter groups, and words on lists. It is helpful for them to reread the lists of decoding words used earlier in the lesson. Emerging readers should practice decodable and partially decodable words on lists and have opportunities for repeated reading in class with teacher guidance. The goal is accurate and fluid reading with adequate speed, appropriate phrasing, and correct intonation. Other activities that aid prosody and fluency include the following:

1. *Sentence completion:* The teacher reads a phrase or phrases. When signaled, a student completes the sentence. Then the teacher reads again and signals another student to complete the next sentence. This activity provides good modeling of rhythm and inflection by the teacher. It also builds reading group skills, as the students must pay attention and follow along in the text while listening to other readers and also anticipate their oral turns.

2. *Round-robin repeated reading:* Each student reads a sentence, paragraph, or page, and then the next student gets a turn. The teacher should expect each student to read with rhythm and fluency.

3. *Readers' theater:* Fiction lends itself to role playing, in which someone is designated narrator and others read the parts of different characters. Nonfiction can be used as students assume the roles of narrators or reporters. This activity may be a group rereading for fun or for a performance for an audience.

4. *Choral reading:* The teacher and the class all read a sentence, paragraph, or page aloud. Some teachers use this activity when introducing books to beginning readers, but this activity can also be used to promote oral reading fluency. However, in this group setting, the teacher may miss the oral reading dysfluencies of some students.

5. *Partner reading:* Paired readers choose a quiet, cozy spot to practice reading to one another. This activity provides additional practice in reading to a classmate after reading in small groups. This is not a substitute for reading with the teacher.

6. *Monitored reading:* The teacher can ask an aide or parent volunteer to listen to a student's oral reading. This activity requires that the teacher build the listening skills of the monitor. It may be necessary for the teacher to help the monitor understand that fluent reading does not necessarily mean fast reading. It means reading with good phrasing, rhythm, and without hesitation.

7. *Repeated reading:* Parents may assist with repeated reading at home by asking students to read orally the same 150- to 200-word passage repeatedly over several days. Students do not have to spend more than 10 minutes rereading each night.

Repetition and review in functional reading situations gradually brings about independence. After guidance through the first two or three paragraphs or pages, students may be able to study the final page or two by themselves. Before asking students to read independently, teachers should provide structure for successful independent reading by reminding them to decode when possible, to use good phrasing or chunking, and to reread to be sure they understand each sentence. When students have studied and completed the whole paragraph or story, they should reread the whole story orally. Group rereading of the story should be for pleasure and fluency.

TEACHING TIP 5-2U: Integrate reading and writing.

Bonnie Meyer, a colleague and teacher trainer, has suggested an interesting activity to practice phrase recognition and prepare students for independent report writing: Use consumable text, such as a book from Reading A–Z (http://www.readinga-z.com). With teacher guidance (e.g., "Highlight the phrases that name a bird"), students highlight the phrases that provide the answers to comprehension questions. This strategy reinforces the concept that the phrase may be more than just the name of the bird and can include a noun marker as well. "Use a green marker to underline phrases describing what each bird eats." "Use a blue marker to underline the phrases that tell where the bird eats." Even young students who have had the instruction with prepositions discussed previously will have success and visual reinforcement of the phrase concept in written text. Another effective approach to link writing with reading comprehension is to ask students to write a summary of the main idea and supporting details in the passage they just read.

TEACHING TIP 5-2V: Provide independent reading activities.

The following general principles should be kept in mind in designing meaningful independent activities:

1. Activities may be related to any skills previously taught. In general, worksheets can provide additional practice and/or enrichment (extension or stretching) of those skills.

2. Activities should be meaningful, and worksheets that ask students to fill in the blanks should be avoided because they do not encourage students to apply new learning to constructing meaning or text. Asking students to reread previously read text or to choose a book of interest at the student's independent reading level is likely to do more to reinforce taught reading skills. Asking students to write their own sentences or text about what they have read is more likely to foster development of their writing skills and integration of writing and reading skills to communicate ideas.

3. Tasks with functional utility are desirable. For example, students might alphabetize words on the decoding list for the day, copy them into a personal dictionary, and illustrate them. Phrases might also be copied and illustrated and used in booklets students write and use for further reading practice. See Sanderson (1985, 1988) for examples of this kind of independent activity with instructional materials that can be duplicated.

4. Activities that encourage students to develop metalinguistic awareness of their own learning are helpful. Teachers can give students newspapers and magazines and ask them to circle the words they can decode with a green marker and the words they cannot decode with a red marker. Then, the teacher can use those words for further teacher-guided instruction. The sports pages or the front page often have the easiest vocabulary words for students. This activity helps students build awareness of their own abilities to attack unfamiliar words.

5. Activities that encourage students to apply new learning to a variety of real-world applications are helpful. Alternatively, the teacher can ask students to search newspapers or magazines for phrases with particular words, such as nouns, verbs, or prepositional phrases. Using real-world reading material may stimulate their interest in reading on their own and not just when they have to read in class.

TEACHING TIP 5-2W: Provide varied experiences in written expression.

Written expression begins when words are combined to convey meaning in written language. In daily spelling lessons, students should be given practice in spelling not only single words but also phrases. Sentence building is an integral part of the daily writing and spelling lesson. The phrases created as part of the daily lesson can be combined to form sentences. Students love to anticipate what the sentence will be and add multiple phrases or rearrange them in novel ways. In planning, the teacher creates the sentence first, using words from the spelling lesson, and then identifies phrases to be written before assembling them into a sentence in a text. Begin by combining spelling words, partially decodable words, and familiar words into phrases (e.g., *when spring comes, in the sun, some students*). Then combine phrases into sentences (e.g., "Some students have fun in the sun when spring comes"). Discuss ways to add details to sentences by answering more of the editorial questions (who? what? where? when? why? how?). This instructional step is followed by opportunities for students to spell their own sentences.

After students begin to understand how to organize and compose sentences to express an idea, they are ready to write paragraphs. Paragraph writing requires integration of several tasks that lead toward eventual independent written work. The student must not only organize his or her thoughts and retrieve the language for each sentence to produce a cohesive sequence of ideas that expresses the thoughts but also spells conventionally and uses capitalization and punctuation appropriately. A good paragraph should have a clear topic sentence that tells the reader what the paragraph will be about. The body of the paragraph gives specific details that support and strengthen the topic sentence. The concluding sentence provides closure or leads the reader to the next paragraph. The goal is to develop proper paragraph writing with organization of thought and functional use of spelling, punctuation, and correct placement on paper. This approach allows students to integrate cognitive and language processes in writing. Guidelines for teaching written expression include the following:

1. Point out to the students during the Question of the Day that their answers to a three-part question can be the basis for a paragraph.

2. Ask them to brainstorm ideas on specific topics (e.g., what they do on a rainy day). Create a topic sentence to use in step 3.

3. As part of the Question of the Day, provide a topic sentence and ask students to create two or more sentences for the body of the paragraph and a concluding sentence.

4. Students may add to a teacher-generated topic sentence to create their own paragraphs. Class discussion of individual paragraphs can help students develop understanding of cohesion in written language.

5. Continue these oral activities until all students are secure with the concept of topic sentences. Daily practice with writing sentences leads to weekly practice in constructing clear, well-organized paragraphs independently. Writing multiparagraph papers provides a structure for note-taking and multipage reports.

Meaningful independent writing activities for instructional groups can be done in groups or individually. For example, students can do the following:

1. Brainstorm lists of words and create class charts or lists students can keep in their notebooks for use during independent writing lessons. This activity will help add variety to writing and eliminate the worry of incorrect spelling.

2. Compile a list of synonyms for the words *speak* or *said*.

3. Compile a list of synonyms for the word *movement*.

4. Compile a list of synonyms for the word *hungry*.

5. Add suffixes or prefixes to base words or start with the whole word and identify root, prefix, and suffixes (the teacher provides lists of base words, prefixes, suffixes, and whole words).

6. Practice with parts of speech is a practical application of written language skills. Even beginning writers can sort nouns, verbs, and adjectives if they understand that nouns are naming words and verbs are action words. Begin by providing lists. Then have students write their own sentences.

7. Use activities for constructing sentences that include the following parts of speech: noun markers, adjectives, and nouns; prepositions, adjectives, nouns; articles and nouns; articles, adjectives, and nouns; prepositional phrases; spatial (where) phrases; and temporal (when) phrases.

8. Provide a matched list of homonyms. Students copy the paired words on folded, half-ruled paper and then illustrate both spellings (e.g., *sale, sail; pane, pain; plane, plain; pale, pail; pare, pair, pear; cell, sell*).

9. The teacher provides a list of base words and points out the list of known prefixes and suffixes that are posted in the room. Students copy the base word, the prefix, and the suffix they are using in the appropriate columns. The whole word they have created is written in the last column.

Story starters allow students to apply their writing skills. They may be more effective for some students if they are allowed to verbalize their ideas before writing.

Written expression of ideas when students can write letters and spell words may be as simple as the completion of a sentence begun by the teacher or as complex as a complete story or written report. Between those two accomplishments come the instruction and guided practice that develop thought patterns and lead to successful independent written language. That guided instruction starts with teaching students to produce automatic and fluent handwriting. Students should be taught to write letters, then the letter or letters that spell the sounds used to spell the words. They will also benefit from activities that help them learn how complex words are formed from adding prefixes and suffixes to base words. Daily, guided practice in writing phrases and sentences from dictation is also helpful. Teacher modeling and teacher guidance in constructing well-formed paragraphs are also beneficial. As is the case for reading, well-planned, structured, sequential, and systematic lessons are necessary for developing writing skills.

TEACHING TIP 5-2X: Never assume that students understood the teacher's instructional talk.

One of the challenges of teaching is that teachers not only use oral language to teach but also they have to teach students to understand instructional talk. Such instructional talk is often in academic register and not the conversational register that students use outside school and during informal interactions with peers and others in school (Silliman & Scott, 2009). See Table 5.5.

Table 5.5. Dyslexia and oral and written language learning disability

What students heard and wrote down	What was dictated
Row musnt bill tinted "a."	Rome wasn't built in a day.
Turnip outs fir ply.	Turnabout is fair play.
Hum tedium tea set honor wall.	Humpty Dumpty sat on a wall.
Al waits beep a light.	Always be polite.
Diamond died weight for nome ann.	Time and tide wait for no man.

Note: Examples are from B. Wolf's classroom.

TEACHING TIP 5-2Y: Provide a language arts section with structured oral language and written language instruction.

In the elementary grades, teachers can provide explicit oral and written language instruction at the word (Chapter 4) and syntax/text (Chapter 5) levels through walk-abouts and differentiated instruction; however, in middle school and high school, special sections of language arts have helped many students with persisting oral and written language problems. Such sections do not have the stigma of the pull-out programs, but they do allow teachers to provide the structured language instruction many students with SLDs still require in an intellectually engaging way so that the students do not perceive it as being for "babies"—that is, just a repeat of instruction in the earlier grades. Rather, the content is grade-appropriate but tailored to the need of students who benefit from systematic, explicit, structured language lessons. For examples of such lessons with students in middle and early high school, see Berninger and Wolf (2009b) and also Chapter 7 in this book.

Assessment of Listening and Reading Comprehension, Oral and Written Expression, and Related Skills

Assessment tools are organized by skills and within skills in alphabetical order by first author surname (or test name after first use). Note that an asterisk (*) means individual assessment is required; otherwise the assessment tool is designed to be used in a group or can be adapted for group administration.

AURAL/ORAL LANGUAGE (LANGUAGE BY EAR AND MOUTH)

Oral Vocabulary

*Wechsler, D. (2003). *Wechsler Intelligence Scale for Children, Fourth Edition (WISC-4)*. San Antonio, TX: Pearson.
  Vocabulary subtest.

Aural-Oral Syntax

*Wiig, E.H., Semel, E., & Secord, W.A. (2013). *Clinical Evaluations of Language Fundamentals, Fifth Edition (CELF-5)*. San Antonio, TX: Pearson Education, Inc.
  Formulated Sentences.

Aural-Oral Text Comprehension

*Woodcock, R.W., Mather, N., & McGrew, K. (2008). *Woodcock-Johnson III Tests of Achievement (WJ III ACH)*. Rolling Meadows, IL: Riverside.
Following Directions and Oral Comprehension.

Pragmatics

*Phelps-Terasaki, D. & Phelps-Gunn, T. (2007). *Test of Pragmatic Language, Second Edition (TOPL-2)*. Austin, TX: Pro-Ed.

Word Finding

*Delis, D., Kaplan, E., & Kramer, J. (2001). *Delis-Kaplan Executive Function System (D-KEFS)*. San Antonio, TX: The Psychological Corporation/Pearson.
Verbal Fluency subtest.

ORAL READING (LANGUAGE BY EYE AND MOUTH)
Oral Text Reading

*National Assessment of Educational Progress (NAEP) ratings for fluency (https://nces.ed.gov/nationsreportcard/)

*Wiederholt, L., & Bryant, B. (2011). *Gray Oral Reading Test, Fifth Edition*. San Antonio, TX: Pearson.
Score for accuracy and rate.

READING COMPREHENSION (LANGUAGE BY EYE AND MOUTH)
Reading Comprehension: Text Accuracy

*Wechsler, D. (1991). *Wechsler Individual Achievement Test, Third Edition (WIAT III)*. San Antonio, TX: Harcourt Assessment.
Reading Comprehension.

*WJ III
Passage Comprehension.

SILENT READING
COMPREHENSION (LANGUAGE BY EYE AND HAND)
Silent Reading Comprehension:
Words, Morphology, and Syntax in Sentences

Berninger, V.W. (2007b). *Process Assessment of the Learner, Second Edition (PAL-II): Diagnostic for Reading and Writing (PAL-II RW)*. San Antonio, TX: Pearson.
Sentence Sense (Accuracy and Fluency) and Does It Fit? (Choose pseudowords with suffixes to fit in blank in sentences.)

Silent Reading Comprehension of Content

Wagner, R.K., Torgesen, J., Rashotte, C.A., & Pearson, N. (2010). *Test of Silent Reading Efficiency and Comprehension (TOSREC)*. Austin, TX: Pro-Ed.

Reading Vocabulary Meaning:
Word Level and Reading Comprehension: Text Level

MacGinitie, W., MacGinitie, R., Maria, K., Dreyer, L., & Hughes, K. (2000, norms updated 2006). *Gates-MacGinitie Reading Tests (GMRT), Fourth Edition*. Rolling Meadows, IL: Riverside.

COMPOSING

Composing: Word Finding

WIAT III
  Word Fluency.

Composing: Sentences

Typically given individually but could be adapted for group administration.

WIAT III
  Sentence Combining.

WJ III
  Writing Fluency.

Composing: Texts

Typically given individually but could be adapted for group administration.

PAL-II RW
  Narrative prompts for length and fluency (and handwriting and spelling during composing). Note taking and expository writing.

KTEA-3
  Written Expression subtest with cross-genre writing activities.

Curriculum-Based Assessment and
Intervention for Integrated Oral and Written Language

*Nelson, N.W., Plante, E., Helm-Estabrooks, N., & Hotz, G. (2016). *Test of Integrated Language and Literacy Skills™ (TILLS™)*. Baltimore, MD: Paul H. Brookes Publishing Co.
  Intended for children 6–18 years, the TILLS™ has been standardized 1) to identify language and literacy disorders, 2) to document patterns of relative strengths and weaknesses, and 3) to track changes in language and literacy skills over time. The 15 subtests of this curriculum-based language

assessment and intervention are based on a model of two language levels (sound/word and sentence/discourse) by four modalities (listening, speaking, reading, and writing).

Planning Instruction Based on Assessment Results and Progress Monitoring

- Identify individual students who fall below the lower limit of the average range ($-2/3$ standard deviation or 25th percentile or standard score of 90 on a test with a most average/mean score of 100 or a scaled score of 8 on a test with a most average/mean score of 10 or a z-score of -.66z on a research measure with a most average/mean score of 0). In some schools, the interdisciplinary team may decide to also identify any students who fall below the most average/mean score (50th percentile).

- Go to Appendix 5B and choose an instructional tool for each skill that meets the first or second criterion above.

- For progress monitoring, readminister the assessment tool after the instructional program is completed.

Instructional Resources for Listening and Reading Comprehension, Oral and Written Expression, and Related Skills at the Vocabulary, Syntax, and Text Levels

CHILDREN'S BOOKS THAT HELP WITH LANGUAGE LEARNING

Homonyms

Alda, A. (2006). *Did you say pears?* Toronto, Canada: Tundra Books.

Barretta, G. (2007). *Dear deer: A book of homophones*. New York: Henry Holt.

Cleary, B. (2005). *How much can a bare bear bear? What are homonyms and homophones?* Minneapolis, MN: Lerner Publishing Group.

Gwynne, F. (1976). *Chocolate moose for dinner*. New York, NY: Simon & Schuster.

Gwynne, F. (1980). *The king who rained*. New York, NY: Simon & Schuster.

Gwynne, F. (1988). *A little pigeon toad*. New York, NY: Simon & Schuster.

Hambleton, L., & Turhan, S. (2007). *Telling tails: Fun with homonyms*. London, UK: Milet Publishing.

Terban, M. (1982). *Eight ate: A feast of homonym riddles*. New York, NY: Clarion Books.

Idioms

Arnold, T. (2004). *Even more parts.* New York, NY: Scholastic.

Terban, M. (1983). *In a pickle and other funny idioms.* New York, NY: Houghton Mifflin.

Terban, M. (1987). *Mad as a wet hen! and other funny idioms.* New York, NY: Houghton Mifflin.

Terban, M. (1990). *Punching the clock: Funny action idioms.* New York, NY: Houghton Mifflin.

Play with Language

Scieszca, J. (1991). *Knights of the kitchen table.* New York, NY: Viking.

Terban, M. (1993). *It figures! Fun figures of speech.* New York, NY: Houghton Mifflin.

Also, any titles by Dr. Seuss.

Word Play

Bourke, L. (1991). *Eye spy.* San Francisco, CA: Chronicle Books.

Gwynne, F. (1976). *Chocolate moose for dinner.* New York, NY: Simon & Schuster.

Gwynne, F. (1980). *The king who rained.* New York, NY: Simon & Schuster.

Gwynne, F. (1980). *The sixteen hand horse.* New York, NY: Simon & Schuster.

Gwynne, F. (1988). *A little pigeon toad.* New York, NY: Simon & Schuster.

Juster, M. (1961). *The phantom tollbooth.* New York, NY: Random House.

Sweet, M. (2013). *Little red writing.* San Francisco, CA: Chronicle Books.

Terban, M. (1988). *The dove dove.* New York, NY: Clarion Books.

Parts of Speech

Adverbs

Cleary, B. (2003). *Dearly, nearly, insincerely: What is an adverb?* Minneapolis, MN: Lerner Publishing Group.

Heller, R. (1998). *Up, up and away: A book about adverbs.* New York, NY: Penguin Young Readers Group.

Adjectives

Brown, M. (1949). *The important book.* New York, NY: Harper & Row.

Cleary, B. (2001). *Hairy, scary, ordinary: What is an adjective?* Minneapolis, MN: Lerner Publishing Group.

Cleary, B. (2007). *Quirky, jerky, extra-perky: More about adjectives.* Minneapolis, MN: Lerner Publishing Group.

Heller, R. (1989). *Many luscious lollipops.* New York, NY: Grosset & Dunlap.

Hubbard, W. (2003). *C is for curious.* New York, NY: Scholastic.

Viorst, J. (1971). *Tenth good thing about Barney.* New York, NY: Simon & Schuster.

Viorst, J. (1987). *Alexander and the terrible, horrible, rotten, no good, very bad day.* New York, NY: Simon & Schuster.

Yagoda, B. (2007). *When you catch an adjective, kill it: The parts of speech, for better and/or worse.* New York, NY: Broadway Books.

Nouns

Heller, R. (1998). *Merry-go-round: A book about nouns.* New York, NY: Penguin Young Readers Group.

Terban, M. (1986). *Your foot's on my feet and other tricky nouns.* Minneapolis, MN: Lerner Publishing Group.

Pronouns

Cleary, B. (2004). *I and you and don't forget who: What is a pronoun?* Minneapolis, MN: Lerner Publishing Group.

Heller, R. (1999). *Mine, all mine: A book about pronouns.* New York, NY: Penguin Young Readers Group.

Prepositions

Cleary, B. (2002). *Under, over, by the clover: What is a preposition?* Minneapolis, MN: Carolrhoda Books.

Heller, R. (1998). *Behind the mask: A book about prepositions.* New York, NY: Penguin.

Punctuation

Truss, L. & Timmons, B. (2006). *Eats, shoots & leaves: Why, commas really do make a difference!* New York, NY: Putnam.

Truss, L. & Timmons, B. (2007). *The girl's like spaghetti: Why, you can't manage without apostrophes!* New York, NY: Putnam.

Truss, L. & Timmons, B. (2008). *Twenty-odd ducks: Why, every punctuation mark counts!* New York, NY: Putnam.

Days of the Week

Carle, E. (1981). *The very hungry caterpillar.* New York, NY: Philomel.

Months of the Year

Sendak, M. (1976). *Chicken soup with rice.* New York, NY: Harper Collins.

LISTENING COMPREHENSION: AURAL TEXT LEVEL

Opitz, M., & Zbarachki, M. (2004). *Listen hear! 25 effective listening comprehension strategies.* Portsmouth, NH: Heinemann.

ORAL AND WRITTEN WORD-LEVEL
VOCABULARY AND TEXT-LEVEL COMPREHENSION

Beck, I.L., & McKeown, M.G. (2004). *Elements of reading: Vocabulary.* Austin, TX: Harcourt.

Beck, I.L., & McKeown, M.G. (2004). *Text talk.* New York, NY: Scholastic.

Beck, I.L., & McKeown, M.G., (2006). *Improving comprehension with questioning the author: A fresh and enhanced view of a proven approach.* New York, NY: Scholastic.

Beck, I.L, McKeown, M.G., & Kucan, L. (2013). *Bringing words to life: Robust vocabulary instruction* (2nd ed.). New York, NY: Guilford Press.

Cain, K., & Oakhill, H. (Eds.) (2007). *Children's comprehension problems in oral and written language: A cognitive perspective.* New York, NY: Guilford.

Carlisle, J. (2003). *Vocabulary in reasoning and reading.* Cambridge, MA: Educators Publishing Services.

Prescott-Griffin, M., & Witherell, N. (2004). *Fluency in focus: Comprehension strategies for all young readers.* Portsmouth, NH: Heinemann.

Stahl, S., & Nagy, W. (2005). *Teaching word meaning.* Mahwah, NJ: Lawrence Erlbaum.

ORAL READING FLUENCY LINKED TO READING COMPREHENSION

Denton, C., Vaughn, S., Wexler, J., Bryan, D., & Reed, D. (2012). *Effective instruction for middle school students with reading difficulties: The reading teacher's sourcebook.* Baltimore, MD: Paul H. Brookes Publishing Co.

Hiebert, E.H. (2003). *Quick reads.* Parsippany, NJ: Pearson Learning.

Read Naturally. (2006). *Read Naturally Masters Edition.* Saint Paul, Minnesota: Read Naturally.

READING COMPREHENSION: WRITTEN TEXT

Carlisle, J. (2000b). *Beginning reasoning and reading, reasoning and reading level one, reasoning and reading level two.* Cambridge, MA: Educators Publishing Service. See the paragraph understanding activities.

Carlisle, J., & Rice, M. (2002). *Improving reading comprehension: Research-based principles and practices.* Timonium, MD: York Press.
See the research-supported paragraph and discourse comprehension activities.

PLAY WITH LANGUAGE

Spector, C. (2009). *As far as words go: Activities for understanding ambiguous language and humor* (Rev. ed.). Baltimore, MD: Paul H. Brookes Publishing Co.

WRITING INSTRUCTION

Carlisle, J. (1996). *Models for writing: Levels A, B, and C.* Novato, CA: Academic Therapy.

Nelson, N., Bahr, C., & Van Meter, A. (2004). *The writing lab approach to language instruction and intervention.* Baltimore, MD: Paul H. Brookes Publishing Co. Offers practical suggestions for teachers to use in scaffolding instruction for students with language learning disability.

Troia, G.A. (Ed.) (2009). *Instruction and assessment for struggling writers: Evidence-based practices.* New York: Guilford.

MORPHOLOGICAL AWARENESS AND VOCABULARY

Bear, D., Invernizzi, M., Templeton, S., & Johnston, F. (2000). *Words their way: Word study for phonics, vocabulary, and spelling instruction* (2nd ed.). Upper Saddle River, NJ: Merrill.

Carlisle, J. (2000b). *Beginning reasoning and reading, reasoning and reading level one, reasoning and reading level two.* Cambridge, MA: Educators Publishing Service.
See the vocabulary activities (analogies, using in another context, inferring from context, etc.).

Carlisle, J., & Rice, M. (2002). *Improving reading comprehension: Research-based principles and practices.* Timonium, MD: York Press.
See the research-supported vocabulary strategies.

Fifer, M., & Flowers, N. (1993). *Vocabulary from classical roots: Strategic vocabulary instruction through Greek and Latin roots. Grades 7–11.* Cambridge, MA: Educators Publishing Service.

Hodkinson, K., & Adams, S. (2000). *Wordly wise 3000. Systematic, sequential vocabulary development.* Cambridge, MA: Educators Publishing Service.

Lubliner, S. (2005). *Getting into words: Vocabulary instruction that strengthens comprehension.* Baltimore, MD: Paul H. Brookes Publishing Co.
Includes strategies and cue sheets for clarifying (in encounters with unknown words), mining memory, all in the family (studying word structure, negative prefixes, root webs, root detectives, word trees), considering

the context, signal words for sequence, cause and effect, compare and contrast, stop for, substituting synonyms, etc.

Remedia. *Quizmo: Structural Skills*. Scottsdale, AZ: Author.
Provides five games in one—a bingo style game that develops understanding of the word formation process (bases, affixes) with application to vocabulary and spelling.

SYNTACTIC AND TEXT AWARENESS AND PROCESSING

Brandon, L. (2006). *Sentences at a glance*. Boston, MA: Houghton Mifflin.

Carlisle, J. (2000b). *Beginning reasoning and reading, reasoning and reading level one*. Cambridge, MA: Educators Publishing Service.
See the paragraph understanding activities.

Carlisle, J. (2000b). *Beginning reasoning and reading, reasoning and reading level one, reasoning and reading level two*. Cambridge, MA: Educators Publishing Service.
See the sentence activities.

Carlisle, J., & Rice, M. (2002). *Improving reading comprehension: Research-based principles and practices*. Timonium, MD: York Press.
See the research-supported paragraph and discourse comprehension activities.

Ehrenworth, M., & Vinton, V. (2005). *The power of grammar: Unconventional approaches to the conventions of language*. Portsmouth, NH: Heinemann.

Goldstein, B., Waugh, J., & Linksky, K. (2004). *Grammar to go: How it works and how to use it*. Boston, MA: Houghton Mifflin.

Institute of Learning. *Word shapes for teaching syntax*. Tacoma, WA: ARK Institute of Learning.

Mar Ban Industries. (2004). *Sentence says: The quick thinking sentence creation game*. Chatsworth, CA: Mar Ban Industries.
This game can be played by children in Grades 3–12. Children are dealt cards with letters that represent the first letter in words they choose, and must construct grammatically acceptable sentences that contain a word for each letter in cards they are dealt.

Opitz, M., & Zbarachki, M. (2004). *Listen hear! 25 effective listening comprehension strategies*. Portsmouth, NH: Heinemann.

Remedia. *Build a sentence: Who, what, where, when. Grades 1–5*. Scottsdale, AZ: Author.

Terry, B. *The sentence zone*. Retrieved from http://www.highnoonbooks.com

Wong, L. (2002). *Sentence essentials: A grammar guide*. Boston, MA: Houghton Mifflin.

GAMES FOR PARENTS, TEACHERS, AND OLDER STUDENTS TO DEVELOP LANGUAGE SKILLS

LinguiSystems. *Grammar scrabble and other games*. Retrieved from http://www .linguisystem.com

SCOTTISH RITE

The Scottish Rite organization provides free assessment and treatment services for children with dyslexia in some states, as well as free assessment and treatment for oral language disability (in children aged 2–8 years) in other states. Because oral language disability typically leads to oral and written language learning disability if not treated, this is a wonderful free resource. Individuals with language learning disabilities may have exceptional talents in nonverbal expression of ideas by hand; thus, teachers should strive to create learning environments in schools that are nurturing of hands-on learning and not just verbal learning.

Teacher Resources for Listening and Reading Comprehension, Oral and Written Expression, and Related Skills

At the beginning of the school year teachers can send home questionnaires that include questions about listening and reading comprehension and oral and written expression and related skills that will help them identify those students who may need extra help and ongoing monitoring with these skills. Each student should keep a portfolio to collect samples of books they have read and written reports about and oral presentations they have given at school. In addition, students can keep a homework folder in which they organize the assignments they do at home but bring to school for the teacher to review with them. Finally, parent conferences in person and over phone and e-mail are helpful ways to reach out to parents to help their child in developing oral and written language comprehension and expression skills.

PARENT QUESTIONNAIRE

1. At what age did your child start to talk in single words? Word combinations? Sentences?

2. Did your child have difficulty putting words together in conversation during the preschool years?

3. Does your child have difficulty following directions?

4. Does your child now or in the past have difficulty with understanding oral instruction at school?

5. Does your child now or in the past have difficulty with expressing ideas in oral language?

6. Does your child now or in the past have difficulty with oral reading of passages?

7. Does your child now or in the past have difficulty understanding what she or he reads?

8. Do you have any concerns about your child's listening or reading compre-
    hension or oral or written expression this year or last year?

9. Is there family history of listening or reading comprehension or oral or
    written expression problems in your family?

READING AND WRITING PORTFOLIOS

Keep monthly samples of reading and writing activities at school that are representative of the student's work and can be examined across the school year.

HOMEWORK

Keep samples of the student's homework to review whether assignments are
completed as expected, meet expectations, and are turned in on time.

PARENT CONFERENCES

Please indicate your preferred mode(s) for communicating with the school.
Please understand that the teacher is busy with your child and others, so he or
she cannot reply to your texts during the school day. However, concerns and
information you share will be discussed at interdisciplinary team meetings to
address your child's educational needs.

In person:

Over phone:

Over e-mail or web site:

Assessment–Instruction Links for Math Concepts, Computations, and Problem Solving

 ## Research Lessons

Chapter 6 presents three Research Lessons. The first two each have one associated Teaching Tip, and the third has two associated Teaching Tips.

COMPLEXITY OF MATH
Research Lesson 6-1

Many concepts, symbols, procedures, and applications are involved in learning math, which is a shorthand nickname for mathematics. That may be why in the United Kingdom, the nickname is the plural word *maths*! In reality, much of the curriculum in kindergarten and the elementary grades has historically focused on arithmetic in the United States. *Arithmetic*, a Greek word, means "number" and is the most elementary branch of mathematics that focuses on the study of numbers—their properties and their operations (addition, subtraction, multiplication, and division). Number theory is the most elementary branch of mathematics, but it informs the top level branches of math including algebra, geometry, and calculus, which historically have been taught in the secondary grades in the United States.

Key number concepts include counting, internal quantitative concepts versus external visual symbols for representing quantity and its distributions along a number line, place value, and part–whole relationships. Key operations for operating on numbers include addition, subtraction, multiplication, and division. Both simple math facts for each operation and procedures for performing these operations contribute to learning math calculation, which can be performed on single-place or multiplace numbers (whole numbers with or without decimals) or fractions (with or without whole numbers). Math problem solving is often taught with word problems, with key words signaling one of the four basic operations, but it can also be taught with a focus on everyday math problem solving (application to the real world).

Counting   Rote counting emerges first, but with hands-on experience in counting objects in the real world, students develop one-to-one correspondence. That is, they learn that as numbers increase in counting order, they stand for more quantity.

Internal Concepts Versus External Symbols   Each individual *number* (the internal quantitative concept that represents an amount linked to counting order) has a *numeral* (the external visual symbol that stands for the internal number concept).

Internal Versus External Number Line   Increasing quantity in counting order is represented in the mind and brain as an internal number line (e.g., Dehaene, 2011). This internal line and counting play a major role in proving theorems in higher mathematics, as illustrated in the story of Erdős, the man who only loved numbers, told by Hoffman (1998). Teachers can use an external number line to represent counting order of sequential numbers to teach math facts for the four basic operations early in the mathematics journey (see Chapters 4 and 5 in Berninger, 2015).

Place Value   A small number of numerals (0, 1, 2, 3, 4, 5, 6, 7, 8, and 9) stand for an infinite number of numbers in base 10. Both whole numbers and parts of numbers can be represented by place value. The place in which a numeral or digit (to reflect the historical origin in the 10 digits of five fingers on two hands) appears indicates the value by which the numeral has to be multiplied—for example, the ones place, the tens place, the hundreds place etc.—to determine its quantitative value. Zero is used as a place holder to indicate the absence of a quantitative value. Place value can be used to represent mixed numbers with whole numbers to left of zero and decimals to right of zero.

Part–Whole Relationships   Numbers may also have relative rather than absolute values, as in counting order along the number line. That is, the value is related to the number of parts into which a whole has been divided.

Understanding part–whole relationships depends on understanding relative versus absolute number concepts—the quantity is related to the number of parts the whole has been divided into rather than the absolute quantity. Parts of numbers can be expressed by fractions or decimals (fractions based on tenths of a whole). Knowledge of part–whole relationships contributes to understanding fractions and mixed numbers (wholes plus fraction or a decimal based on tenths of a whole).

Key Operations   Numbers can be added together—that is, combined, as in addition. Numbers can be taken away—that is removed, as in subtraction. Numbers can be combined through multiple, repeated additions—that is, multiplied together. Numbers can be taken away through multiple subtractions—that is, they can be divided by removing them from the starting number by a constant increment until zero is reached. Understanding these four basic operations conceptually should be taught along with the basic math facts for each of the four operations. These facts are best taught through multisensory-motor touching and orally counting along the external number line, followed by writing the math fact in visual numerals, and using multimodal methods (look-say, look-write, hear-say, hear-write) to review the math facts until they are accessed automatically. It is also important to teach the steps of computational operations in reference to both time (ordered steps or procedures) and space (arranged in columns, diagonals, and other spatial displays). See Chapters 4 and 5 in Berninger (2015) and the Teaching Tips in Chapter 6. In the United States, the National Mathematics Advisory Panel (2008) concluded that understanding number concepts and operations is essential for effective use of computer tools for calculation; the computer tools alone are not a substitute for understanding the quantitative basis of math facts and operations. See Chapter 11 for use of technology tools in math instruction and assignments.

Math Problem Solving   Learning to apply math to a variety of problems in the real world is often taught using word problems. These require teaching math-specific vocabulary that cues the kind of operations needed to solve the problem, listening comprehension if the teacher presents the problem orally, reading comprehension if the teacher presents the problem visually in words, writing skills for producing legible and automatic numerals and other math symbols, using appropriate place value, performing math calculations in correct sequential steps across time, and correct movement and placement in dimensional space along right-left, left-right, top-down, up-down, and diagonal axes. Also needed are the appropriate use of writing tools (which draw on sensory-motor skills), self-regulation and self-monitoring, positive emotion/ motivation, and cognitive and working memory processes. That is, all brain systems involved in language learning are also involved in math problem solving (see Research Lesson 6-3 later in Chapter 6).

Algebra   The National Mathematics Advisory Panel (2008) has set second-level algebra as the goal for all students to achieve by high school graduation and has noted the importance of understanding fractions in learning algebra. Thus, teaching students to understand the part–whole relationships underlying fractions should be a high priority in the elementary grades (e.g., Bailey, Hoard, Nugent, & Geary, 2012). Students also need to be taught how to read algebra problems (Hinsley, Hayes, & Simon, 1977). Algebra contributes to cognitive development by helping students learn that multiple rather than single variables may be involved in concepts, the same whole can vary on each side of the equals sign as to the number of parts the whole is divided into, and some variables have quantities that distribute continuously but others are constant.

Geometry and Measurement   These skills can be taught using hands-on learning activities, such as through building two-dimensional and three-dimensional shapes using blocks, LEGOs, or other manipulatives. Learning to tell time is still an important skill even in the digital age. The circular clock face helps students understand the concept of circular number lines (not all lines are linear) and circular time (seconds within minutes within hours within days within months and years). Circular clock faces can also be used to teach fractions of whole. Once students understand the concepts in measuring time, they can then be taught how digital clocks represent the same time information using place value. Hands-on activities also support learning to recognize a variety of two-dimensional and three-dimensional shapes and measuring them using different measurement scales. There has been renewed interest in outdoor education as a way to learn the geometric concepts based on the three-dimensional space of nature that contrasts with the three-dimensional space of the buildings that house computers and classrooms. In nature and higher mathematics, fractals (irregular lines like on coast lines) and motion (moving across space and time) play important roles.

Calculus   Two important lessons are learned from calculus. First, what is on the left and right of the equal signs is not always equal. What is on the left may be transformed into what is on the right. Second, not all relationships between variables are linear—a line represents how changes in one variable are related to change in a second variable. Some are nonlinear—a curved line may be needed to represent how changes in one variable are related to changes in a second variable.

TEACHING TIP 6-1: Link math instruction to evidence-based assessment at the beginning of the year and response to instruction to evidence-based assessment at the end of the year.

The goal of Chapter 6 is therefore to provide an evidence-based model of which math concepts and skills to assess at which grade level (see Appendix 6A) and resources for linking assessment findings with math instruction. In the text, examples of assessment tools for specific kinds of math skills are described, organized by grade levels and referred to by their abbreviated titles by which they are known in the schools. In Appendix 6A, specific math assessment tools are provided along with their full names spelled out and citations for locating the assessment tools. If assessment shows there is a weakness in one or more specific math skills at a specific grade level, instructional resources (Appendix 6B), other teacher resources (Appendix 6C), and Teaching Tips in Chapter 6 are provided to plan and implement individually tailored math instruction. Thus, the text and appendices are designed to use in conjunction with each other for a developmental model of assessment–instruction links for math.

Also see Chapter 13 for a discussion of how a multidisciplinary team can support the general education teacher in 1) conducting the assessments to identify students needing individually tailored instruction for specific math skills, and 2) implement that instruction. Tools for instruction in Appendix 6B also indicate whether the test can be given in a group or require individual administration. The instructional tools can be used in large-group instruction or small-group instruction formed for students with similar instructional needs.

EVIDENCE-BASED ASSESSMENT

These measures are based on studies in Math Trek, a longitudinal study of math development of typically developing and advanced math learners (Robinson, Abbott, Berninger, & Busse, 1996; Robinson, Abbott, Berninger, Busse, & Mukhopadhyay, 1997) and Yates's (1996) dissertation on screening for math disabilities.

Kindergarten

One-to-one correspondence in counting. Because one to one correspondence is the foundation for developing the concept of quantity needed for arithmetic, that is number sense, give PAL-II M Oral Counting. Also this task is sensitive to the early development of the internal number line that supports working memory in learning math facts.

Copy and name numerals from model. Because numerals are the alphabet for writing number concepts, it is important to monitor that every student can write and name each of the 10 numerals (digits). Write one numeral (0 to 9) on each of ten index cards. Shuffle the cards and ask each child to write and name the numeral. Record results on teacher created record form.

First Grade

Auomatic and legible numeral writing 15. Because arithmetic learning depends on writing numerals, it is important to assess legibility and automaticity of not only letter writing but also numeral writing. Give PAL-II M Numeral Writing. Score for first 15 seconds and total legibility.

Navigating the internal number line. Learning number facts requires counting forward or backward by fixed increments or number of steps along the internal number line supported by working memory. Give PAL-II M Oral Counting.

Involving sensory and fine motor systems in math fact retrieval. Automatic retrieval of math facts benefits from alternative approaches to linking sensory input and motor output (e.g., look write or listen say). Give PAL-II M Look and Write for addition facts up to 10 and subtraction math facts up to 10.

Column addition and subtraction without regrouping. In first grade children learn to add and subtract with numbers in a single column and often two columns. Give PAL-II M Computational Operations.

Choosing strategy for problem solving. The first step in solving a word problem is to choose a strategy for solving it. Give PAL-II M Math Problem Solving, in which students decide which of the computation choices provided would be a solution to the visually displayed word problem the teacher reads to them.

Second Grade

Automatic and legible numeral writing. For the same reason as in first grade, give PAL-II M Numeral Writing. Score for 15 seconds and total legibility.

Navigating the internal number line. Learning number facts requires counting forward or backward by fixed increments or number of steps along the internal number line supported by working memory. Learning mental math requires starting at different start points and performing different calculations along the internal number line. Give PAL-II M Oral Counting.

Involving sensory and fine motor systems in math fact retrieval. Automatic retrieval of math facts benefits from alternative approaches to linking sensory input and motor output (e.g., look write or listen say). Give PAL-II M Look and Write for addition facts up to 20 and subtraction math facts up to 20.

Place value for writing multiplace numerals. Place value signifies the quantity a numeral symbolizes depending on which place it is in (ones, tens, hundreds, etc.). Give PAL-II M Place Value.

Column addition and subtraction with regrouping. In second grade children learn to add and subtract with numbers in multiple columns and to use regrouping across places/columns. Give PAL-II M Computational Operations.

Choosing strategy for problem solving. The first step in solving a word problem is to choose a strategy for solving it. Give PAL-II M Math Problem Solving, in which students decide which of the computation choices provided would be a solution to the visually displayed word problem the teacher reads to them.

Third Grade

Automatic and legible numeral writing. For the same reasons, give the same measure as in second grade.

Navigating the internal number line. Learning number facts requires counting forward or backward by fixed increments or number of steps along the internal number line supported by working memory. Learning mental math requires starting at different start points and performing different calculations along the internal number line. Give PAL-II M Oral Counting.

Relating math facts to number line involving sensory and fine motor systems. Give PAL-II M Look and Write for multiplication facts by 2, 3, 4, and 5 and related division facts.

Place value for writing multiplace numerals. For same reason as in second grade, give PAL-II M Place Value.

Column addition and subtraction with regrouping. In third grade, children continue to add and subtract with numbers in multiple columns and to use regrouping across places/columns. They are also introduced to multiplying and dividing by single digit multipliers or divisors. Give PAL-II M Computational Operations and at least one other measure of Math Calculation in Appendix 6A.

Part–whole concept. Learning that numbers can have relative rather than absolute quantitative value underlies learning measurement and fractions. Give PAL-II M Part–Whole.

Choosing strategy for problem solving. For the same reason as in second grade, give PAL-II M Math Problem Solving on which students decide which of the computation choices provided would be a solution to the visually displayed word problem the teacher reads to them. Also give at least one other test of Math Problem Solving in Appendix 6A.

Fourth to Fifth Grades

Navigating the internal number line. Learning number facts requires counting forward or backward by fixed increments or number of steps along the internal number line supported by working memory. Learning mental math requires starting at different start points and performing different calculations along the internal number line. Give PAL-II M Oral Counting.

Relating math facts to number line involving sensory and fine motor systems. Give PAL-II M Look and Write for multiplication facts by 6, 7, 8, 9, and 10 and related division facts, and also switching between addition and subtraction and switching between multiplication and division.

Place value for writing multiplace numerals. For same reason as in second grade, give PAL-II M Place Value.

Calculation. In fourth and fifth grade students continue to learn and review multiplying and dividing by single and multiple digit multipliers and divisors. Give PAL-II M Computational Operations and at least one other measure of Math Calculation in Appendix 6A.

Part–whole concept. Learning that numbers can have relative rather than absolute quantitative value underlies learning measurement and fractions. Give PAL-II M Part–Whole.

Choosing strategy for problem solving. For same reason as in second and third grade, give PAL-II M Problem Solving. Also give at least one other test of Math Problem Solving in Appendix 6A.

Sixth to Eighth Grades

For the same reasons, give the same measures as in fourth to fifth grades. For students who continue to struggle in math, involve the interdisciplinary team in comprehensive assessment.

Ninth to Twelfth Grades

For students who continue to struggle in math, involve the interdisciplinary team in comprehensive assessment.

DEVELOPMENTAL AND INDIVIDUAL DIFFERENCES IN LEARNING MATH
Research Lesson 6-2

Behavioral and brain research has documented the typical developmental trajectories in math learning (e.g., Geary, 1994; Nunes & Bryant, 1996; Siegler & Lortie Forgues, 2014; Watts, Duncan, Siegler, & Davis-Kean, 2014), as well as developmental and individual differences (Geary, 2010). Because of individual differences in math learning, different students may follow different developmental paths in their math learning (Fuchs et al., 2010). For example, students may have difficulty with any of the following:

- Counting (Geary, Hoard, & Byrd-Craven, 2004)

- Math fact retrieval (Geary, Hoard, & Bailey, 2012)

- The four basic arithmetic operations (Rosenberg-Lee, Chang, Young, Wu, & Menon, 2011)

- The internal number line (Geary, Hoard, Nugent, & Byrd-Craven, 2008)

- Part–whole relationships (Mazzocco & Devlin, 2008)

- Working memory (Swanson & Beebe-Frankenberger, 2004; Swanson, Jerman, & Zheng, 2008)

- Exact math (for which there is a correct answer)

- Estimated math (judging whether an answer to a math problem is a reaonable one) (Mazzocco, Feigenson, & Halberda, 2001)

- Mental math (Rivera, Reiss, Eckert, & Menon, 2005)

Other students do not have these difficulties. Student profiles may also vary in which of these skills they may have weaknesses versus strengths. For example, some students struggle with written operations (calculations) but excel at geometry, algebra, or visual-spatial higher-math thinking.

Some individual differences are related to low income or cultural diversity, but research shows there are ways to nurture math achievement in students across income (Siegler & Ramani, 2011) and cultural groups (Greene, 1996; Gutiérrez, 1996, 1999). Regardless of the nature of the specific math skill with which a student struggles or other individual or developmental differences, research has shown the value of explicit, systematic instruction (Mayer, 2005).

Some students may be advanced in their math learning overall or in specific areas of math development (Robinson, Abbott, Berninger, Busse, & Mukhopadhyay, 1997). These students need to be taught math at their advanced instructional levels. Some students with math talent may also have co-occurring specific learning disabilities (SLDs; see Chapter 10).

TEACHING TIP 6-2: Individually tailor math instruction to developmental and individual differences in math learners.

Because of developmental and individual differences in math learning, differential instruction is as important in math as in reading and writing. Just as forming instructional groups within classrooms or across classrooms aimed at students' instructional levels can facilitate learning to read and spell (see Chapter 7), so can they for math instruction. In elementary school, these groups can be formed for skills related to acquiring the concept of numbers, basic facts, operations, and word problem solving. In middle school and high school, differentiated instruction can be provided in math sections that teach at a student's math instructional levels in an intellectually engaging way that also takes into account areas of interest in math and application across the content areas of the curriculum (see Chapter 8). Such differentiated instruction is not the same as ability grouping used in the past. However, with systematic annual assessment and related differentiated instruction, the number of students with persisting problems in math can be reduced significantly.

MULTIPLE SYSTEMS INVOLVED IN MATH LEARNING
Research Lesson 6-3

Effective math instruction draws on all five functional brain systems that are related to the five domains of development: sensory and motor, oral and written language, cognitive and memory, social-emotional, and attention and executive function.

Sensory and Motor   One of the surprises of a neuropsychological study of math was that sensory-motor integration predicted math calculation skill. The measure of sensory-motor integration required identifying a numeral by naming it without any visual input—only by tactile kinesthetic sensation of the sequence of movements the examiner used to produce the numerals on the student's fingertip (Shurtleff, Faye, Abbott, & Berninger, 1988). The ability to use grapho-motor skills to write numerals also plays a role in learning math (Busse et al., 2001; Yates, 1996). Counting objects by touching them and counting on one's fingers can also contribute to learning to count.

Oral and Written Language   Oral discussion is a missing component of math instruction in many classrooms in the United States. However, in China, oral language instruction is fundamental in math instruction (Zhou, Peverly, & Xin, 2006). For example, not only the teacher but the students assume the role of teacher in helping students who do not grasp a math concept and discuss it until all students understand it. Teachers should also provide reading instruction for reading math textbooks, which have domain-specific reading requirements (Bryant et al., 2008).

Cognition and Working Memory   Many kinds of thinking contribute to math problem solving (for examples in middle childhood and adolescence see Chapters 5 and 6 in Berninger, 2015). Different components of working memory may need to be taught for learning specific math skills (Meyer, Salimpoor, Wu, Geary, & Menon, 2010). However, if a student has a working memory problem, it does not appear that teaching cognitive strategies alone will be sufficient (Swanson, 2014).

Social-Emotional   Teacher–student relationships affect math learning (Crosnoe et al., 2010), as does a student's sense of self-efficacy (Midgley, Feldlaufer, & Eccles, 1989). The role of math anxiety in both students (Ma, 1999) and teachers (Sian, Gunderson, Ramirez, & Levine, 2010) has also been demonstrated in research and requires specialized approaches to overcome.

Attention and Executive Functions   Attention is involved in math problem solving (Swanson, 2011). Executive functions are also involved in math problem solving (Swanson & Sachse-Lee, 2001).

TEACHING TIP 6-3A: Design lessons that involve all five developmental domains.

Draw on sensorimotor, attention, and oral language processes in learning to write numerals, number facts, multiplace numbers, and perform math calculations; oral and written language in math vocabulary instruction and in teaching students to read word problems; focusing, switching, and sustaining attention in performing multistep computations and self-monitoring steps and final outcomes in all math work; and cognition in grasping math concepts and engaging intellectually in math problem solving (see Chapter 2). Draw on social-emotional systems in teaching students not to be math anxious but rather to develop self-efficacy and pleasure in solving math problems alone and with others. There are many ways to implement this Teaching Tip; the following five examples are provided to illustrate how teachers can do this.

EXAMPLE 1

Joyce Steeves of the International Dyslexia Association (IDA) teaches to all five developmental domains in the following way with students at all grade levels.

1. *Attention/executive functions:* Joyce emphasizes the importance of organizing the lessons in a manner that will help students self-regulate their own math learning. She recommends beginning with a 5-minute practice session in which one or more previous skills are reviewed to instill confidence. Note that to keep students engaged, each part of the lesson only lasts 5–10 minutes. Frequently varying learning activities provides the novelty the brain seeks and reduces the probability of brain habituation. Yet, a balance between review and practice of old learning and introduction and practice of new learning are provided so that learning is distributed over time and consolidated.

2. *Sensorimotor skills:* Joyce provides space for writing math facts, math computations, or math problems to solve, just as she does for writing instruction. For example, this might be on the board to allow gross and fine motor movements to be integrated with number concepts and numerals that represent them visually. This approach also enables the teacher to observe error patterns and provide feedback when necessary. This activity might last about 5 minutes.

3. *Oral language tied to number concepts:* For about 5 minutes, oral counting is used to reinforce math operations. For example, students count forward for addition or multiplication and backwards for subtraction. They may practice counting beginning at any number or practice skip counting to reinforce multiplication skills.

4. *Cognitive and working memory:* For about 5 minutes, students solve math problems mentally. If the student feels more comfortable with a pencil in

hand to use visual, motor, and kinesthetic cues to help with problem solving, that should be permitted.

5. *Oral language tied to math problem solving:* For the next 5 minutes, students talk about the math problems they just solved mentally. This oral discussion may include discussion of math-specific vocabulary, relevant math concepts, and brainstorming alternative ways to solve the problem.

6. *Oral language to teach a new concept:* For the next 10 minutes, a new concept is introduced.

7. *Written computation or problem solving:* Students then apply the new concept to their own written work for the next 10 minutes. Joyce observes the students closely to give the necessary help for success and feedback as needed.

8. *Oral language to review the important learning*: Some days, Joyce reviews the new learning in the lesson just ending. Other days, she reviews the learning from day to day, for the week, or for a unit on a specific topic.

EXAMPLE 2

Bev Wolf visited a first grade classroom in National City, California. When the students had been writing for a while, the teacher called a break. The class stood and counted to 100, then counted in reverse from 100 back to 1. The counting, coupled with the physical activity, recognized the students' need for activity while ensuring that no time was wasted as they practiced counting, too. What is remarkable about this counting is that it not only involved oral language (and aural language feedback) but also gross and fine motor activity (and kinesthetic and visual feedback). Over the years, Wolf and her students adapted the whole body counting to addition, subtraction, multiplication, and division facts. Figure 6.1 was developed in collaboration with the students.

To also engage the attentional system, it is important for the teacher to monitor that all students are engaged in the oral counting and the associated movements during the exercises. Once the students have mastered counting by increments of one in counting order, vary the activities in the following ways to further learning about the number line:

• Do not always start with 1. Start in different places, such as 73, 22, or 15.

• Start by counting backwards from a given number.

• Skip count by constant increments to link number line to multiplication.

Once the students have mastered these activities, create equations using an agreed-on signal for plus (arms crossed at right angles) minus (one arm held horizontally), and multiplication (two arms crossed like an X). The teacher can silently present the simple equation to the whole class and they can all respond, or a single student may be called on to respond with no words necessary.

These warm-up activities integrating sensory, motor, and quantitative learning can be supplemented with integrating language in math learning in

Single digits

1 hands back

2 hands down, elbows straight

3 hands open
   reach for the stars

4 fists closed

5 hold them tight

6 let them go

7 pat your tummy

8 slap your thigh

9 hands forward,
   shoulders straight

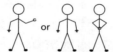   or

10 one hand back (1) and thumb
    and forefinger circle (0)

Number facts
3 + 5 = See top row of figure that follows.
8 − 5 = See second row of figure that follows.
4 × 3 = See third row of figure that follows.
12 ÷ 4 = See bottom row of figure that follows.

Figure 6.1. Expressing basic addition,
multiplication, and division facts through body
expressions of numerals in sequence.

BOX 6.1.   Language of Math

Make sure that students understand the way that this vocabulary is used for math, and guide their understanding of how these terms give clues to help them solve problems. Teach words appropriate to the concepts or computations or problems relevant to a specific lesson. By the end of fifth grade, students should have mastered all these words.

WORDS RELATED TO AMOUNT

between	around	lots	many	a number of	
less	fewer	none	least	not any	digits
even	odd				

COMPARING WORDS

same		equivalent	as many as	some	equal
the same number as		greater	most	extra	different from
exactly		almost	more		

SIZE WORDS

bigger	greater	more	larger	most	above
smaller	less	fewer	smallest	least	below

ORDERING AND POSITION WORDS

first	second	third	fourth	fifth	sixth (etc.)
last	next	next to last	final	before	after
between	every other				

WORDS FOR ESTIMATION

nearly	close to	almost	just under	just over
about	the same as			

GROUP WORDS

set	pair	leave	between	below	above

FRACTION WORDS

whole	half	quarter	third

WORDS FOR ADDITION AND SUBTRACTION

less than	subtract	difference	more than	add	increase	make
together	sum	all together	total	more	leave	left
remove	taking away	remove	remaining	less	remaining	
difference	fewer than	in all	greater than	how many left		

(continued)

BOX 6.1. *(continued)*

MULTIPLYING AND DIVIDING

times	product	for	sets of	times as	groups of
for each	for every	double	triple	big	times as much
twice	again	left	pairs	how many sets of	the same as

GEOMETRY

solid	hollow	round	symmetry	open	closed shapes
edge	curved	straight	corners	surface	match
face	regular	irregular	side	apart	between
mirror	reflection	close	far		
around	angles	slant	diagonal		

MEASUREMENT

about	nearly	enough	approximately	not enough
just over	just under	close to	too much	too little
almost	roughly	big	light	time
how long (time)	how long (distance)			

---

multiple ways. Math-specific vocabulary should be taught both for the main domain and across the content areas of the curriculum. Box 6.1 provides important math-specific vocabulary words to teach during the elementary grades. Strategies for solving story or word problems in math should also be taught. Books written for students on important math concepts are also an effective way to use both oral and written language and pictorial representations to teach math concepts. See Box 6.2 for examples of these books.

TEACHING TIP 6-3B: Teach multiple relevant component math skills close in time.

Multiple relevant math skills should be taught close in time in a given lesson so that students learn to coordinate them in a functional math system.

EXAMPLE 3

This five-part lesson is designed for students in Grade 3.

1. *Warm-up*: Students are asked to write the first 26 numerals starting with 1 in counting order on lined paper in their math folders. The teacher says

BOX 6.2.   Students' Books for Math Concepts

DAYS OF THE WEEK

Carle, E. (1981). *The very hungry caterpillar.* New York, NY: Philomel.

MONTHS OF THE YEAR

Sendak, M. (1976). *Chicken soup with rice.* New York, NY: Harper Collins.

COUNTING

Sendak, M. (1991). *One was Johnny.* New York, NY: Harper Collins.

INVENTIONS, THEORY, AND PLAYING WITH MATH

Davis, G. (2014). *Mr. Ferris and his wheel.* New York, NY: Harcourt Brace.
Lewis, J.P. (2002). *Arithmetical—an even number of odd riddles.* New York, NY: Harcourt.
Lewis, J.P. (2012). *Edgar Allan Poe's pie: Math puzzlers in classic poems.* New York, NY: Harcourt.
Scieszka, J. (1995). *Math curse.* New York, NY: Viking.
Scieszka, J. (2014). *Frank Einstein and the antimatter motor.* New York, NY: Harry H Abrams.

MATH DICTIONARY

Rogers, K. (2012). *First illustrated math dictionary.* Saffron Hill, London, UK: Usborne.

LOVING MATH: THE STORY OF ERDŐS

Heiligman, D. (author), & Pham, L. (illustrator). (2013). *The boy who loved math: The improbable life of Paul Erdős.* New York, NY: Roaring Brook.

"Now!" after 15 seconds, at which point students draw a line after the last numeral they wrote. After everyone has completed this activity, students exchange their papers with their math buddies. Each student in the pair circles the numerals that are not legible for the other student to self-correct. Each student plots on a growth graph how many legible numerals they wrote in the first 15 seconds.

2. *Mental math:* Students close their eyes and silently start counting at 5. They are directed to add 4 and then add 5, then open their eyes and write what the final sum was. The teacher pauses and asks, "Did you write 14?"

If so, the teacher smiles. Students are then directed to close their eyes and silently start counting at 12, take away 6, and then take away 4. Then, they should open their eyes and write what the final sum was. The teacher pauses and asks, "Did you write 2?" If so, smile.

3. *Number line activity*: Each student will need a masking tape (or paper) number line taped to her or his desk. The number line should begin at 0 and have the numerals 0 to 40 marked in black numerals. The goal is to integrate multimodal learning (grapho-motor touches with kinesthetic tactile feedback) with number concepts for quantity in counting order and the basic operations of addition, multiplication, subtraction, and division, and writing the number facts in numerals that represent the numbers added, multiplied, subtracted, or divided. Third grade is when multiplication and division are introduced, but it is important to review addition and subtraction and to make sure students understand how the four operations differ.

   The teacher says, "First, we will add. Adding is counting forward in steps. Put your finger on numeral 5. Then count forward by 5, and as you do, touch each numeral with your finger. What was the last numeral you touched? Yes, 10. Now write the math fact in numerals 5 + 5 = 10. Now we will multiply. Multiplying is fast forward adding. We will multiply 5 times 3. So put your finger on 0. Now move your finger forward 3 times in 5 steps each. What was the last numeral you touched? Yes, 15. Now write the math fact in numerals 5 × 3 = 15. Now, we will subtract. Put your finger on 10. Subtraction is counting backwards a certain number of steps. Count backwards from 10 for 5 steps. What was the last numeral you touched? Yes, 5. Now write the math fact in numerals 10 – 5 = 5. Now, we will divide. Dividing is fast subtraction in backwards direction. Put your finger on 15. Now, divide 15 by 5. Touch each numeral as you count backwards first by 5 steps, then 5 more steps, and by 5 steps until you reach 0. How many sets of 5 steps did you have to take to end up at 0? Yes, 3, now write the math fact in numerals 15 ÷ 5 = 3." The goal is to make sure the students understand the difference between the four operations and how math facts relate to the number line.

4. *Computation*: Students now practice addition, subtraction, multiplication, and division on their grid paper. The teacher says, "Note that we read left to right but write our numerals right to left, beginning with the ones place and then moving to the tens place and so on. Please write 14 + 6 so that 14 is in the top row—with 4 in the ones place and 1 in the tens place. Then, write 6 in the row below in the ones place. Make sure there is only one numeral per square in the grid paper. Did you regroup the sum of 4 + 6 so that on the bottom row below you wrote a 0 in the ones place and regrouped the 1 ten to the one already in the tens place to get the sum of 2 tens? Does your final sum say 20?"

The teacher continues, "Now start with 20 and subtract 14. Write 20 on the top row and 14 on the bottom row. Did you regroup one ten from the tens place and add it to the ones place so you could subtract 4 from 10 rather than 0? Does your final difference say 6? Now, we will multiply 14 × 6. Write 14 on top and 6 below with one digit per square. Now, this time multiply the number in the ones place in the top row times the 6 in the ones place in the second row (multiplier). To multiply the top number in the tens place in the top row times the multiplier in the second row, move along a diagonal line instead of a vertical line. Because the product is a two place number, write the 4 in the ones place and regroup two tens to the tens place. Then after multiplying the 1 in the tens place times the 6 in the second row (multiplier), add that regrouped 2 tens to 6 and write 8 in the tens place. So the final product is 84."

The teacher concludes, "Finally, we will divide 24 by 6. Write the 6 on the left (divisor) and the 24 to its right inside the division symbol (dividend—number to be divided) with curved line on left and horizontal line on top; trace over this with your finger. Write the quotient 4 above the horizontal line over the number in the ones place of the dividend (also 4). Multiply the quotient times the divisor and write the product below the number that was divided (24), the dividend. The quotient is correct if the product of the divisor and quotient is the same as the dividend."

The goal of this activity is to help the students navigate through two-dimensional space for basic operations. They will need to learn vocabulary for vertical, horizontal, and diagonal lines and dividend, divisor, dividend, and quotient and the placement of numerals in space (small squares in grid) to reflect place value with and without regrouping. The teacher should note that these math terms have word origins in Latin and Greek.

5. *Problem solving:* Ask each student to create one problem that will require addition to solve, one that will require subtraction to solve, one that will require multiplication to solve, and one that will require division to solve. Students work in pairs with a math buddy, exchange the problems, and solve the problems their math buddy created for them. The teacher collects these and uses them for designing a follow-up lesson on when to use the four basic operations, why, and how.

EXAMPLE 4

This five-part activity is designed for fourth- or fifth-graders who are working on computation procedures for multiplace multiplication and long division and the part–whole concept underlying fractions. Written computations involve travel through space in lining up numbers to be multiplied or divided and through time in applying the sequential steps of a computational procedure (algorithm).

1. *Warm-Up:* The teacher dictates five numbers in terms of their place value and asks students to write the numerals using correct place value. For example, students can be asked to write in numerals "five ones, no tens or hundreds, two thousands" for a correct answer of 2005. Also, because math errors are often due to inattention to numerals in specific positions or their sequence in a multiplace numeral, show five multiplace numerals, one at a time. First, ask students to look at them carefully for one second, then close their eyes, then open them, and ask them if the multiplace numeral displayed matches the original one. If not, students explain how to fix. For example, show 21,387 followed by 21,837, for which students would have to explain that there should be 3 hundreds and 8 tens to correct it.

2. *Mental math:* Ask students to close their eyes and in their mind solve three problems. For example, the teacher could say, "Start at 11. Add 7 and then subtract 10. Finally multiply that difference by 3. Where are you now on the number line in your mind? Did you end up at 24?" Ask students to solve two oral word problems without paper and pencil, such as the following:

   • Suzie helped her mom make dinner three times this week. Each time she spent about 30 minutes helping. So how many minutes did she help her mom this week?

   • Bob likes to play baseball at lunch. On Monday, he got to first base. On Tuesday, he got to third base. On Wednesday, he struck out. On Thursday, he got to second base. On Friday, he hit a homerun. What was his average daily number of bases?

   Take time to discuss orally not only correct answers, but also the thinking that goes into arriving at solutions.

3. *Math fact fluency:* Use a multimodal approach to review 10 basic multiplication facts with products 35 or higher. First, say a math fact and ask students to give the product orally. Second, say a math fact and ask students to write the product. Third, show a math fact and ask students to give the product orally. Fourth, show a math fact and ask students to write the product. On the next day, practice the corresponding division facts through listen-say, listen-write, see-say, and see-write. This multimodal approach helps code the facts in memory and access and retrieve them.

4. *Explaining and applying sequenced steps of computations:* Use grid paper so that students can write one numeral per square and arrange the numerals appropriately in rows and columns for multiplying two multiplace numbers (three numerals on the top row and two numerals on the bottom row). Before performing the calculation, ask each student to explain to his or her math buddy the steps (time sequence) for performing the computation of multiplying multiplace numerals. Then, both students perform the operation. Finally, to teach how multiplication and division

are related and multiplication can be used to check division answers, ask the other student in the pair to explain the steps for performing the long division problem before both students perform it. Remind students that although we read left to right and do addition and subtraction of whole numbers right to left (and top down and bottom up when regrouping is involved), for multiplication we also go diagonally and have to sum the products for each place in the multiplier. Also point out that for long division we begin on the left and go up, then diagonally and down, and then subtract top-down, and then repeat the process dividing a number below instead of at the top. Many students get lost in space and/or time in performing these multistep calculations, but they can learn to do them if they take time to talk about the direction for movement and sequence of steps.

5. *Linking part–whole relationships to writing fractions.* For this lesson, you will need 10 small food items. Be sure to check on dietary restrictions or allergies, or use ten nonfood items. Ask students to group them in different ways. For example, start by asking them to create two groups on a piece of paper, with four grapes in one group and six grapes in the second group. The teacher then asks, "If you can have one grape, do you have relatively more in the group of four or in the group of six?" To help students think about this, also ask them to use numerals to write a fraction showing the parts of the whole in each group: ¼ or ⅙. Discuss why 6 is more than 4 on the number line, but one of four is more than one of six for fractions. Make sure they understand that part–whole relationships means that the quantitative value of numbers also depends on how many parts a whole is divided into—that is, numbers have relative quantity as well as absolute quantity in counting order on a number line. Then, ask students to create a group of three and a group of six grapes. Ask students how many of the group of six they would need to have the same amount as one of the three in the other group. Write a fraction for both (⅓ and ²⁄₆) and discuss how sometimes there are different numerals in the top and bottom of a fraction, but overall the parts to whole relationships are equivalent.

EXAMPLE 5

The following 11-step sequence was developed by Bev Wolf and Rita Lowe, when she was math consultant for the Renton School District in Washington, to teach the language of math and steps in solving story problems. This approach has been used effectively with students with SLDs that interfere with their ability to understand a teacher's instructional talk to learn the language of math. The approach is illustrated with addition, but it can be adapted to any of the operations. Note that items 1–4 are acted out, whereas items 5–8 use pictures, and 9–11 are abstract.

1. *Act out number statement.* The teacher makes a number statement, such as "Rita gave three peanuts to Helen." Students act it out.

2. *Show the number statement with pictures and manipulatives.* Students make the picture that illustrates a number statement, such as "There are four cars on one side of the street and three cars on the other side. Make that picture." Then, ask students to show it with counters and tell the story back.

3. *Act out the statement and answer question about it.* The teacher makes a number statement and asks a question about it, such as "Sue gave four peanuts to Helen and three peanuts to Bev. How many did she give away?" Students act out the statement and the answer to the question.

4. *Use manipulatives to represent the number problem, identify the operation, and answer it.* The teacher makes a number statement and asks a question, such as, "The Easter Bunny brought three chocolate eggs and four real eggs. How many eggs are there in all?" Students use counters to represent the problem and answer the question about it.

5. *Discuss a picture showing a math story problem visually.* Students tell what they see in the picture.

6. *Tell the story about the picture in a number statement.* For example, the story might be, "There are three red apples and two green apples. There are five apples all together."

7. *Tell the story, ask questions, and record in numerals.* The teacher or student tells a story and asks a question. (This is an opportunity to develop use of key math words.) "There are three red apples and two green apples. How many apples are there in all?" The teacher records the story in numerals on board so all can see.

8. *Tell the story now in pictures or objects to show the equation in numerals that solved the problem.* Students draw pictures or manipulate objects to show the equation that shows the number statement and answer.

9. *The teacher gives an equation and students tell the story.* The teacher gives a verbal problem with no pictures. Students tell the story orally.

10. *Students write story problems.* Students first write their own equations, and then they write the story problems. They may illustrate the problems if desired.

11. *Identify the operation in the teacher-provided story problem and solve it.* The teacher reads or tells a story problem. The students identify the operation to be used and then solve it and write the answer. Encourage students to use manipulatives or pictures if they wish before writing the problem and answering with numerals.

These five examples illustrate how math can be taught with sensorimotor, language, cognitive and memory, social interaction, and attention and self-regulation in mind. Teachers are encouraged to create their own lessons for the curriculum used at their grade levels in their schools that also teach math to multiple systems involved in math learning. Not only students with SLDs but also their classmates often benefit. Finally, to instill positive affect and persuade students that math can be fun, teachers are also encouraged to read with the students the story of Erdős (Heligman, 2013; Hoffman, 1998), who loved numbers!

Assessment of
Math Concepts, Computations,
Problem Solving, and Related Skills

Assessment tools are organized by skills and within skills in alphabetical order by first author surname. Note that an asterisk (*) means individual assessment is required; otherwise the assessment tool is designed to be used in a group or can be adapted for group administration.

MATH CONCEPTS: COUNTING

*Berninger, V. (2007a). *Process Assessment of the Learner Diagnostic for Math (PAL-II M)*. Boston, MA: Pearson.
Oral Counting, Math Concepts, Place Value, and oral, written, and problem response written for Place Value.

MATH CONCEPTS: PART–WHOLE

*PAL-II M
Part–Whole Concepts.

DEVELOPMENTAL MATH CONCEPTS

*Connolly, A. (2008). *Key Math Third Edition (Key Math 3) Diagnostic Assessment*. Boston, MA: Pearson.
Concepts.

MATH: WRITING

*PAL-II M
  Numeral Writing; Look and Write—Addition, Subtraction, and Switching Addition and Subtraction Facts.

MATH: CALCULATION

*PAL-II M
  Computation Operations.

*Key Math 3
  Operations.

*Kaufman, A., & Kaufman, N. (2012). *Kaufman Test of Educational Achievement, Third Edition (KTEA-3).* San Antonio, TX: Pearson.
  Math Computation.

*Wechsler, D. (1991). *Wechsler Individual Achievement Test, Third Edition (WIAT III).* San Antonio, TX: Harcourt Assessment.
  Numerical Operations.

*Woodcock, R.W., Mather, N., & McGrew, K. (2008). *Woodcock-Johnson III Tests of Achievement (WJ III ACH).* Rolling Meadows, IL: Riverside.
  Math Calculation.

MATH: PROBLEM SOLVING

*PAL-II M
  Multi-Step Problem Solving.

*Key Math 3
  Applications.

*KTEA-3
  Math Concepts and Applications.

*WIAT III
  Math Problem Solving.

*WJ III
  Applied Problems.

MATH: SELF-MONITORING

*PAL-II M
  Finding the Bug.

PLANNING INSTRUCTION BASED ON
ASSESSMENT RESULTS AND PROGRESS MONITORING

- Identify individual students who fall below the lower limit of the average range (-⅔ standard deviation or 25th percentile or standard score of 90 on a test with a most average/mean score of 100 or a scaled score of 8 on a test with a most average/mean score of 10 or a z-score of -.66z on a research measure with a most average/mean score of 0). In some schools, the interdisciplinary team may decide to also identify any students who fall below the most average/mean score (50th percentile).

- Go to Appendix 6B and choose an instructional tool for each skill that meets the first or second criterion above.

- For progress monitoring, readminister the assessment tool after the instructional program is completed.

Instructional Resources
for Math Concepts, Computations,
Problem Solving, and Related Skills

EARLY CHILDHOOD MATH

Early mathematics: A key topic resource (http://www.researchconnections.org)
A partnership of the National Center for Children in Poverty, the Interuniversity Consortium for Political and Social Research, the Child Care Bureau, and the Office of Planning, Research, and Evaluation.

Ginsberg, H. (2002). *Big math for little kids kindergarten classbooks*. San Antonio, TX: Pearson Education.

Greenes, C. (n.d.). *Big math for little kids*. Retrieved from http://gse.buffalo.edu/org/conference/ConfWritings2/Greenes.pdf

Greenes, C., Balfanz, R., & Ginsburg, H. (2004). Big math for little kids. *Early Childhood Research Quarterly, 19*, 159–166.
A description of Big Math for Little Kids, a research-based, comprehensive mathematics program for preschool and kindergarten.

Jump Math (http://www.jumpmath.org)

ELEMENTARY AND MIDDLE CHILDHOOD MATH

Boaler, J., & Humphreys, C. (2005). *Connecting mathematical ideas: Middle school video cases to support teaching and learning*. Portsmouth, NH: Heinemann (http://www.heinemann.com).

Coggins, D. (Ed). *A mathematics sourcebook for elementary and middle school teachers.* Novato, CA: Arena Press (http://www.highnoonbooks.com).

Fosnot, C., & Dolk, M. *Young mathematicians at work, preK–Grade 3.* Professional development materials. CDs developed by M. Dolk and C. Fosnot; Facilitator's Guides developed by A. Cameron, S. Hersch, & C. Fosnot. Portsmouth, NH: Heinemann (http://www.heinemann.com).

Fosnot, C., & Dolk, M. *Young mathematicians at work, Grades 3 to 5.* Professional Development Materials.CDs developed by M. Dolk; Facilitator's Guides developed by A. Cameron, S. Hersch, & C. Fosnot. Portsmouth, NH: Heinemann (http://www.heinemann.com).

Math Their Way (http://www.center.edu/)

Ramani, G.B., Siegler, R.S., & Hitti, A. (2012). Taking it to the classroom: Number board games as a small group learning activity. *Journal of Educational Psychology, 104,* 661–672. doi:10.1037/a0028995.

Siegler, R., Carpenter, T., Fennell, F., Geary, D., Lewis, J., Okamoto, Y., Thompson, L., & Wray, J. (2010). *Developing effective fractions instruction for kindergarten through 8th grade: A practice guide* (NCEE #2010-4039). Washington, DC: National Center for Education Evaluation and Regional Assistance, Institute of Education Sciences, U.S. Department of Education. Retrieved from http://ies.ed.gov/ncee/wwc/publications/practiceguides

MATH FACT FLUENCY

Arena Press. *More Make-A-Games.* Novato, CA: Author.
Design board games to reinforce memorization.

Arena Press, High Noon Books. *Designs in math.* Novato, CA: Author (http://www.highnoonbooks.com).
Addition, division, subtraction, multiplication.

Johnson, P. *Math scramble!* LinguiSystems. Retrieved from http://www.linguisystems.com

Remedia. *Addition and subtraction, multiplication and division, multiplication songs.* Scottsdale, AZ: Author (1-800-826-4740).
Uses "cool" songs and action-packed videos to help children commit math facts to memory.

Remedia. *Timed math flash cards.* Scottsdale, AZ: Author (1-800-826-4740).

COMPUTATIONAL ALGORITHMS

The following materials are available from Remedia (Scottsdale, AZ; 1-800-826-4740):

Math for fun: Mazes and other puzzles can only be correctly solved if answers to computations are correct.

Math practice: Plenty of sequential practice on addition and subtraction.

Multiplication and division practice: Practice activities for mastering multiplication and division.

LINKING LANGUAGE WITH MATH PROBLEM SOLVING

Arena Press, High Noon Books. *Multiplication and division: Book 3.* Novato, CA: Author (http://www.highnoonbooks.com).

Arena Press, High Noon Books. *Solving math word problems: Book 4.* Novato, CA: Author (http://www.highnoonbooks.com).

Arena Press, High Noon Books. *Sums to 99: Book 1.* Novato, CA: Author (http://www.highnoonbooks.com).

Arena Press, High Noon Books. *Sums under 1000: Book 2.* Novato, CA: Author (http://www.highnoonbooks.com).

Koepke, H. *The Math Language Game.* LinguiSystems. Retrieved from http://www.linguisystems.com

Remedia. *Math puzzles.* Scottsdale, AZ: Author (1-800-826-4740).
Crossword puzzles are solved by completing computations correctly.

REAL-WORLD MATH PROBLEM SOLVING

The following materials are available from Remedia (Scottsdale, AZ; 1-800-826-4740):

Clocks and calendars

Personalized math

Real life math: Menu math (Grades 1–3)

Real life math: Department store math (Grades 4–8)

Real life math: Market math (Grades 3–6)

Time line math

Time concepts

THINKING WITH NUMBERS FOR MATH PROBLEM SOLVING

Algebra word problems I. Retrieved from http://www.criticalthinking.com
Books with reproducible activities for Grades 7–8.

Brain stretchers: classic math, logic, and word problems. Retrieved from http://www.criticalthinking.com
   Book with reproducibles for Grades 5–9.

Cranimum crackers critical thinking activities in math. Retrieved from http://www.criticalthinking.com
   Book with reproducibles for Grades 3–8.

Designs in math: Decimals. Novato, CA: Arena Press, High Noon Books (http://www.highnoonbooks.com).

Designs in math: Fractions. Novato, CA: Arena Press, High Noon Books (http://www.highnoonbooks.com).

Dr. Funster's quick thinks math. Retrieved from http://www.criticalthinking.com

Loose, F. *Decimals and percentages*. Novato, CA: Arena Press, High Noon Books (http://www.highnoonbooks.com).

Loose, F. *Fractions: Books 1 and 2 and teacher manual*. Novato, CA: Arena Press, High Noon Books (http://www.highnoonbooks.com).

Math detective. Retrieved from http://www.criticalthinking.com
   Book with reproducibles for Grades 3–8.

Mathematical reasoning through verbal analysis. Retrieved from http://www.criticalthinking.com
   Book with reproducibles for Grades 2–8.

Math word problems. Retrieved from http://www.criticalthinking.com
   Book with reproducibles for Grades 4–8.

Mind building math K–1. Retrieved from http://www.criticalthinking.com
   Book with 40 activities and reproducibles.

Revenge of the math spiders develops mental math. Retrieved from http://www.criticalthinking.com
   CD-ROMs for Grades 4–8.

Scratch your brain. Retrieved from http://www.criticalthinking.com
   Book with reproducibles for Grades 2–8.

Teacher Resources for
Math Concepts, Computations,
Problem Solving, and Related Skills

At the beginning of the school year teachers can send home questionnaires that include questions about math and related skills that will help them identify those students who may need extra help and ongoing monitoring with these skills. Each student should keep a math portfolio to collect samples of his or her math work at school across the school year. In addition, students can keep a homework folder in which they organize the assignments they do at home but bring to school for the teacher to review with them. Finally, parent conferences in person and by phone and e-mail are helpful ways to reach out to parents to help their child in developing math skills.

PARENT QUESTIONNAIRE

1. Did your child have difficulty learning to count?

2. Does your child have difficulty writing numerals so that others can recognize them?

3. Does your child have difficulty with paper and pencil written calculations? If so, please explain.

4. Is there anyone in your family who has history of difficulty with math?

5. Is there anything you would like to share with the school to help your child succeed in math this year?

MATH PORTFOLIOS

Keep representative samples of math assignments in a math portfolio to review periodically with the student and also with parents at parent conferences.

HOMEWORK

Note if student keeps up with homework assignments in math. If not, analyze whether there is a pattern as to which aspects of math prove difficult.

PARENT CONFERENCES

Which is the best way to contact you to keep you informed about your child's progress and to discuss any issues that may arise to help your child succeed in school this year, including math homework? Please understand that the teacher, who is busy with your child and others, cannot reply to your texts during the school day. However, concerns and information you share will be discussed at interdisciplinary team meetings to address your child's educational needs.

In person:

Over the telephone:

Over e-mail or web site:

Systems Approaches to Schools, Families, and Learners with Specific Learning Disabilities

In "Trouble at the Bottom" (1998) Pete Seeger, who wrote the words and lyrics of this song, raises the question "Where's the trouble at the bottom?" He observes that some say it may be the principal, some say the kids, some say the curriculum, some say the textbooks, some say the class, and some even say the system, including the upper, not the bottom!

In this book, which was written at a time in the history of education when it is often assumed that the teacher and schools are the problems, we adopt a systems approach but reframe the issues. Instead of focusing on the troubles in the system, we propose that the solutions are in the system. We discuss a systems approach in which all of the above levels have important roles in creating solutions to optimize the learning of students with and without specific learning disabilities (SLDs). In contrast to Section II, which focused on the multiple, multileveled language systems that contribute to learning and assessment–instruction links for preventing SLDs, Section III focuses on other kinds of relevant systems. Chapter 7 considers the classroom systems—the organization and role of the classroom in creating positive social emotional climate. Chapter 8 covers issues in teaching language and math skills across the content subjects of the curriculum. Although these are often considered distinct content domains, a system approach to curriculum is also needed because all areas of the curriculum draw on language and math skills. Chapter 9 deals with the multicomponent system for self-governing learning in complex functional language and math systems. Chapter 10 applies the system approach to understanding the students with co-occurring SLDs and the students with talents and SLDs. Chapter 11 calls attention to system issues in technology user–technology interfaces for both explicit instruction and accommodations for students with SLDs.

Classroom Organizational and Social-Emotional Climate Issues

Learning occurs within social systems. Individual developing children live with others in homes or other shelters. Their caretakers, who are often family members, play a big role in the child's learning and development beginning at birth. However, so do other members of society, including the teachers who may work with the student, often in preschool programs for 3- to 5-year-old children, and then in classrooms in schools from K–12. Children learn not only from adults—parents or caretakers outside school and teachers and other professionals and paraprofessionals in school—but also from each other. This chapter calls attention to the classroom organizational issues for creating a social environment at school that supports learning during the school year and the ways in which schools can reach out to parents and caretakers to create positive home–school relationships. The social-emotional climate both at school and home can influence students' learning and and development (Berninger, 2015).

In keeping with the overall goal of offering solutions rather than criticisms, this chapter offers seven guidelines to inform translational science (reduction of research to educational practice) for classroom systems.

1. Organizing the classroom learning environment

2. Differentiating instruction for individual students within group learning environments

3. Creating a positive learning environment for all

4. Planning, implementing, and evaluating lessons at students' instructional levels

5. Designing independent work

6. Creating inclusive learning environments

7. Creating positive school–home relationships

Individualizing instruction for students with dysgraphia, dyslexia, oral and written language learning disability (OWL LD), and dyscalculia in a general education classroom may initially seem like a daunting challenge. However, other students can also benefit from differentiated instruction, even if they do not have biological risk for specific learning disabilities (SLDs). For example, a student's parents may have little formal education and provide few literacy or related activities in the home or the student may not be fully proficient with English. In addition, ways of reaching out to parents and caretakers that have been used successfully by some schools are described to provide inspiration and guidance in creating those positive relationships.

ORGANIZING THE CLASSROOM LEARNING ENVIRONMENT

Classrooms can be organized as social organizations with rules and procedures to meet the needs of individuals and the group. Seven guiding principles can be helpful in creating such supportive learning communities.

Principle 1: Students Are Motivated to Learn

Do not assume that lack of motivation is the cause of a student's struggles in learning to read and write. Most students want desperately to learn, even though they may camouflage their fear of failure with reluctance (avoiding or not completing assignments), aggressive displays (acting out), or humor (assuming role of class clown). With the correct learning tools, students with dysgraphia, dyslexia, OWL LD, and/or dysgraphia can succeed and gain confidence in their own abilities to learn, even if they need to work harder than others. Teachers should provide encouragement so that these students do not give up on themselves. Linking instruction in basic reading, writing, oral language, and math skills to their interests and to intellectually engaging content helps students with dysgraphia, dyslexia, OWL LD, and/or dysgraphia sustain hard work over time. Students with SLDs are also embarrassed by their learning problems; their positive strengths should be pointed out to them and their classmates so that they are recognized for their successes.

Principle 2: Oral Language Is Related to Written Language Development and Remains Important During All Schooling

Teaching reading, writing, and math requires more than written language instruction. Daily instruction should be organized to include instruction in oral language as well because developing both oral and written language can be mutually facilitative. Students need to develop awareness of sounds, the meaning of word parts, and syntax in oral language in order to learn to decode unfamiliar words and comprehend text. They also need to process the teacher's instructional language in order to learn academic subject matter and to produce oral language in order to answer questions and participate in class discussions (see Chapters 5 and 6).

Principle 3: Never Assume that What Was Taught Is Necessarily What Was Learned

The goal for teachers is to bring teaching and learning together. Simply covering the required material is not enough.

Principle 4: Teach Students at a Level at Which They Can Appropriately Learn, Which Varies Across Students

The writers of curriculum materials follow grade-level guidelines, which often do not reflect the normal variation of learning in most classrooms; observant teachers often know their own students best and know where they are functioning along the path to reading, writing, and math development. However, keep in mind that students may have relative strengths and weaknesses across the curriculum. A student may struggle with oral language but have strengths in nonverbal learning, or they may not be able to express their intelligence and thinking in oral language but may, for example, by building or drawing. The teacher's goal is to pace instruction to student needs and reteach, restructure, and review as needed within specific content domains of the curriculum. This kind of developmentally tailored instruction is best accomplished using three to four instructional groupings, based on instructional levels for reading, writing, or math within the general education classroom. Such approaches to differentiated instruction have also been successfully implemented by teams of teachers offering language arts or math at the same time of the instructional day.

Principle 5: One Exposure Is Not Enough for Many Kinds of Learning and Learners

Although students may learn some skills through one exposure (lesson), all students—including those with and without reading and writing problems—tend to require multiple exposures (lessons) and practice. However, students with SLDs may need more repeated exposures and practice than other students. Repeated practice over time often is needed to acquire mastery and confidence to apply learning to a variety of situations. "We cannot teach them everything they need to know, but we can teach them how to learn" (B. Slingerland, 1980, personal communication).

Principle 6: Teach How to Learn

Remembering letters and words is not the same skill as thinking. Teachers should acknowledge and celebrate evidence of thinking and problem-solving ability in students with dysgraphia, dyslexia, OWL LD, and/or dyscalculia. This kind of praise boosts students' self-esteem and creates self-concepts that they are bright learners so that they do not get discouraged and give up.

Principle 7: Flexibility Is the Key to Master Teaching and Effective Learning

A wise teacher knows when to let go, try another strategy, let it rest, or change direction to take advantage of teachable moments. For example, if a student does not readily grasp what is being taught that day, do not push him or her to do so. Reintroduce the concepts or procedures on another day. With a fresh start, the student may grasp what is being taught.

DIFFERENTIATING INSTRUCTION FOR INDIVIDUALS WITHIN A GROUP

The challenge teachers face, in addition to teaching academic skills, is creating a social community that supports all students who differ in their instructional or social-emotional needs. How can a teacher meet the needs of all students when their needs are not identical? How can instruction be individually tailored and yet meet the needs of the whole group? Providing differentiated instruction during part of the school day in small groups is helpful, but so are opportunities for the whole group to learn together during other times of the day to create a community of learners.

When the general education classroom teacher is aware of the needs of students with SLDs and provides structured, sequential, systematic instruction for these students while meeting the needs of other students in the class, fewer students are likely to be referred for special education. To meet the needs of all students, teachers need to couple carefully planned lessons with daily and weekly monitoring of students' responses to instruction. The observant teacher seeks a balance between challenging and overloading students. When tasks do not demand much intellectual energy, students may become bored; however, when tasks are too difficult, students may become discouraged and frustrated and may misbehave. For example, when teachers observe a student misbehaving, they should ask how the instructional and learning environment might be structured differently so that the student is successful rather than discouraged and frustrated. Rather than jumping to the conclusion that the student has an emotional or behavioral problem or that the parents are not supportive, teachers should consider whether a behavior may be a signal that the student is frustrated because he or she so wants to succeed.

After initial instruction in any new concept, a skilled teacher individualizes instruction by adjusting the difficulty of the task so that each student finds success while continuing to move forward. For example, the teacher might form a small instructional group for those students who need reteaching of a concept and form another group for the students who mastered the concept very quickly and need enriched learning opportunities to extend and elaborate the initial learning (Delisle, 1984). When students have sufficient time to practice and review concepts, they often become firmly fixed in long-term memory. All students can learn, but some need more instruction and practice, and even further enrichment, than others. A few simple adjustments to the daily plan, such as selection of words with a range of difficulty for the daily reading and spelling lessons, are typically all that is necessary to allow the teacher to keep the stronger students challenged while providing appropriate input, modeling, and practice for those with weaker skills. Teachers can also adjust classroom and homework assignments to reflect individual needs, whether or not a student has a formal, legal Accommodation Plan based on section 504 of the Rehabilitation Act of 1973.

CLASSROOM GROUPING PLAN FOR DIFFERENTIATED INSTRUCTION

Differentiating instruction does not mean one-to-one tutoring. Providing small-group or one-to-one instruction for every student in need of individualization is not feasible or even desirable; however, it is possible for the teacher to organize the class to provide instruction tailored to the range of instructional levels in most general education classrooms. Several informal reading inventories are available commercially (e.g., Leslie & Caldwell, 2005; Woods & Moe, 2003) or can be designed for the specific textbook(s) used in a school. These inventories can be administered at the beginning of the school year to identify the instructional levels of students and then to form three to four small instructional groups. The teacher can meet daily with each of these groups for 20–30 minutes of teacher-guided instruction while other students do independent work designed for their group (e.g., practicing and applying skills learned from instructional time with the teacher, reading new stories, rereading stories to develop fluency).

The informal inventory can be readministered in the middle of the year to assess whether any students need to be moved to a different group. This kind of assessment of response to instruction increases the probability that instruction remains differentiated throughout the school year. When students are grouped by instructional level, the teacher can pace instruction to the students' rates of learning and adapt students' response to instruction as needed. Even within groups formed on the basis of similar instructional levels, teachers may have to provide additional individualization because instructional levels are rarely identical. Variation in levels of learning, profiles of learning skills and achievement, and strategies for learning are normal. Normal variation in reading and writing acquisition is the rule rather than the exception. Teachers must flexibly adapt to these individual differences within the larger and smaller instructional groups in the classroom.

If students cannot recognize at least 90% of the words, they are unlikely to understand what they read (Juel, 1994) or make progress (Honig, 1996). Without challenge, students are also unlikely to grow in reading. If a book is too easy, students are likely not to make progress. A perceptive teacher provides balance between ease and challenge. The key to effective reading instruction is to match the level of instruction to a student's reading level with the right book at a level for their current word decoding and word identification skills but also to challenge the student to keep learning. Small-group instruction will also allow each student more opportunities to respond when the teacher provides feedback. It will also provide the teacher with opportunities for informal daily evaluation of response to instruction that leads to more refined instruction. As one student told Beverly Wolf, "It's just plain stupid to try to teach a kid to read in a book that's too hard." Sigmund Freud said it in a different way: "Understanding becomes impossible once reading becomes difficult" (qtd. in Henry, 1999, p. 17).

By forming three or four instructional groups, the teacher can also provide differentiated instruction for the oral and written language skills at the syntax/sentence and discourse levels (see Chapter 5 and Appendices 5A and 5B) or for math skills (see Chapter 6 and Appendices 6A and 6B). However, doing so requires careful choosing and integrating of instructional components.

Many federal initiatives have specified the components of science-supported reading instruction. Major textbooks for reading and instructional materials for writing are incorporating these elements in their materials, and many school districts adopt a particular textbook or program for all teachers to use at a specific grade level to implement science-supported reading instruction. For example, the National Reading Panel (National Institute of Child Health and Human Development, 2000) identified five critical areas for early reading skills: phonemic awareness, phonics, oral reading fluency, reading comprehension, and vocabulary. Regrettably, orthographic awareness and morphological awareness were left behind (see Chapter 4). Based on other research on oral language (Silliman & Scott, 2009) and writing (Hooper, Knuth, Yerby, Anderson, & Moore, 2009), a complete language program for all students—and especially those with OWL LD, dyslexia and/or dysgraphia—should include instruction and practice in oral language, including morphological and syntactic awareness, and orthographic awareness, handwriting, spelling, and written composition. See Section II, Appendices 3B, 4B, and 5B in Chapters 3, 4, and 5, respectively, for instructional tools that can be used to develop these other skills not addressed by the National Reading Panel. Henry (2005) also provided a conceptual framework to apply in choosing supplementary instructional material for students with dyslexia, OWL LD, and/or dysgraphia.

CREATING A POSITIVE LEARNING ENVIRONMENT

Emotional climate is defined by a teacher's attitude toward students and students' attitudes toward one another. Teachers provide the emotional safety that encourages students to take risks and allows students to make mistakes. Freedom to make mistakes is necessary for learning. Teachers should praise good performances judiciously—students know when praise is false—and commend hard work as well as the accuracy of performance. Students with dyslexia, OWL LD, and/or dysgraphia appreciate teachers understanding how much effort it may take for them to learn to process, pronounce, and spell written words compared with their classmates. Teachers can build the concept that an error is not failure by helping students to self-correct and discover the correct response rather than turning immediately to another student to answer. Students should be guided through the steps to success, given clues if necessary, and given information in order to perform accurately and feel the satisfaction that comes as a result of their efforts. If a student misspells a word, for example, the teacher can repeat the word clearly and ask the student to repeat it as well. "What sounds do you hear? How do you spell that sound?" Teachers should discourage guessing and teach strategies for cues to figuring out an unknown word. Students who have more difficulty spelling than the majority of students in the class may simply need reteaching and more guided practice. Likewise, students with dyscalculia can benefit from structured guidance, flexibility, and honest feedback and support for their math work.

Teachers can also build the concept that an error is not failure by using a team approach to decoding or spelling unknown words or solving math problems, which minimizes the stigma of not knowing a word instantly and calls attention to the fact that the student is not alone—other students may face similar challenges. Using such a team approach helps to create an atmosphere of support and acceptance. Few things are as gratifying as the applause of fellow classmates when a student, alone or through teamwork, is finally able to read or spell a word or do a math calculation. The inner satisfaction of the successful student who has finally mastered a new skill is a powerful motivator. Teachers can help build a spirit of support and cooperation by helping students to help one another. Taking responsibility for one's own learning, recognizing one's own efforts, and helping others all contribute to building self-esteem. In addition, teachers need to recognize that what is a good performance for one student may be less acceptable for another. Although teachers set the standards of students' expected, appropriate level of performance, levels may need to be adjusted for certain students so that their levels are within reach.

Thus, teachers can provide a more positive environment for students with a variety of learning requirements when physical, learning, and social-emotional needs are considered. Some students may be easily distracted, confused, or disorganized. They may need order to work effectively. Their classroom should be well organized, neat, and clutter free.

Neuhaus (2002) found that some students were still learning the alphabet in fourth grade. A readily accessed alphabet with manuscript and/or cursive letters at the students' desks provides reinforcement for those with insecure recall. Prefix and suffix charts and vowel pattern charts should be clearly visible as well, perhaps on a wall or in a personal dictionary at each student's desk, as these will help students with encoding and decoding. Teachers should encourage students to refer to these learning aids whenever they do not have immediate recall.

Display areas in the classroom should also reflect the interests and ideas of the students. Such areas are a valuable tool for building self-esteem and motivation when they are used to display student work. Desks and aisles must be spaced to allow the teacher easy access to all students. On occasions when the whole class is reading content area materials, the teacher must circulate throughout the classroom to ensure that all students are keeping their places and are on task, providing assistance as needed. Having easy access to every student allows teachers to circulate and check writing during practice times and to help prevent errors before performance. Student desks should be oriented to the front of the room during written language instruction to allow ready reference to wall displays and the teacher's nonverbal and verbal instructional cues. Teachers should ensure that students have access to visual displays without distortions due to distractions in the classroom.

During small-group reading sessions, students in the group should be seated so that they all have a clear view of the board or charts. For example, seating students in an arc or semicircle allows students to see and allows the teacher to easily assist all students, helping them with keeping their places and following along in the story. While working with a small group, the teacher should also have a clear view of the whole class, and the whole class should have a clear view of the teacher. In this way, without speaking, the teacher can manage the students who are working independently and provide guidance with just a smile, a nod, a shake of the head, or a gesture. Teachers should establish a rule that no one should interrupt while the teacher is with a reading group. Instead, teachers can take a few minutes between groups to reinforce independent standards and to give extra help.

Left-handed students might be grouped together so that they have space to move their writing arms comfortably without bumping others. This grouping may also reduce confusion for students who are uncertain about which is their dominant hand. (Teachers can determine hand preference by asking the student to perform the series of tasks described in Chapter 3.)

Providing preferential seating may not always mean front-row seating. Students are often the best judges of what works best for them. Some need to be in front or near the teacher. Others work best when seated off to the side or in the back, away from distractions. Students as early as first grade come to understand that as much as they would like to sit by their friends, they may not be able to manage their behavior if they do. It is the teacher's responsibility, however, to help students recognize their own classroom needs.

PLANNING, IMPLEMENTING, AND EVALUATING INSTRUCTION AT STUDENTS' INSTRUCTIONAL LEVELS

Teachers need time to plan their teaching at students' instructional levels, implement those plans, assess student response to the implementation of the plans, and reflect on implementation of those plans and student progress.

Planning

The grade level of the reading material should be matched with the assessed instructional level—for example, through an informal reading inventory that takes into account ability to identify words on a list without context clues, ability to identify words in passages with context information, and comprehension based on answering factual and inferential questions.

Instructional levels can also be informed by the assessment results for handwriting (see Chapter 3 and Chapter 3 appendices), word reading and spelling (see Chapter 4 and Chapter 4 appendices), and listening and reading comprehension and oral and written expression (see Chapter 5 and Chapter 5 appendices). Basal readers and literature readers are designed to provide a variety of experiences that will allow students to read library materials. They differ in the difficulty of the material in terms of decoding requirements for unfamiliar words, vocabulary level, sentence syntax structures, and other factors that affect readability for ease of reading the materials. Likewise, textbooks used at a particular grade level in math, science, and social studies can differ in these requirements.

Although many students can handle the decoding requirements of grade-level textbooks, students with dyslexia typically have difficulty with decoding unfamiliar words or with automatic recognition of familiar words. They may benefit from extra practice in decoding. For a modest fee, grade-level books can be downloaded from http://www.readinga-z.com and used to provide extra practice with decoding and comprehension at a student's instructional level. Another web site, http://www.starfall.com, offers free phonological awareness lessons and other instructional materials. At the same time, however, grade-level reading materials may be a better match with a student's vocabulary development or thinking ability. Newsela (http://newsela.com) is an innovative way to build reading comprehension with nonfiction that is always relevant: daily news is presented at five different reading levels. Unfortunately, comparable programs aimed at the instructional levels for writing and math are not available and require teachers to develop their own differentiated instruction (see Section II).

Implementing

Across the content areas of the curriculum, students should work with reading materials that are as close to their instructional level as possible in all content areas of the curriculum. Science, social studies, and other content area materials are written at a reading level appropriate for the grade level that will be using them; therefore, students reading below grade level will have difficulty accessing information in the texts. Some textbook publishers are now providing textbooks with the same content written at a reading level below the grade level for which the textbook is designed. Many textbook publishers are now also providing electronic versions of textbooks in the content areas that can be accessed through special computer programs that read the text orally to students reading below grade level while they follow along reading the text displayed on the monitor. Computer programs also exist that scan in pages in whatever text is being used so that students who are reading below grade level can have the text read orally to them while they follow along with the visual display on the monitor (see Chapter 11).

Pacing lessons and using predictable routines are keys to success in specialized instruction. Teachers should plan lessons in detail and be fully prepared to move through the lesson with no wasted time. For example, when the class follows a routine of passing out papers, heading their papers, and preparing to listen, the teacher is relieved of constant redirection that wastes time. Successful pacing requires knowledge of the group, understanding of the material, and careful planning for both 1) longitudinal needs related to the sequential progression through curriculum materials and recognition of where the students are in relation to the goals for the year and 2) horizontal needs for movement from instruction to guided practice and functional use of material within a given lesson.

Teachers should plan horizontal learning lessons as they look ahead to the next curriculum goal. The teacher must be a manager who recognizes each student's strengths, weaknesses, and needs, knows the curriculum, responds to school or district requirements, expectations, and schedules, and manages time for the planned and unexpected needs of the students. Knowledge of each student's needs also allows the teacher to guide the class as a whole through new learning.

One 11-year-old boy wrote about unprepared teachers, saying that his teachers could have ridden with Jesse James because of all the time they stole from him while he waited for them to prepare (Delisle, 1984). A well-planned lesson will protect both teachers and students from stolen time. Some elements for well-planned handwriting, word decoding and spelling instruction, and reading comprehension and written expression include the following:

- Work on critical procedural skills such as letter writing, word decoding, and spelling across the year until they are automatic.

- Integrate new learning with the old. With thorough teaching and practice, students will build patterns for success and synthesize learning to allow them to move forward longitudinally at ever-increasing rates.

- Overteach using varied approaches because one exposure in only one lesson is seldom enough for all students. Presenting the same material in a variety of ways helps build success before introducing additional new concepts.

Evaluating

Teachers need to allocate time on a daily and weekly basis to assess whether students have learned what teachers intended for them to learn. The assessment might include daily probes of accuracy or time; unit tests that accompany text-books; teacher-designed tests that assess skills or content taught; schoolwide curriculum-based assessment at the beginning, middle, or end of the school year; schoolwide group-administered standardized, normed achievement tests or high-stakes tests; or portfolios with work samples across the school year (see Berninger, 1998a). Members of the interdisciplinary team should support teachers in this effort to monitor response to instruction (see Chapter 13).

DESIGNING INDEPENDENT WORK

Independent activities can provide valuable reinforcement for skills taught and practice with self-regulated learning for students with or without dys-graphia, dyslexia, OWL LD, and/or dyscalculia. Art or work stations that have taped materials, games, and skill-building activities create a stimulating learning environment. Such stations, however, should be considered a supplement to independent work that provides practice in taught skills.

Reading and writing activities aid in the development of thought processes for independent functional use of skills. Use of (duplicated) worksheet forms with blanks to fill in or choices to circle is strongly discouraged because such sheets make the student's task too simple. Students need practice in organizing and placing their own work on the page—something they do not get if all they are required to do is fill in the blanks (Slingerland, 1976).

Providing opportunities for students to apply language skills in content areas such as social studies and science can improve motivation through high-interest activities, which can stimulate creativity. Any independent work should be interesting and meaningful. It will allow students at various levels to practice skills and can turn the classroom into a creative space where structured learning takes place.

Completed independent activities provide teachers with an additional tool for evaluating response to intervention and with documentation of performance while requiring less time for testing. Intervention can be immediately provided as the teacher plans for subsequent lessons for students' small instructional groups. These lessons may involve reteaching or reviewing skills, individualizing instruction, and adjusting the amount or kind of performance expected from an individual student.

Students should be given some open-ended assignments that allow them to work within the limits of their time, interests, and abilities. Teachers should begin independent work by setting clear standards of behavior and performance and by teaching the proper use of materials, expectations, and rules. Each activity—whether it is art, writing, or use of the computer or listening station—should be carefully structured. Providing time for free choice of reading material for reading for pleasure allows students to practice reading skills, helps to instill pleasure in reading, and increases the likelihood that students will read independently on their own.

It is also important for teachers to provide written directions in addition to oral directions. Written directions (e.g., on the board, on a worksheet) provide a sequence that aids recall. Students who may have difficulty with assignments can be asked to repeat directions so it is clear that they understand an assignment. In addition, providing alternatives to written assignments may give students who do not write well alternate avenues to success. Teachers should always remember to give credit for content as well as for written performance.

Because students work at different rates, some will complete assignments and need enriching or stretching activities, while others may not complete the work at all. A few well-done examples may be all that some students can produce. If a student has been on task throughout the independent work period, the teacher should accept the parts of the assignment that are completed even if the whole assignment is not complete. At the same time, the teacher should continue to raise standards for a student who is careless or hurries through an assignment. When evaluation takes place with the student, the teacher can clarify expectations and make suggestions. Some teachers, recognizing that correction is most valuable with a student present, may take time to correct before the independent period is over. Other teachers may offer brief daily conferences. More detailed evaluation can occur at the teacher's discretion.

Having peers correct other students' work should be a method that is used judiciously. Students who are learning new skills can be frustrated or intimidated when peers question, criticize, or even make inappropriate comments about their work. For example, one student with whom Beverly Wolf worked said that he discontinued using his clear, readable cursive writing when a fellow student said, "I can't read cursive, and no one writes that way." At some stages of learning when students have more confidence, using peer checkers and peer tutors may be helpful. However, it can be motivating for students to read aloud their compositions to a writing buddy in order to share their writing orally as many published authors do.

CREATING INCLUSIVE LEARNING ENVIRONMENTS

For students with impaired executive functions, pull-out, resource-room services in special education may be more confusing than helpful. These students may do better when remaining in an organized, coherent learning environment with consistent teacher guidance for the entire school day without disruption. However, they often respond to before- or after-school tutoring or clubs to supplement the regular instructional program in reading (e.g., Berninger, Abbott, Vermeulen, & Fulton, 2006) and writing (e.g., Berninger,

Rutberg, et al., 2006, Study 2). They also respond to explicit instruction in self-regulation activities (see Appendix 9A).

For many reasons, students with dysgraphia, dyslexia, OWL LD, and/or dyscalculia, who tend to have executive function problems, may learn more effectively in the general education classroom than by being pulled out from the regular program. The critical issue for students with impaired executive functions is to have all of the reading or writing or math instruction provided within the same block of time rather than in separate lessons at different times in the day that are not well integrated. All too often, special education pull-out services are not coordinated with the regular program in general education. Students may not transfer skills taught in the resource room to their reading or writing program in the general education classroom unless the special and general education programs are coordinated and explicit instruction is provided. Rather than pulling students out of the general education program, specialized learning environments can be created within the general education classroom that show students how to integrate the various reading, writing, and math skills. Such specialized learning environments are possible if teachers form instructional groupings based on students' instructional reading, writing, and math levels (as described in Section II and this chapter) or participate in cross-classroom team teaching during common blocks of instructional time.

Private schools for students with learning differences often create such integrated learning environments that support success in learning, but public schools can, too. Often, these specialized learning environments are created within a language arts block or math block offered at the same time by all teachers at specific grade levels. Different teachers assume responsibility for reading groups at different instructional levels within those grade levels. Students go to the classroom that has the group for their instructional level, which might be in the classroom taught by their teacher, another classroom taught by a teacher at the same grade level, or a classroom taught by a teacher at another grade level. The instructional groups do not necessarily correspond to the teacher's grade level. Students are under the impression that they "walk about" for reading or language arts or math so that they have an opportunity to interact with other students in the school. The groups are not identified as good, average, or poor students, and they all engage in interesting activities.

Following a consistent routine often helps reassure students with difficulties in organizing their time and space and builds awareness of how to self-regulate their organizational skills. Teachers should post the class schedule daily and take time at the beginning of the day to discuss any changes. Following a schedule helps students know what to expect, reduces anxiety for students who do not manage change well, and helps students move through the day with assurance. The support of an orderly teacher can increase confidence and pattern behavior and can help students understand when and how assignments are expected.

Students of all ages can use a calendar or weekly planner. Teachers can encourage students to use such tools by allowing time for them to copy assignments, if of an age to do so, and to check each morning to see what is due. Some teachers eliminate the need for copying assignments by publishing a weekly calendar with a schedule, special events, assignments, and deadlines printed on it for students' notebooks. Teachers should also educate parents about the importance of learning to organize one's self-management of the learning process. Organizational patterns can be established if parents and teachers consistently use a calendar and help students to use their own as management tools. Students should follow timelines for outline, rough draft, and final written reports, with specific due dates for each. Teachers should monitor student work completion for long-term projects and assignments to help students follow the timelines.

CREATING POSITIVE HOME–SCHOOL RELATIONSHIPS

One way schools can create positive working relationships with parents is to reach out to them in a proactive way. Appendices 3C, 4D, 5C, and 6C in Section II contain practical suggestions for doing so. Sending home parent questionnaires to find out about developmental, medical, family, and educational history, and current issues; coordinating homework assessments; collecting work samples for parent-teacher conferences; and opening communication links through phone or e-mail can contribute to positive home–school relationships. Parents are invited to share information that may help the school better teach their child or personal stressors the student may be facing outside school. Parents are asked at the beginning of each school year about their preferred modes of communication. Above all, schools should remember that SLDs occur more frequently in some families than others. The parent may be reliving the struggles he or she experienced in school through his or her child. Educational professionals who can connect with these parents and assure them they will do all they can to help their child succeed will go a long way in helping these parents feel supported. In turn, the parents will be more able to support their child's learning outside of school when feeling connected to the teachers and school routines and practices.

To summarize, this chapter offers a systems approach for organizing differentiated instruction in inclusive settings and creating a positive classroom climate. Practical guidelines are provided for implementing this systems approach.

Teaching Across the
Content Areas of the Curriculum

General education teachers have an important role to play in developing the cognitive and multiple language skills (listening, speaking, reading, and writing) of all students, with and without specific learning disabilities (SLDs), across all content areas of the curriculum. This is true in both the elementary grades (when the teacher spends most of the day with the same class, unless the school uses team teaching for walk-abouts or other cross-classroom approaches) and in the secondary grades (when most teachers teach five to six sections a day in specific content areas of the curriculum). In this chapter, examples from teaching experience and research studies are provided to illustrate how collaborations among teachers across classes and other members of the interdisciplinary team in the system can facilitate learning across the content areas of the curriculum.

The weaknesses of students with dysgraphia, dyslexia, and/or oral and written language learning disability (OWL LD), frequently deprive them of the classroom experiences in skills at which they may excel, such as creative and insightful thinking outside the box (Arieti, 1976). Instead, their instructional program may overemphasize drill and practice of the written language skills with which they struggle. As a result, these students may be cheated of opportunities to explore, discover, and create, which are normal avenues toward motivated, self-directed learning and thinking.

An integrated curriculum, using material from across content areas, may set the stage for intellectual engagement and provide a context within which students with SLDs can both develop their thinking skills and learn the more difficult written language and/or math skills. Working with high-interest materials may allow these students to use their intellectual skills to find success apart from written language weaknesses or written math calculation weaknesses. All students may benefit from hands-on learning, beginning during the concrete operational stage (Piaget, 1952). As explained in Chapter 1, multimodal teaching may be necessary to help students with and without SLDs link sensory input or motor output modes with internal language systems. At the same time, in addition to multimodal instruction, intellectually engaging material in content areas of the curriculum, including language arts, may capture and maintain students' attention and increase academic engagement in learning in students with SLDs and support transfer to improved academic performance (Torrance, 1963).

Immersing a class in new material by involving as many curriculum areas and modalities of input and output as possible also offers students opportunities to make new and creative cognitive connections. For instance, the letter *m* became memorable when beginning readers sang the folk song "Miss Mary Mack" and learned about machines. They created the sounds of machines during music and rhythm, created their own machines during art, and developed oral language skills as they described the purpose and operation of their inventions. This immersion made them acutely aware of the letter *m* while they were moving, creating, and learning about science.

In another class, when the letter *a* was introduced, each student received an apple and was instructed to draw pictures of the different things they could do with apples. Then, the students took their apples home to use in some way and then bring back to show the class. The following day, they produced turkeys and clowns made of apples and marshmallows. One student recited "Peter, Peter *apple eater*" and showed Peter's house made of an apple. The food was also exciting because the students brought apple pies, apple cakes, apple cookies, apple sauce, and apples and dip to share, making a memorable experience. Also, having so many good things to eat motivated the class to assemble an apple cookbook, which included apple pictures and apple poems created from a class-generated vocabulary cache of words to describe apples. They also sang Malvina Reynolds's apple tree song, "If You Love Me" (1974), planted an apple tree at their school, tasted a variety of apples, and graphed their preferences. The students found books about apples and watched *The Legend of Johnny Appleseed*. Learning about the letter *a* had generated science, nutrition, math, art, music, and oral language activities!

Second-grade students in another class, who were learning that the letter combination *ow* sounds like /ow/ as in *cow*, were motivated to practice and remember by learning about clowns. Each student created his or her own clown face on paper, and then parent volunteers painted the student's faces. Some students designed costumes and others planned the funny things that they would do. Students also practiced decoding /ow/ words during independent activities. They added the suffixes -*ing* and -*ed* to /ow/ verbs (e.g., *bowed, frowning, howled, vowed, plowing, crowned*) and used them with /ow/ nouns (e.g., *cow, frown, town, sow, crown*) to build their own sentences, which began, "A clown came to town and...." Some clowns fell down or turned upside down, and others put on fancy gowns.

MULTIMODAL INSTRUCTION ACROSS THE CURRICULUM

Primary grade teachers commonly bring a sense of fun and exploration to the language curriculum. Unfortunately, as students grow older or as they are confronted with weaknesses in written language, these adventures in learning typically are neglected. They need not be, however.

For example, one sixth-grade activity in a school for students with dyslexia began with a social studies lesson about food production. The teacher, recognizing that food is a motivator for many students, used chocolate to demonstrate the steps involved in bringing a product from its source to the home. During a math lesson, she gave each student a chocolate bar and used the candy to lead the class through a simple fraction lesson. The bars were easy to break on the dividing lines and easy to manipulate. After the lesson, while students were eating their chocolate bars fraction by fraction, the teacher led a discussion of the origins of chocolate and students' favorite chocolate foods. In another lesson M&M's were sorted by color for a graphing activity. Such approaches create positive associations between pleasurable tastes and math!

This theme was also used in reading and writing instruction. During a reading lesson, students read *All About Chocolate,* an upper elementary/middle school nonfiction booklet (http://www.readinga-z.com). This consumable, high-interest book allowed the teacher to develop comprehension and note-taking skills that were appropriate for the students' reading level. The students used many words related to the production of chocolate for decoding practice and a vocabulary discussion, which prepared them for the text. The words also allowed them to practice the new skills of decoding multisyllable words with both open and closed syllables and those with suffixes, with an emphasis on words that are changed when a suffix beginning with a vowel is added. The students also practiced reading many phrases that appeared in the book. The teacher guided the students through reading the book, helped them to make connections to prior knowledge, and related the information in the text to the information in the time lines, illustrations, and charts in the booklet. The students also used comprehension extensions (see proposal by Bonnie Meyer in Chapter 5) to prepare for note-taking and written reports.

The students then reread the book and, with teacher guidance, selected phrases from the book to answer comprehension questions. Instead of writing in the book, however, the students used transparent overlays on the text, highlighting certain phrases with different colors and numbering processes. For example, the teacher directed the students to use yellow to highlight phrases describing cocoa beans, use light green to highlight phrases describing the process, and number the order in which the processes took place. On another occasion, with different materials, the students used colored markers to identify noun phrases, descriptive phrases, and prepositional phrases while the teacher led them through the beginning steps of outlining. The week's spelling lesson was also about chocolate. The teacher wrote the following paragraph, which included often-troublesome words, on a chart for students to copy:

> People around the world love chocolate. Have you ever wondered where chocolate comes from? Chocolate grows on trees. You can't pick a chunk of chocolate from a tree branch and eat it. Chocolate starts from cocoa beans, but getting from beans to chocolate is a very long and complicated process.

Each day's lesson also included practice with phrase and sentence writing using some of the words the students generated for decoding practice. After the students practiced writing independently, they were paired; then, using their highlighted booklets, the students wrote a paragraph about one step in the process of bringing chocolate to market. The paragraph the teacher provided during the spelling lesson became the introductory paragraph of the students' papers, followed by their own paragraph and a concluding paragraph the teacher supplied. After the students gained more experience following this model and writing multiparagraph papers, the teacher planned to have the students follow the same steps for generating notes and writing multipage reports.

In addition to writing activities, the students participated in oral language activities, including an oral report on their homework assignment to make something from chocolate. Some students discussed the physical changes as milk, cocoa, and sugar became fudge. One student thought the gases that make a cake rise were most interesting, and he demonstrated cake baking in class. Others wrote poetry or used candy wrappers for a collage. The week's lesson also provided review and practice with phonic elements used in spelling such as short vowels, letter combinations, soft *c*, multisyllable words and partially phonetic words (e.g., *come, from, people*), and contractions.

Teachers should always consider the specific goals to be accomplished when planning integrated activities across the curriculum:

- How will each activity help move the lesson forward?

- How will the activity provide success for the range of students in the classroom?

- What adjustments are necessary to meet all student needs?

- Is there enough flexibility for different skill levels?

- Is the activity engaging for all students?

Teachers should not expect students with reading problems to acquire all of their information through reading assignments, nor should they expect those with difficulties in written expressive language to submit only written assignments. Subject knowledge can also be acquired through teacher-guided, hands-on activities and oral discussion in which all students participate. Students can also demonstrate what they have learned by recording or dictating their oral productions. Content areas not only contain new vocabulary and concepts to expand knowledge but also introduce students to known vocabulary in new ways (e.g., math vocabulary uses the words *times* and *into* in ways that may confuse students). Student activities, tied to content, are limited only by teacher and student imagination. Students do not need apples or chocolate if they can be drawn into the search for knowledge through imagination alone.

INTEGRATING LANGUAGE INSTRUCTION
ACROSS THE CONTENT AREAS OF THE CURRICULUM

Over the course of his career, Alvin Liberman (1999) had a groundbreaking insight: Because language has no end organs of its own in the brain, it teams with the sensory input and motor output systems of the brain. In other words, language is an internal code. When language teams with the ears, a functional system for listening develops for receiving information from the environment on the aural channel (ears). When language teams with the mouth, a functional system for speaking develops for acting on the environment via oral-motor movement of mouth in speech, which produces oral language. When language teams with the eyes, a functional system for reading develops. Finally, when language teams with the hands, a functional system for writing develops for producing written language via grapho-motor movements of the hand. All four of these language systems are called upon in the content areas of the curriculum, although in somewhat different ways.

General education has increasingly adopted oral discussion as an effective instructional tool for reading, writing, and math instruction (e.g., Beck & McKeown, 2001, 2007; Nussbaum, 2002; Reznitskaya et al., 2001). However, students with relative weaknesses in listening comprehension and oral expression may need instructional activities to develop these language skills sufficiently to be able to participate in these discussions (see Chapter 3 for suggestions). Also, teaching oral language skills is often relevant to developing reading comprehension (Cain & Oakhill, 2007; Carlisle & Rice, 2002; see also Chapter 5). Alternatively, some students with dyslexia may have relative strengths in listening and/or oral expression despite their relative weaknesses in reading and writing, so they can learn and actually shine in front of classmates in these oral discussions.

In addition, a writing-across-the-curriculum movement has influenced mainstream general education practices since at least the 1980s. Students are expected to write in all content areas including math and science, not just in language arts. Many states' annual tests yoked to Common Core or other standards require that students write answers or describe their thinking processes and not just choose multiple-choice answers.

LANGUAGE ARTS CONTENT AREA

Language learning does not occur only when adults explicitly teach oral and written language skills. Language learning also occurs as the result of play with language. Some students with SLDs benefit from activities that use humor to help them gain insight into the use of language.

Humor

Plays on words and puns require instant recognition of multiple meanings of words and recognition of intonation for understanding exaggeration or to indicate teasing. Donald was such a student in Beverly Wolf's classroom. In fourth grade, he was feeling isolated and left out of classroom friendships. The "joke of the day" helped him to understand what made people laugh. Each day, during snack time, the teacher or students read or told a joke. Then, they explained why it was funny. Soon the whole class, including Donald, was checking joke books out of the library. Everyone benefited from the analysis and explanations of the nuances of language and the motivation for reading.

Figurative Language

Students also benefit from discussing and practicing figurative language. Books such as Fred Gwynne's *Chocolate Moose for Dinner* (1976) provide a good introduction to figurative language. (See Chapter 5 for additional book titles that can help with language learning.) Teachers can read these books to the class and discuss them with students. Teachers can also ask students to illustrate figures of speech, such as "You drive me up the wall!" or "It's raining cats and dogs." Also, Melissa Sweet's *Little Red Writing* (see Box 5.2) can be used for word play, illustrating parts of speech, teaching composition processes, and rethinking the value of handwriting in the computer era.

Choosing Children's Literature and Other Books

Reading quality literature to students also provides language stimulation that enriches vocabulary, introduces new language constructions and story grammar, and allows students to discover the joy of language and reading. Reading to students and discussing books with them helps them develop vocabulary and organization of language (Whitehurst et al., 1988). Discussing the text also aids in understanding and prediction (e.g., "What do you think will happen next?" "Why do you think the character did that?"). These open-ended questions promote language and vocabulary growth that is a factor in written language performance. Rhyming stories and poetry develop phonological awareness and can foster a love of the rhythm of language. Reading to students not only opens a world of literature but also improves listening skills; skilled readers listen better and skilled listeners read better. Literature also provides information to those students who are unable to access it themselves—not just factual information but also information about feelings, points of view, and interpersonal relationships. Literature can give pleasure, provoke thought, teach skills, and provide understanding of other cultures. When introducing literature to students, teachers should begin with illustrated books.

Many picture books, such as Patricia Polacco's *Pink and Say* (1994), are written with concepts most suited for 10- to 12-year-olds. Pictures can aid in clarifying vocabulary, developing comprehension of the text, and illustrating difficult ideas, which is especially important for students with weak auditory skills. Pictures help the audience focus and provide clues to action. Text in picture books comes in shorter chunks than in chapter books, but it expresses ideas with economy and richness of vocabulary. Picture books are tools to help students of all ages to tie words to pictures—to interpret, imagine, visualize, and understand what the author is saying.

A good children's book appeals to adults as well as children. Reading to children helps develop vocabulary, inflection, phrasing, and prosody—all of which may help to develop effective listening. Adults should help children to visualize and be actively involved by asking editorial questions, such as *who, what, where, when, why,* and *how.* Students learn to understand the structure and organization of books by regular informal discussion of such things as author, illustrator, characters, and setting: "How did the characters feel?" "What emotions made them act as they did?" "What words make you think this?" Motivation is the *why* of the story—the source of critical actions. Time and place and mood are all part of setting. Discussing the plot leads to clarification of motivation, sequence, action, and resolution. Were issues resolved? Could the same problems occur again? The level of a discussion will vary with the age of the students in the group. Older students should have many opportunities to develop vocabulary and an understanding of the difference between narrative language that tells a story and expository language that may describe, explain, predict, argue, or convey ideas. All of these experiences contribute to competence and confidence in reading.

Oral Language in the Language Arts Reading and Writing Curriculum and Other Content Areas

Reading, handwriting, spelling, and composing are all language skills and should be taught in the language arts curriculum (see Section II). Oral language development is the natural basis for instruction for all of these skills. If students are allowed to be imprecise or to use oral language incorrectly, they are being denied the tools for learning and for higher level thinking skills across the curriculum. When students do not use oral language correctly, teachers should model correct usage through instructional activities. See Chapter 5.

ALTERNATIVE DELIVERY OPTIONS
FOR STRUCTURED LANGUAGE INSTRUCTION

In this section, we discuss the following models, which schools might consider on a schoolwide basis to provide explicit, structured, and integrated instruction in reading, writing, and related oral language skills for the content area of language arts. Cross-grade instructional groups during the language arts block in which all classes at one or several grade levels offer reading and writing instruction at the same time, and in which students are grouped by instructional level and taught by the teacher assigned to that instructional level (rather than to a particular classroom); specialized language arts sections in which specialized systematic, structured instruction is provided for students with SLDs as an alternative to pull out programs; explicit language instruction in all areas of the curriculum K–12; before- or after-school tutoring in reading and/or writing; and summer school programs. All these organizational plans require collaboration among educators across individual classrooms within a school building in order to staff them.

Cross-Grade Instructional Groups During the Language Arts Block

This model, which is often adopted in the elementary grades, requires a team approach in which all teachers at one or several grade levels agree to teach reading and writing at the same time every day. To implement this walk-about model, the teachers collaborate in the following:

1. Identifying each student's instructional level

2. Forming instructional groups for students with similar instructional levels

3. Assigning these groups to specific teachers

4. Having students leave their regular classroom and go to another classroom for reading and writing instruction (unless the group to which they are assigned happens to be in their regular classroom)

By teaming with colleagues, teachers are able to offer differentiated instruction on a larger scale than if they attempted to do so only in their own classrooms. Students benefit because more students at a particular instructional level are likely to exist across classes than in a single class; thus, students receive instruction more closely tailored to where they are in their literacy development without the stigma of being pulled out of the general education program. This model does not preclude teachers also providing some literacy enrichment activities for all students in their class at other times of the day.

This walk-about model requires an initial assessment to determine instructional levels at the beginning of the school year and reassessment at midyear to determine if adjustments in instructional groups are needed. Paraprofessionals (if supervised) and other professionals in the building (e.g., school psychologists, special education teachers, speech-language pathologists [SLPs]) may assist classroom teachers in the initial and midyear assessment (see Chapters 9, 10, and 13).

The walk-about model seems to be growing in popularity and is being used increasingly in many schools. Although it requires commitment, communication, and professional collaboration among all building staff and preplanning, the payoff in terms of student learning outcomes and professional satisfaction can be great. Teaching load is more manageable and teachers can provide instruction for more students at their appropriate instructional levels.

Specialized Language Arts Sections

In middle school and high school, students generally are required to take at least one language arts course per year. This course may cover reading and writing but also literature. Because instruction in the upper grades is delivered by multiple teachers as students switch from class to class during the day, multiple sections of language arts are typically scheduled. Not all sections for the same subject are taught at the same time; students, by necessity, have to sign up for a section of a required course. In this model, one of these sections can cover the same content as the others but provide all instruction in more explicit, structured, and systematic lessons, which students with dyslexia, OWL LD, and/or dysgraphia require more than their peers without these SLDs. This way, there is no stigma attached to attending special pull-out classes for those in the more explicit language arts section—it happens during a regularly scheduled section and is equally intellectually engaging. Other students may also choose this alternative approach. Also, providing such explicit language arts instruction within the general education program is more cost effective than small-group pull-outs at this age level. This model can be so popular among students, parents, and teachers that, depending on schoolwide needs, more than one section of language arts may be designated for explicit, structured, systematic, intellectually engaging language arts instruction. However, the success of this model depends on assigning teachers who are well trained, knowledgeable, and effective in providing this kind of language arts instruction.

Continuous, Structured Language Arts Classes

Continuous, structured language arts classes in general education Grades 1–12 are an innovative adoption of the special language arts section. These classes have been used in a few school districts in Washington State since the 1960s. The model is based on the recognition that some students require explicit language-based instruction in all areas of the curriculum, throughout the school day and throughout their public school years. At each grade level, one class is set aside in which the teacher provides highly explicit, language-based instruction across the curriculum. Parents can request that their child be assigned to this class, which is open not only to students with learning disabilities but also to other students who may benefit from this kind of instruction for a variety of reasons; for example, students who come from low-literacy homes or who are English language learners also benefit from explicit, intellectually engaging instruction. The other classes at the same grade level provide traditional language arts instruction.

Both parents and students with learning disabilities may like the option of choosing a class that offers structured language instruction rather than a special education pull-out program, which requires that the student miss some of the regular program. Students with SLDs often fail to respond to piecemeal, fragmented instruction in pull-out classes, which does not help them to integrate their language arts instruction with the regular curriculum. Especially if appropriate professional development is provided for the teachers in this classroom, this approach may be an effective, resource-efficient way to provide appropriate services for students with SLDs.

Before- or After-School Tutoring

Some schools have instituted before- or after-school tutoring to assist those students who struggle more than classmates in reading, writing, or math. In some schools, extra tutoring is provided by paraprofessionals or parent, grandparent, or community volunteers under the supervision of a general or special education teacher, reading specialist, or school psychologist. If a school is located near a college or university, tutors from the university training programs may be available to provide tutoring under the supervision of a designated university official. The biggest challenge with before- and after-school tutoring is providing transportation for students to arrive at school earlier or leave later. Sometimes, the parent-teacher association raises money to provide transportation for students whose families cannot afford it. Sometimes, transportation is provided as part of after-school child care for working parents.

Tutoring does not have to be one-to-one, with one tutor for each student. In fact, students often enjoy working in small groups more than being singled out for individual assistance. It can be reassuring to them that others need special help, too. Also, students typically enjoy social interactions with others during the learning activities. Research studies showed that second-graders who participated in after-school reading clubs did better than controls on the state standards in reading fluency, and fourth-graders who participated in writing clubs did better than controls on the state's high-stakes test. The club interventions have been translated into lesson plans (see Lesson Sets 9 and 10, respectively, in Berninger & Abbott, 2003, which also links the lesson plans to the published research).

Tutoring may occur at school or in other settings. Some parents, for example, choose to hire private tutors. However, asking parents to hire a private tutor is not an acceptable alternative to providing free appropriate public education for students with educationally disabling conditions under the Individuals with Disabilities Education Improvement Act of 2004 (PL 108-446). Whenever students receive instruction outside of their usual classrooms, teachers and the remediation specialists should maintain close communication to ensure their understanding of specific learning needs and consistent classroom follow-up.

Special Summer Programs

Some school districts offer summer programs for students who are not at grade level in reading or writing. These can be as effective as extra help during the regular school year. Some students do require extra time to learn the same skills as their classmates. They also benefit from practicing them over the summer, which prepares them for a strong start in the fall when the new school year begins.

Issues Related to Implementing These Alternative Language Arts Models

Each individual school or school district will need to decide how to allocate professional resources to implement the model chosen to serve students with SLDs affecting written language acquisition. Schools vary greatly in access to special kinds of professional expertise, such as school psychology and speech-language pathology, for assistance in implementing these models. Many schools have reading specialists. However, as pointed out by Barbara Efrè at the University of Padua (B. Arfé, personal communication, September 21, 2008), the schools she observed during her graduate student global exchange experience in the United States had reading specialists, but none had writing specialists; moreover, SLPs have more training in oral language than in written language or literacy. Thus, effective implementation of these models requires a system approach involving members of the interdisciplinary team and not just classroom teachers, in keeping with the position that a multilevel system offers solutions to the challenges in educating students with SLDs.

Linking Assessment to Instruction

Another issue is that, in general, teachers are trained to teach rather than perform diagnostic or individualized assessments, and psychologists are trained to assess individuals but not usually to provide instructional interventions. As a result, links between assessment and intervention are not always clear to an interdisciplinary team. One staffing model that might facilitate schoolwide implementation of the four models would be to create positions for more broadly prepared learning specialists to integrate assessment and instructional interventions for oral language, reading, writing, and math. Learning specialists would receive preservice training in oral and written language, psychology, and curriculum and instruction across content areas and acquire supervised experience in both assessment and teaching. These individuals would have to demonstrate at least 5 years of successful teaching experience before being appointed as the learning specialist in a school. Both preservice and in-service professional development would equip them with professional skills to provide group and individual assessments in oral language, reading, writing, and math and to plan, conduct, and evaluate individualized instruction in group settings in the same domains. Sometimes, these interdisciplinary learning specialists would supervise the teachers or paraprofessionals in providing assessment and instructional services. Interdisciplinary learning specialists would also be available for ongoing consultation with any teacher for any student as learning problems in literacy (and numeracy) arise during the school year.

If a school is located near a college or university, administrators may be able to create partnerships with universities to secure additional help in serving students with learning disabilities. For example, if a teacher training program is nearby, part of the student teaching experience could include supervised practica in local schools for teaching students with SLDs. An experienced teacher with expertise in the kind of specialized instruction needed would supervise the practica. As a result of such partnerships, students with SLDs benefit from extra help while the student teachers are better prepared after graduation to teach students with SLDs in their own classrooms. Some states are developing model programs that partner special university-based centers with local schools.

SOCIAL STUDIES CONTENT AREA

Students will not necessarily generalize what they learn about language in language arts to the social studies content area of the curriculum without specific instruction on how to do so. The preparation activities for guided reading activities described in Chapters 4 and 5 can be adapted for social studies instruction. See Ervin (2001) for graded lessons for teaching reading across the content areas, including social studies.

Begin the lesson by teaching vocabulary specific to the content to be covered in a particular lesson or unit. Provide purpose-setting questions for reading the material that provides the content for a lesson or unit. Students might first read the material silently and then discuss it using a two-part strategy guided by the teacher. First, the teacher poses a question and students offer answers. Second, the teacher asks them to read orally the sentence or sentences in the reading material that supports that answer.

Alternatively, the teacher guides the students in writing a summary of what has been read. To begin, the students are asked to write the main idea or ideas and then make a list of supporting details for each idea. Next, they are asked to integrate the main idea(s) and supporting details in a paragraph so that someone who did not read the material could learn what they learned from reading it.

Also, when written reports, homework, or other written assignments are created for the social studies curriculum, teachers should provide strategies for how to complete the written reports and other assignments. These strategies can be specific to the nature of the assignment but should cover making a plan for content and organization, generating a first draft, reviewing it (for content, organization, spelling, capitalization, punctuation, etc.), and making necessary revisions.

MATH CONTENT AREA

As explained in Chapter 6, students with dysgraphia will need special instruction during math lessons in writing numerals legibly and automatically, using place value correctly to represent numbers, and placement of multiplace numbers correctly in two-dimensional space with numerals aligned correctly in columns and rows. Students with dyslexia and OWL LD will need special instruction in reading word problems. Students with OWL LD will need special instruction in math-specific vocabulary and listening to instructional talk during math instruction.

At the same time, some may have special strengths in math concepts and thinking that should be nurtured, along with providing the supports to assist with the oral and written language requirements for math skills.

SCIENCE CONTENT AREA

Language is a system that not only makes contact with the external world through end organs (sensory and motor systems) but also makes contact with the internal mental world of cognition. Some refer to this mental world as *intellect*. Language supports the translation of ideas in this mental world into a code that can be communicated with the outside world by mouth (speaking or oral expression) and/or by hand (writing or written expression). Effective instruction must engage multiple modes of language and intellect. Two instructional strategies for creating and sustaining intellectual engagement, which can be integrated with literacy instruction involving listening, speaking, reading, and writing, are 1) thematic units in science on developmentally appropriate topics of interest, and 2) embedding hands-on science activities (e.g., building models of the brain, conducting science experiments, solving virtual reality problems in oceanography, observing natural phenomenon in the out of doors, learning cross-cultural anthropology on linguistics; see Berninger & Wolf, 2009a). In addition, themes of hope can be used to inspire struggling learners that they, like others, can overcome obstacles and succeed. For example, a lesson can be organized around the life story of a person who overcame numerous challenges to become successful and make contributions to society (e.g., Albert Einstein, Mark Twain, John Muir, Sequoyah; see Berninger & Wolf, 2009b).

TRANSLATIONAL SCIENCE

In programmatic research at the University of Washington, early intervention studies of assessment–intervention links K–4 were first conducted in school settings to show that early identification and intervention aimed at all levels of language can prevent reading and writing problems (e.g., Berninger, 2009; Berninger & Richards, 2010). These were translated into lesson plans (Berninger & Abbott, 2003, at specific grade levels for specific language skills). Other assessment–intervention links were validated on the bases of genetics, brain, and behavioral data and response to instruction for students with diagnosed SLDs in a family genetics study on the basis of both behavioral and brain data (e.g., Berninger, 2000; Berninger & Richards, 2010). The interventions were aimed at all levels of multiple language systems and their multiple sensory and motor links, cognitive engagement, and themes of hope. These too were translated into lesson plans (Berninger & Wolf, 2009a). First, the citation for research showing changes in brain and behavioral data and then translation of the instructional research into lesson plans are provided to illustrate translation of science into educational practice.

In the Word Detectives curriculum (Richards et al., 2000; Berninger et al., 2003; Berninger & Wolf, 2009b, Unit I), two themes are used to intellectually engage students with dyslexia in the curriculum designed to improve their reading: Einstein's uncle's advice that he overcome dyslexia by becoming a word detective and Sherlock Holmes solving word mysteries and aliens learning about language on earth. In the Mark Twain's Writers' Workshop (Berninger, Winn, et al., 2008, Study I; Berninger & Wolf, 2009b) the story of Mark Twain as a writer, public speaker, and humorist was used to spur interest in linking oral language to writing and learning how one can become a successful writer and orator even if one has struggled in learning to spell. A science writers' workshop (Berninger, Winn, et al., 2008, Study 2; Berninger & Wolf, 2009b, Unit III) used the story of John Muir—a scientist and writer who survived an accident, then founded the American National Park system and the environmental movement—to spur interest in writing about science. Another workshop, The Sequoyah Writing Readers Workshop (Berninger, Stock, Lee, Abbott, & Breznitz, 2007; Berninger & Wolf, 2009b, Unit IV), introduced the science of linguistics and cultural anthropology through the story of Sequoyah, the Cherokee who at age 50 gave his people written language and for whom the giant redwoods in California are named. Sequoyah's life accomplishments, despite his physical disabilities.

Instructional studies have also informed brain research. Students with dyslexia have trouble paying attention to written words on orthographic tasks but not to spoken words on phonological tasks (Thomson et al., 2005). Thomson and colleagues proposed that the visual motion detection region of the brain, which had been shown to differ in individuals with and without dyslexia (Eden et al., 1996), might be disrupted by attentional mechanisms; in turn, the visual motion region disrupts nearby regions involved in orthographic processing. Winn and colleagues (2006) found that individual differences in the visual motion region of the brain were related to individual differences in the rate of performing orthographic tasks in students with but not without dyslexia.

Richards and colleagues (2007) found that, following hands-on virtual reality training in navigating the Puget Sound to find Luna, a lost orca whale, the brain normalized in the visual motion region on a task that required students to pronounce written pseudowords. The normalization occurred in a region associated with touch sensation of the hands, which is near a center for phonological processing. Thus, hands-on, intellectually engaging activities may help overcome the visual motion impairment and related impairment in phonological decoding of written pseudowords, which requires initial orthographic processing followed by phonological recoding of graphemes, via the touch sensation.

HELPFUL GUIDELINES TO SUPPORT MULTIMODAL INSTRUCTION ACROSS CONTENT AREAS

Continual opportunities to respond should be built into the lessons to maintain attention to and engagement in the task at hand. Attention has three components: 1) focusing on the relevant and ignoring the irrelevant, 2) staying on task, and 3) switching between tasks. Engagement is presence of mind or mindfulness as opposed to detachment from what is happening. Sometimes, the response is oral and sometimes it is written. Maintaining attention to and engagement in instruction is often very difficult for students with impaired executive functions. Also in the lessons, the teacher frequently provides feedback or reinforcement to students for paying attention and staying on task.

For example, when a student habituates, which is common in students with impaired executive functions, the student fails to pay attention to or respond to the task at hand after continual exposure to the same stimuli or task. To overcome habituation within a lesson, tasks should be of brief duration and vary frequently; however, within each lesson, the variation should occur in a predictable routine for the order and nature of activities.

Collectively, short duration, constant change that introduces novelty, and predictable routine across lessons can help students attend, engage, and self-regulate their learning. An instructional study showed that attentional training prior to spelling and composition instruction led to greater improvement in writing than did the control treatment, possibly because attention training improved the ability to pay attention to written words during instruction (Chenault, Thomson, Abbott, & Berninger, 2006).

CONCLUSION

Both teaching experience and research findings support the conclusion that effective instruction for students with dysgraphia, dyslexia, OWL LD, and/or dyscalculia includes instruction to develop oral (listening and speaking) and written (reading and writing) language systems in the mind as well as high-interest, intellectually engaging, hands-on activities across content areas of the curriculum. One study even showed that students without these SLDs benefited from and enjoyed these lessons. The lessons can be implemented in general education classes across the curriculum, and hopefully they will encourage others to develop such lessons aimed at multiple levels of four language systems and high intellectual engagement.

A Systems Approach
to Teaching and Learning

On the one hand, the developing learner requires considerable other regulation—that is, structured guidance and support from adults, such as parents and teachers. On the other hand, individual students also need to learn to self-regulate—that is, self-govern their complex minds (Posner & Rothbart, 2007). In Section I, the multimodal, multilevel, multiple-language systems supporting language learning and aspects of math learning were discussed. In Section II, a developmental model of assessment–instruction links for identifying weaknesses and planning and implementing instructional interventions at each grade level to prevent specific learning disabilities (SLDs) was presented. In Chapter 9, in keeping with the focus of Section III on organizational issues required to support the goals of Section II, mental self-government, which draws on both other regulation of teachers and parents, and self-regulation of learning and behavior by the developing student are discussed.

COORDINATING MULTIPLE,
MULTILEVEL SYSTEMS OF THE LEARNING BRAIN

The transition from other (teacher) to self-regulation of learning is fundamentally important for students with SLDs, who often have weaknesses or significant impairments in executive functions (Berninger & Richards, 2002, 2010). Not all students in the general education classroom require the same level of teacher guidance and orchestration of instructional components as do students with dysgraphia, dyslexia, oral and written language learning disability (OWL LD), and/or dyscalculia. Effective instruction for students with impaired executive functions may need to be specially designed to overcome the associated impaired timing of component processes in working memory: word form coding for storage and processing, phonological and orthographic loops, and supervisory attention/executive functions (Berninger, Abbott, Thomson, et al., 2006) as well as syntax buffer for accumulating words (Berninger, Richards, Abbott, 2015). The goal of Chapter 9 is therefore to teach oral and written language with working memory in mind.

Teaching to students' instructional levels is necessary but not sufficient—instruction may also have to be individually tailored to students' impaired or weak working memory components, especially executive functions required to focus, switch, and sustain their attention (see Appendix 9A). Students who have strong executive functions are self-regulated learners who can generate their own strategies for managing the learning process. Teachers who adapt their instruction to the individual differences in students for self-regulation also need well-honed executive functions to plan ahead, monitor student response to instruction, and be exceptionally well organized!

ROLE OF WORKING MEMORY IN COORDINATING MULTIPLE, MULTILEVEL SYSTEMS

Many functions of the human mind occur outside of conscious awareness in what psychologists call *implicit memory*, supported by an episodic buffer in working memory that abstracts patterns in environmental exposure to stimuli. Conscious awareness of thinking requires explicit memory and goal-related working memory (Baddeley & Hitch, 1974). Working memory has limited resources to support storage and processing of information; thus, working memory can only make a fraction of one's mental processes available to consciousness at a particular moment in time. Three instructional approaches for coordinating unconscious and conscious language and math processes are discussed next. These include cross-code mapping, integrating internal and external modes, and self-government of working memory components.

CROSS-CODE WORD FORM MAPPING

The early pioneers in teaching students with dyslexia knew intuitively that both auditory and visual processes were involved in creating connections between heard and read words as well as kinesthetic (touch) sensation from writing words. Hence, they emphasized the multisensory aspects—auditory, visual, and kinesthetic—of teaching reading to students with dyslexia (see Chapter 1 for an overview with relevant references). However, years later, research has made it clear that although the primary sensory brain regions are involved, so are the other brain regions. These include association areas in the brain that transform sensory auditory input into higher level phonological representations, transform sensory visual input into higher level orthographic representations, and integrate the phonological and orthographic representations, as well as the motor regions involved in producing written language—letters, words, and sentences. Thus, multimodal, sensorimotor instructional approaches informed by contemporary psycholinguistics are needed for teaching students with dysgraphia, dyslexia, OWL LD, and dyscalculia.

Linguistic awareness (Mattingly, 1972) helps students learn to store and process words in conscious memory for the goal of creating maps of the relationships between spoken and written words, their sounds and morphology, or their spellings and morphology, or among their phonology, orthography, and morphology that can be accessed consciously. Such maps specifying interrelationships are essential for reading and spelling words in a morphophonemic orthography (see Chapter 4). For example, phonological awareness of the small sound units called phonemes helps students associate them with graphemes (one- and two-letter spelling units) in learning to decode words. Orthographic awareness of graphemes in written words also contributes to learning to apply grapheme–phoneme correspondences in decoding. Morphological awareness of word parts that signal meaning and grammar also contributes to conscious awareness of written and spoken words in learning to decode written words (Nagy, Berninger, Abbott, Vaughan, & Vermeulen, 2003).

The greater one's conscious linguistic awareness of the task-relevant levels (units) of language, the fewer working memory resources are needed to complete a reading task in explicit memory. Likewise, if some parts of a reading task can be completed automatically in implicit memory outside of conscious awareness, then fewer of the limited working memory resources will be needed to complete the task in explicit memory. However, research has also shown that students with SLDs have impaired working memory, which may interfere with their access to the unconscious language processes (e.g., Siegel, 1994; Swanson, 1999, 2006; Swanson & Ashbaker, 2000). That is why explicit instruction aimed at linguistic awareness, which facilitates conscious access to the episodic buffer in implicit memory that records exposure to words at an unconscious level, may be particularly important in teaching students with SLDs to form these maps across word form codes.

Explicit instruction is not the same as direct instruction implemented with fixed teacher scripts, although lesson plans for teacher-guided instructional activities are used. For example, words sorts may create conscious linguistic awareness without teaching specific rules. As illustrated in Section II, the teacher guides by questioning and gives students ample opportunities to construct responses and practice skills. Many of the illustrated examples of teacher-guided prompts for processing at different levels of language show that teachers are expected to respond flexibly to student response to instruction and adapt instruction as necessary for individuals. Also, in the recommended approach, the teacher is well prepared ahead of time so that he or she can respond flexibly and responsively to the students' instructional needs, as observed in the unfolding teaching–learning interaction cycles.

Students with SLDs will vary in the degree of explicit instruction, modeling, and teacher-guided student-response construction they require. Other students in other instructional groups may require minimal to moderate degrees of explicit instruction and may even benefit from student-generated and self-guided learning (e.g., Connor et al., 2004). Differentiated instruction that meets the instructional needs of all students in the classroom provides the appropriate mix of teacher-directed instruction and student-generated learning for each student. Such a mix can be accomplished, but it requires the flexible cognitive and language processes of not only the student but also the teacher (Deák, 2001).

For historical reasons, phonological awareness received more attention than orthographic and morphological awareness at the end of the 20th century and beginning of the 21st century. The importance of phonological awareness was discovered at a time when the prevailing view was that dyslexia was a visual perceptual disorder. However, Vellutino (1979) presented data to debunk that view, making a compelling case that dyslexia is a language-based disorder, which is now the prevailing view.

Just because the eye and visual regions of the brain play a role in the initial processing of written words, it does not follow that dyslexia is a visual perceptual disorder that requires visual perceptual training. Rather, individuals with dyslexia need specialized language instruction. However, individuals with and without dyslexia differ in the brain regions (e.g., fusiform gyrus) that integrate letters with sounds in speech to create orthographic representations of written words; thus, reading written words involves visible language (orthography) but not primarily nonlinguistic visual processes (Berninger & Richards, 2002). Chapters 2 and 4 provide a further discussion of the roles of morphological, orthographic, and phonological awareness in learning to read English—a morphophonemic orthography. Semantics (understanding vocabulary meaning, such as deciding if two words such as *baby* and *infant* or *son* and *father* are synonyms) is also involved in creating maps linking word-level language, but it is not synonymous with morphology (word form structure rather than word meaning; Stahl & Nagy, 2005).

Two kinds of mapping across written words and spoken words may be involved in learning to read and spell:

1. *Fast mapping*, which is based on one or two exposures, such as in naming visual objects and acquiring semantic concepts in oral vocabulary (McGregor, 2004) and beginning reading and spelling (Apel et al., 2006)

2. *Slow, effortful mapping*, which requires many more exposures, more practice, and explicit instruction

Fast mapping may explain how students acquire automatic sight word vocabulary. In contrast, slow mapping is based in large part on the alphabetic principle and its transfer to phonological decoding. Both fast and slow mapping may contribute to the creation of an autonomous orthographic lexicon (mental dictionary for written spellings), which has links to pronunciations and word meanings.

Early intervention with at-risk first-grade readers showed that a whole-word strategy (in which every letter was named and the whole word was pronounced; fast mapping) and the alphabetic principle (slow mapping) were both effective. No relative advantage for onset-rime strategies was observed for at-risk readers at this stage of reading development (Berninger, Abbott, et al., 2000).

In many readers, fast-mapping orthographic representations are refined by slower mapping during self-teaching, which is decoding words while reading (Share, 2008), or by teacher-guided, explicit instruction during reading lessons. Students with dyslexia or OWL LD may have problems in fast mapping, so they have to rely greatly on slow mapping to create the maps for translating written words into spoken words or spoken words into written words.

Word origins are also important in teaching cross-word mapping (Balmuth, 2009; Henry, 2003). Henry (1993) showed the importance of teaching Latin and Greek phonemes and morphemes as a word decoding strategy for developing readers beyond the initial stage of word decoding. Explicit reading instruction, however, should not end after the third grade. In fourth grade and above, instruction should focus on mapping strategies related to morphology as well as orthography and phonology and to reading specific words that are likely to be of lower frequency, longer length, and greater complexity than words encountered in previous grades.

The most frequent words in oral language are Anglo-Saxon, a version of English based on old German and English. Compared with the total number of English words, these high-frequency words total only about 1,000 words, and many of them are function words. These function words include conjunctions, prepositions, pronouns, articles, and helping verbs (e.g., *is*), which have no meaning of their own apart from the sentence context in which they occur, but they glue the content words (e.g., nouns, verbs, adjectives, adverbs) of the sentence together. Most of the written words in textbooks used in Grades 1–3 contain Anglo-Saxon words, which tend to be of one or two syllables; the first syllable is typically accented.

Henry (1990) summarized the important differences in the phonology, orthography, and morphology of words of different word origin. For example, the letters *ch* may stand for the /ch/ phoneme at the beginning of *children* or *chalk* in Anglo-Saxon words; however, in Greek words, it stands for the /k/ phoneme as in *chorus* or *psychology*. Although *sh* is the only spelling for the /sh/ phoneme at the beginning of *should* or *shall* in Anglo-Saxon words, in words of Latin or French origin the /sh/ phoneme can be spelled with *ch* as in champagne, *ti* as in *nation*, *ci* as in *ancient*, or *si* as in *mission*. The morphology is also different across word origins. Many of the suffixes in Anglo-Saxon code inflection (past tense, plural, comparison of two or more than two), contractions involving function words, or ownership (possessive). Many of the suffixes in Latin or French words code derivation that marks parts of speech and therefore syntactic clues for using a word in sentence context. Greek morphemes, on the other hand, contribute jointly rather than modifying bases, such as in *automobile* (a self-driven motion machine).

In contrast, the content area subject textbooks in Grades 4 and above have an increasing numbers of words of Latin or French (romance languages) and Greek origins. Individual words of Latin, French, or Greek origin are lower in frequency than words of Anglo-Saxon origin and tend to have three to five syllables with accents beyond the first syllable, and contain schwas (reduced vowels); their spelling has to be memorized for specific word contexts, and they are generally longer and more complex than words of Anglo-Saxon origin. For example, multiple suffixes can be added to a word, as in transforming *inform* (a verb) to *information* (a noun) to *informational* (an adjective).

Latin and Greek words are used in the written language of formal schooling, and individuals who have more schooling have more opportunities to learn them (Beeler, 1988). Thus, as Beeler pointed out, students whose parents have more formal schooling are more likely to hear those words spoken in the home than students whose parents have had less schooling. That is why students of less-educated parents are likely to be at an academic disadvantage at fourth grade and above. They have less oral exposure to the kind of words that increasingly appear in written texts in the upper grades. However, the contribution of morphology to word formation in longer, more complex words can be taught at school even if students do not hear those kinds of words at home. Thus, the instructional significance of morphology extends beyond its benefits for students with dyslexia or OWL LD. As Nagy (2007) proposed, teaching morphological awareness and decoding in school may be the way to narrow the achievement gap between students whose families differ in education and income levels and ethnic or racial backgrounds.

See Henry (1990) and Berninger and Richards (2002, Chapter 7) for pseudowords from Anglo-Saxon and Latin word origins to use in professional development workshops to expand teachers' linguistic awareness related to word origin, as well as how knowledge of the three kinds of word-level linguistic awareness might be applied to instruction. See Berninger and Wolf (2009b) for the POM certificate to award teachers who grasp the importance of phonological, orthographic, and morphological (POM) awareness in teaching word reading and spelling and how these may be unique for words of different origin.

RAPID AUTOMATIC CROSS-CODE MAPPING

When a skill can be performed only with application of explicit, controlled strategies (Schneider & Chein, 2003; Schneider & Shiffrin, 1977; Shiffrin & Schneider, 1977), it is said to be strategic. Examples of skills that require strategic processing include decoding unknown words, which may be words never encountered before or words that were encountered but are not remembered, and reading comprehension.

When a reading skill becomes automatic (Samuels, 1985), it executes outside conscious awareness in implicit memory. An example of a reading skill that might become automatic is recognition of a previously encountered word without the reader consciously devoting strategies to decode it. Learning new skills typically requires strategies. Once the skill is practiced and mastered, it may become automatic (direct access without conscious awareness) or fluent (executed quickly and in a coordinated, efficient manner). However, reading comprehension typically requires strategies and cannot be performed completely automatically outside of conscious awareness.

Ehri (1992) provided a conceptual framework for how phonics are coordinated with word-level processes in developing automatic recognition of words. Although automatic recognition of written words is often referred to as a *sight vocabulary* or *sight words,* the use of the word *sight* is somewhat misleading because the visual code is not the only one involved; at least two different codes—phonological and orthographic—are involved. Automatic word recognition also draws on word-specific representations of written words in long-term memory. These orthographic representations have links to other language (phonological and morphological word forms and their parts) and cognitive (semantic associations and concepts) representations in long-term memory.

When students can recognize single words automatically, use sentence syntax to combine words in meaning units, and comprehend the text they are reading orally or silently, their reading is likely to be fluent—smooth, coordinated, effortless reading at the appropriate rate for the task at hand. Fluency is not just fast reading. The appropriate speed depends on the task at hand—for example, skimming for information, initially reading before receiving explicit comprehension instruction, subsequently reading and reflectively discussing, preparing a written summary with main ideas and supporting details, taking notes for preparing a written report, or studying for a test.

Biemiller (1977–1978) provided the first evidence that the reading rate across multiple levels of language, ranging from letters to words to text, contributes to reading fluency. Dowhower (1987) showed that, in reciprocal fashion, reading comprehension contributed to fluency. Biemiller and Siegel (1997) demonstrated that vocabulary instruction contributed to accurate and fluent reading in students at risk for reading for environmental reasons.

Research supports a number of teaching approaches for developing reading fluency. Repeatedly reading the same text improved the reading fluency of at-risk second-grade readers (Dowhower, 1987). Prior word-level training for single words that would appear in the text also improved some aspects of reading fluency (Levy, Abello, & Lysynchuk, 1997). For students with dyslexia who had not yet developed adequate knowledge of the alphabetic principle and decoding, combining instruction directed to the automatic alphabetic principle as well as repeated readings was more effective than repeated readings alone (Berninger, Abbott, Abbott, Graham, & Richards, 2002).

EXECUTIVE FUNCTIONS FOR SELF-REGULATING COMPLEX FUNCTIONAL ORAL LANGUAGE, READING, WRITING, AND MATH SYSTEMS

Approaches to teaching self-regulation of multiple processes should aim instruction at all levels of language or all developmentally appropriate concepts, procedures, and applications of math close in time with working memory in mind. Such an approach creates functional connections that support all of the components of the systems functioning in concert, just like the musical instruments in an orchestra led by a conductor (Posner, Petersen, Fox, & Raichle, 1988). Examples of the subword and word levels of language relevant to learning to read and spell words include sounds in spoken words (phonological awareness); letters in written words (orthographic awareness); and word parts that mark bases, modify meaning, and mark tense, number, comparisons, and parts of speech (morphological awareness). Examples of the levels of language relevant to learning to understand and produce spoken and written words consisting of multiple words includes awareness of syntactic structure, and schema for the higher order organizing structures.

The National Reading Panel of the National Institute of Child Health and Human Development (2000) concluded that both vocabulary and reading comprehension should be taught. Stahl and Nagy (2005) and Carlisle and Rice (2002) have reviewed the research evidence for effective ways of teaching vocabulary and reading comprehension. Even though dyslexia is a disorder in word decoding, word reading, and spelling, students with dyslexia need more than phonics instruction. They also need to receive instruction in transfer of those phonics to the actual decoding process and repeated practice in applying decoding until word recognition becomes automatic. Students with dyslexia or OWL LD also benefit from systematic instruction in developing vocabulary meaning and reading comprehension because they tend to have impairments in word and text meaning across language systems by ear and by eye. To comprehend a variety of texts, these students need instruction and practice in coordinating the multiple modes of input, output, and their integration and the multiple codes within levels of language in working memory so that they work in concert. That is, they need explicit instruction in their impaired skills but also all the skills needed for a functional reading system

A similar case can be made for writing. To facilitate the transfer of transcription skills to composition and to integrate the various writing components in resource-limited working memory, which may have reduced storage or processing capability in students with dysgraphia, transcription, and composition instruction should be taught together in the same lesson so that they become functionally integrated (Berninger et al., 1995; Berninger et al., 1997, 1998; Berninger, Rutberg, et al., 2006; Berninger, Vaughan, et al., 2000). The fifteen lesson sets, all based on published research in Berninger and Abbott (2003) provide examples of teaching across all levels of language to create functional reading and writing systems, while at the same time remediating impaired skills that identified the student for specialized instruction.

Explicit Strategy Instruction

Explicit strategies should be used for not only the transcription skills but also high-level cognitive processes of composing (Auman, 2003; Berninger et al., 1995, 2002; Carlisle, 1996; Graham & Harris, 2005; Graham & Perrin, 2007a, 2007b). Examples of explicit composition instruction are teacher modeling of the Plan, Write, Review, Revise strategy (Hayes & Flowers, 1980); for example, thinking aloud as the teacher plans, translates, reviews, and revises and models each of these processes for the students and teacher guidance in constructing well-formed paragraphs, which includes asking questions and offering suggestions as students plan, compose, review, and revise. Following this kind of explicit writing instruction, below-average writers at the transition between third and fourth grade improved in their composing; in addition, they self-reported fewer writing avoidant behaviors when they could write better (Berninger et al., 1995). This transition is critical because the writing requirements of the curriculum increase and become more complex in fourth grade and above. Students need to be monitored and given supplementary instruction if needed during this transition.

Students also benefit from explicit strategy instruction in learning different writing genres, such as narrative and expository—informational, compare and contrast, and persuasive. For a review of research, especially the programmatic research of Wong, on this topic with middle school and high school students, see Wong and Berninger (2004). Berninger and colleagues (2002) showed that third-graders at risk for writing improved in expository writing when they were explicitly taught how to plan, translate, and review and revise this genre. (For translation of the research into a teaching plan, see Lesson Set 7 in Berninger & Abbott, 2003.)

For students with dyslexia, OWL LD, and/or dysgraphia—many of whom have problems in executive functions for self-regulation of the writing process (Graham, 1997; Hooper, Swartz, Wakely, de Kruif, & Montgomery, 2002; Hooper, Wakely, de Kruif, & Swartz, 2006)—and for other students in Grade 4 and above, simply engaging in the authentic communication process is not sufficient (Graham & Perrin, 2007a, 2007b). Students benefit from explicit instruction (raising cognitive awareness of the processes) and strategy instruction (Graham & Harris, 2005) in each of the cognitive processes of writing. They also benefit from explicit instruction in the six traits of writing (Culham, 2003), which some states' high-stakes tests use in evaluating whether students meet state standards in writing. *The Writing Lab Approach to Language Instruction and Intervention* is a valuable source of writing instruction activities and software to support the composing process for general education teachers; it is based on research that included students with a variety of language problems, including OWL LD (Nelson, Bahr, & Van Meter, 2004; see also http://wmich .edu/speech-audiology/wlop).

Learning to write (or read) English should not be delayed until oral, conversational English is mastered. In fact, written language can support learning a second language in its oral as well as written format. (See http://www .techno-ware-esl.com for resources for teaching writing to English language learners.)

Research has shown that by directing instruction to all levels of language close in time, struggling writers may be able to overcome working memory inefficiencies in writing.

Grouping Issues Related to Reaching Self-Regulated Learning

In order to group students for instructional purposes, it is important to know whether individual students have difficulties in handwriting only, spelling only, or word reading and spelling only or syntax and text for oral and written language comprehension or expression or some combination of these. The students' profiles across these language systems inform issues in teaching across levels of language to create functional language systems. In addition, gender differences occur in writing rather than reading (Berninger, Nielsen, Abbott, Wijsman, & Raskind, 2008): Boys tend to have more difficulties than girls in handwriting, spelling, and executive functions for self-regulation of composing, and girls are more likely than boys to compensate for both reading and writing problems in their adult years (Berninger, Nielsen et al., 2008). Nevertheless, many boys respond to instruction designed to overcome their writing problems (e.g., Berninger et al., 2014; Tanimoto et al., 2015).

At the same time, teachers should always keep in mind that the learner is a person with emotions and motivations and incorporate motivation-enhancing components into the instructional activities (Hidi & Boscolo, 2006) so that students will persist and sustain efforts in their educational journeys.

Thus, from a systems perspective, teachers may be challenged by how to teach to all levels of language—each of which is leveled—with social-emotional, cognitive, sensorimotor, and attention/executive functions in mind to create functional reading and writing system, while at the same time tailoring instruction to an individual student's impairments in specific levels of language within specific language systems. A similar case can be made for teaching math across the multiple concepts, procedures, and applications to problem solving (see Chapter 6). This daunting task requires a team effort involving multiple professionals on interdisciplinary teams in schools. (For more information on cross-disciplinary collaboration and communication, see Chapter 13 in this book and Berninger, 2015.)

Instructional Resources for Executive Functions

For assessment of attention and executive functions consult with school psychologists for the evidence-based rating systems and normed measures available in the school and request an assessment of students exhibiting difficulty with self-regulation of attention, learning, and behavior in the classroom. If problems are identified the following instructional resources are helpful for classroom teachers.

Dawson, P., & Guare, R. (2010). *Executive skills in children and adolescents: A practical guide to assessment and intervention.* New York, NY: Guilford.

Juarez, B., Parks, S., & Black, H. (2000). *Learning on purpose: A self-management approach to study skills.* North Bend, OR: Critical Thinking Co.
Available at http://www.criticalthinking.com/learning-on-purpose-book.html

Levine, M. (1990). *Keeping a head in school: A student's book about learning abilities and learning disorders.* Cambridge, MA: Educators Publishing Service.
For helping students understand and manage their attentional and learning difficulties. Other titles by M. Levine are also available from Educators Publishing Service: *All Kinds of Minds, The Myth of Laziness,* and *A Mind at a Time.*

Co-occurring Specific Learning Disabilities and Twice-Exceptional Students

Epidemiological studies investigate the incidence of disorders in the general population. A series of epidemiological studies at the Mayo Clinic showed that reading (Slavica, Colligan, Barbaresi, Schaid, & Jacobsen, 2001), writing (Slavica et al., 2009), math (Barbaresi, Katusic, Colligan, Weaver, & Jacobsen, 2005), and oral language (Stoecke et al., 2013) disabilities with and without attention-deficit/hyperactivity disorder (ADHD; Katusic et al., 2005) occur in about one in five children and youth. However, how the various specific learning disabilities (SLDs) are defined affects the incidence. Definitions can affect whether reading disabilities are more likely to include dyslexia or oral and written language learning disability (OWL LD). Nevertheless, epidemiological studies showed that SLDs and ADHD may co-occur. If so, it is important that educational professionals identify which of these conditions an individual may have so that the student receives specialized instruction for each SLD that may be affecting his or her learning (see Chapter 9) as well as ADHD if relevant.

CO-OCCURRING SPECIFIC LEARNING DISABILITIES

Although many students appear to have only dysgraphia, only dyslexia, or only OWL LD, other students show signs of having more than one disability (Berninger, Raskind, et al., 2008; Berninger et al., 2015). Some students with dyslexia also have dysgraphia (handwriting subtype), but others do not. Some students are thought to have dyslexia when they really have OWL LD. Not all reading disabilities are the same (see Chapters 2, 4, and 5). Many students with

OWL LD have lower verbal comprehension scores than nonverbal reasoning scores because of difficulties in translating their thoughts into oral language, but some have high verbal comprehension skills (Berninger, Raskind, et al., 2008). Some students have both reading and math disabilities (Jordan, Hanich, & Kaplan, 2003). Other students may have both writing and math disabilities (Busse et al., 2001; Yates, 1996).

TWICE-EXCEPTIONAL STUDENTS

Some students are twice exceptional—they may be intellectually gifted but also have learning disabilities (Craggs, Sanchez, Kibby, Gilger, & Hynd, 2006). These students need intellectually stimulating instruction, as well as specialized instruction for their SLDs in the general education program. Some students have language talent and score in the superior or very superior ranges on measures of verbal comprehension but they also may have co-occurring reading disabilities (Berninger & Abbott, 2013). Some students have mathematic talent (Hoard, Geary, Byrd-Craven, & Nugent, 2008) but have co-occurring math disabilities (Brody & Mills, 1997; Busse, Berninger, Smith, & Hildebrand, 2001; Yates, 1996). Students who have talent and SLDs are referred to as *twice exceptional*, sometimes abbreviated as 2E. Twice-exceptional students need specialized instruction aimed at both their talents and their SLDs.

OTHER CO-OCCURRING CONDITIONS

Some students have co-occurring ADHD and SLDs. Occasionally, what appears to be ADHD turns out to be absence seizure disorder. Some students with SLDs have co-occurring medical conditions or injuries that need to be taken into account when individually tailoring their educational programs. In one sample, students who met evidence-based criteria for SLDs based on test scores and history also had inborn errors of metabolism (hypothyroidism), autoimmune disorders, sleep disorders, or concussions (Wingert, Del Campo, & Berninger, 2015). Other co-occurring conditions have included diabetes, anxiety disorder, and depression. (For further information on consideration of medical and other conditions in educational planning, see Chapters 10 and 11 in Berninger, 2015.)

INSTRUCTIONAL IMPLICATIONS OF CO-OCCURRING SPECIFIC LEARNING DIABILITIES

The following case study (Berninger & Niedo, 2014) illustrates why it is important to identify all the relevant SLDs and provide specialized instruction that addresses each of them.

A seventh-grade girl had been identified in the early elementary grades as having dyslexia. She received special education services for reading in Grades 3–5. The school provided specialized instruction for the reading problems associated with dyslexia. The good news is that she learned to read, enjoyed reading, and read for pleasure before going to bed. The bad news was that she continued to have significant academic problems and was getting failing grades.

At the transition from elementary to middle school in sixth grade, she was referred for comprehensive assessment. The assessment showed that she was twice exceptional. As often happens with 2E students, her superior to very superior cognitive abilities (on average at the 99th percentile) masked her dysgraphia and dyscalculia.

Dysgraphia was diagnosed based on an impaired orthographic loop using a rapid alphabet writing task assessing the number of legible letters during the first 15 seconds in alphabetical order, on a rapid numeral writing task assessing the number of legible digits during the first 15 seconds in counting order, and imitative finger sequencing. Even though the girl's dyslexia had been remediated, her previously unidentified and untreated dysgraphia was interfering with her spelling, which in turn was interfering with her completion of written work in both language arts and math. Her grades suffered because she could not complete writing assignments. Instructional recommendations based on research (e.g., Berninger & O'Malley May, 2011; Berninger, Winn, et al., 2008) included the following:

1. Forming legible letters until she reached age-appropriate automaticity and speed for sustained writing

2. Self-monitoring the legibility of her letter writing in her own written work

3. Spelling using a systematic spelling program at her instructional level

4. Explicit self-regulation strategies for grade-appropriate composing tasks

5. Frequent feedback when the quality of the content and organization of her compositions was grade appropriate so that she thinks of herself as a capable writer

Of note, the girl had strengths in phonological, morphological, and syntactic coding in sixth grade, as expected for a compensated dyslexic without OWL LD, but she had significant difficulty with orthographic coding (border between low average and below average). Orthographic coding affects both numeral and alphabet letter storage and processing in working memory.

The girl's dyscalculia was identified on the basis of her extreme difficulty in writing numerals legibly and automatically alone, in multiplace numbers, and in written computations and math fact fluency (all but addition below average). She reported that a teacher told her she could never learn long division. When asked to show us how she did long division, she had no concept how to arrange the number to be divided and the number to divide it by in two-dimensional space. Based on interventions with clinical and research samples who were both math talented and had math SLDs (e.g., Busse et al., 2001) and math teaching experience, we recommended instruction and practice in the following:

1. Forming the numerals

2. Writing numerals in multiplace numbers to express place value both to the right and left of the decimal point

3. Counting along the number line to model fast forward adding (multiplication) or fast backward subtracting (division), and then writing the math fact and graphing accuracy and time for progress monitoring

4. Self-monitoring strategies to pay attention to operation signs and check answers to written computations

5. Strategies for writing math facts, computations, and equations in left-right and top-down/bottom-up orientation in space, and applying the sequential steps of computation algorithms in two-dimensional space (see Chapter 6)

This girl illustrates the puzzle of 2E students in the math domain. On the one hand, this student struggled with the language of math through the hand: writing numerals (subword level), writing place value notations for whole and mixed numbers (word and syntax level), and writing computations that require travel across horizontal and vertical planes of two-dimensional space and sequential steps in time in calculations. On the other hand, in answering one of the questions on the test assessing cognitive ability, she explained to the examiner through language by mouth the importance of taking into account space and time in solving science problems. Thus, expression of cognitive understanding may depend on the nature of SLDs and instructional history. Teachers who adopt a systems approach to linking assessment and instruction within a student's whole learning profile, including possibly co-occurring SLDs, are more likely to meet all of the learning needs of a student (see Section II for skills-specific linked assessment and instruction).

Use of Technology in Teaching

In the information age the interface between computer tools and student computer users is relevant to students with and without specific learning disabilities (SLDs). Although computer tools are often recommended for accommodations for students with SLDs, they can also be used for explicit instruction in oral and written language and math as discussed in Chapter 11.

TEACHING STUDENTS TO USE COMPUTERS

The computer is an invaluable tool for writing activities—it can be used to produce letters, detect and fix spelling errors, and generate and revise written texts. Several decades ago, Logan (1986) predicted that computer technology would enhance literacy. However, whether students with dysgraphia or with or without other SLDs benefit from use of computers in written expression may depend on whether they receive explicit, systematic instruction in keyboarding, spelling, and composing with the computer. The same graphomotor and orthographic coding processing skills that interfere with their learning to write with a pencil or pen could interfere with learning to use a keyboard to write (Berninger, 2007b). Therefore, multidisciplinary team assessments should evaluate the processes related to both handwriting and keyboarding in designing individually tailored instruction for a specific student. A recent study showed that students learned to form letters equally well by finger formation on a tablet and stylus (Tanimoto et al., 2015) but another dissertation study showed sizable individual differences in whether stylus or keyboard resulted in longer compositions; these individual differences varied with writing task within the same student as well as across students. Moreover, elementary school students tend to hunt and peck on keyboards. Of concern is the lack of explicit instruction in touch typing in the upper elementary and middle school grades in many schools.

NEED FOR EXPLICIT HANDWRITING INSTRUCTION

For students with severe dysgraphia, a decision has to be made as to whether instruction should focus on just manuscript and cursive handwriting or on keyboarding to use in operating a computer for written assignments. Increasingly, research is pointing to the value of teaching both handwriting modes and keyboarding to students with and without SLDs (Alstad et al., 2015; Berninger, 2012, 2013). Research has shown that typically developing writers often use a mix of cursive and manuscript or revert to manuscript (Graham, Berninger, & Weintraub, 1998; Jones, 2004).

Even if students with dysgraphia struggle to write manuscript letters, they should be taught to read them. Most printed matter is displayed in manuscript, and other people use manuscript in their personal writing that students may need to be able to read. Likewise, even if students with dysgraphia struggle to write legible cursive letters, they should be taught to read cursive letters that others still use. If a decision is made that a student with dysgraphia should, as an accommodation, be allowed to use a computer for all written assignments, then explicit instruction in keyboarding should be provided. See Appendix 3B for resources on teaching touch typing. In addition, styluses and other writing tools are now available for writing on tablet computers.

Research shows that manuscript instruction transfers to improved word reading (Berninger et al., 1997), cursive instruction contributes to spelling (probably because connecting strokes link letters into word units; Alstad et al., 2015) in typically developing writers, and computers can teach students with dysgraphia to improve both their manuscript and cursive handwriting (Berninger, Nagy, Tanimoto, Thompson, & Abbott, 2015). Also, typically developing writers in elementary school write more words, write words faster, write more complex syntax, and express more ideas when writing by pen than by keyboard (Berninger et al., 2009; Hayes & Berninger, 2010). Manuscript and cursive contribute to the development of keyboarding skills from middle childhood to early adolescence in typically developing writers (Alstad et al., 2015). Thus, the keyboard is not a substitute for handwriting, and quality handwriting instruction and practice in composing with pencil or pen, as well as keyboard, are important for writers with and without writing disabilities.

NEED FOR EXPLICIT SPELLING INSTRUCTION

The need for explicit instruction in spelling continues even in the technology era with spell check, which flags possible spelling errors that can only be fixed if the computer user knows the correct spelling to select from the menu of possibilities offered. Often, students with dysgraphia, dyslexia, and/or oral and written language learning disability (OWL LD) do not have grade-appropriate spelling skills. Appendix 4B provides evidence-based approaches for teaching spelling without a computer, which can improve the ability of students to proof and correct their spelling errors when using a technology tool to communicate in written language.

NEED FOR EXPLICIT WRITTEN COMPOSITION INSTRUCTION

Charles MacArthur has conducted long-standing programmatic research on the use of computers in teaching written composition (e.g., MacArthur, 2000, 2006, 2008, 2009; MacArthur, Ferretti, Okolo, & Cavalier, 2001). Computers have been shown to help both those who do and do not struggle with writing. As MacArthur's research has shown, computers can be used to teach strategies for planning, translating, reviewing, and revising a written composition. Spelling problems can be addressed during the revision of multiple drafts of compositions.

An important skill to learn beginning in middle childhood is to read source material and write about it, that is, to integrate reading and writing. Some source material is hard copy of traditional reading material but increasingly students are accessing posted entries online through search engines for use as source material. Students in middle school and high school benefit from systematic instruction in strategies for using both kinds of source material in school assignments, including the need to paraphrase and cite sources so as not to plagiarize.

USE OF COMPUTERS IN CONTENT AREAS OF THE CURRICULUM

An ongoing topic of interest in educational technology is whether computers deliver more effective instruction than human teachers. For example, see the research activities at the Assistive and Instructional Technology Lab in the College of Education at the University of Texas at Austin (http://www.edb.utexas.edu/ATLab/index.php). Other research has shown that using both visual and verbal information in designing and writing technology-supported instructional tools is more effective than verbal alone (Mayer, 2009). For a review of the research literature showing how computer games can enhance motivation for learning but not necessarily attention and engagement for language learning and evidence that computerized instruction aimed at all the multileveled, multimodal, multiple-language systems with human teacher monitoring can improve oral and written language skills and attention to and engagement in language learning for students with SLDs, see Berninger and colleagues (2014) and Tanimoto and colleagues (2015).

Another controversial topic has been use of computer tools in taking notes. Most of the research to date has been done with college students (e.g., Peverly, 2006; Peverly, Ramaswamy, Brown, Sumowski, Alidoost, & Garner, 2007) and points to the conclusion that handwriting plays a very important role in note taking. More research on note-taking in developing students with and without SLDs, beginning in middle childhood, with a variety of letter production tools for varied purposes is needed. For students who have difficulty with the pace of class discussions or lectures, Smartpens and other audio recording devices may provide assistance. With these pens, students need only to replay the recorded lecture to add to the written notes what was not written during the oral lecture. This technology can remove the stress of missing out on important notes or having to catch up with the speaker.

The use of calculators has also been a controversial topic. The National Math Advisory Panel (2008) recommends that students first learn math facts and computational procedures using paper and pencil. Once those skills are mastered conceptually and procedurally, the use of calculators can be taught for problems that will require more complex calculations that build on the basic skills. The use of calculators allows these more complex calculations to be performed more quickly and efficiently by computer users who understand conceptually and procedurally the calculations involved.

Technology can also be used to create classroom economies. One of the reasons the business community has advocated for accountability of teachers is the perception that schools are not preparing students for the world of work. Therefore, some schools are preparing students for the future world of work by creating classroom economies to teach math, social studies about local and global economies, and science lessons related to science, technology, engineering, and mathematics (STEM) careers.

Technology tools have been developed to guide classroom teachers in designing and implementing classroom economies as part of the instructional program. For example, Talbot Hill's MicroSociety Program simulates a functioning community, with student-run businesses and services. Together, students run businesses, banks, a marketplace, and a government with branches for taxation, licensing, and dispute resolution. Each student earns "cool cash," which can be used to purchase student-made goods at the marketplace. This model is based on the MicroSociety program (http://www.microsociety.org) used in hundreds of schools nationwide, which is made available and supported by a nonprofit organization.

Students have a chance to practice everything they learn in the classroom during their MicroSociety activities. Reading, math, language, social studies, and technology become practical tools rather than abstract concepts. Running a business teaches the consequences of behavior: students learn they must work in order to be paid, cooperate in order to get a job done, and plan ahead. From the student-written laws to the mediation and court process for enforcing the laws, students learn that they have the power to make a difference in their world. For further information about how the Renton Schools implemented Talbot Hill's MicroSociety Program, contact coordinator Sally Boni at sally.boni@rentonschools.us.

USE OF COMPUTERS FOR BOTH
ACCOMMODATION AND EXPLICIT INSTRUCTION

Computer tools can be used for accommodations as well as explicit instruction for students with SLDs. Assistive technology (AT; Bryant, 2015; Bryant & Seay, 1998; Bryant, Seay, & Bryant, 1999; Mace, 2010) is helpful especially during middle school, high school, and postsecondary education (e.g., Bryant, Bryant, & Rieth, 2002). Simulations of how AT devices can be used across the lifespan and in various contexts for students with and without SLDs have been designed with Universal Design for Learning guidelines and principles (CAST, 2010) in mind; see the work of Brian and Diane Bryant (e.g., Bryant & Bryant, 2012; Bryant, Bryant, & Rieth, 2002; Bryant & Seay, 1998; Bryant et al., 1999; Bryant, Seok, Ok, & Bryant, 2012). They advise that instructional technology tools can be used to enhance the education of students with and without SLDs, but it is always important to find the best match between the technology and the learner. One size does not fit all when it comes to AT tools or apps.

Examples of technology tools that can be used for accommodations and assistance in instruction (Julnes & Brown, 1993) include the following:

- *Scanning:* Desktop scanners or other technology can be used to scan grade-appropriate text into text-to-speech software programs, which can then read the text back to students who cannot read and comprehend the texts well enough on their own. This computer application gives students with dyslexia or OWL LD access to grade-appropriate content, despite reading problems, for completing writing activities.

- *Dictation and speech recognition:* Another computer tool that has proven helpful to some students is dictation and speech recognition technology (e.g., MacArthur & Cavalier, 2004) for creating written assignments. Students can orally express their ideas, bypassing writing problems due to handwriting as in dysgraphia or spelling as in dyslexia. The technology translates the oral language into written language to assist in preparing a written assignment.

Best practices for the use of technology tools include that the accommodation should be linked to the problem it is addressing. For example, if the student has difficulty with accuracy or rate of reading, then computerized tools are recommended that allow teachers to scan any text material into the computer program, which then regulates the reading rate and highlights each word as it is spoken. If the student has difficulty with legible handwriting, then the use of a keyboard may be helpful. However, if the difficulty is with spelling, spell check, which flags typographical errors, may not be an appropriate accommodation. Unless a student has the ability to recognize the correct spelling from a menu of options, the spell checker alone will not be adequate compensation for lack of spelling skills. As Charles MacArthur on the Advisory Panel for Berninger (2015) pointed out, the goal should be to teach students to use spell checkers intelligently. They need to know that spell checkers will not find all errors, and students still need to proofread their work. Students also need to know how to select correct replacements once errors are found. MacArthur's cited research shows it is possible to teach these spelling skills.

No matter how computers are used for accommodation, explicit instruction in the skill area(s) with which a student has difficulty should continue to be provided. Both reading and writing skills, even if they are behind the typical developmental stepping stone schedule (see Chapters 4, 5, and 6 in Berninger, 2015) trajectory, can still be remediated in students without developmental disabilities during early childhood, middle childhood, and adolescence.

More research is needed on which technology tools may be most beneficial for students in general, as well as for accommodation of students with SLDs. For example, tracing with the index finger on a tablet involves forming a letter without a pencil grip, whereas writing with a stylus on a tablet involves forming a letter with a pencil grip and may help in early childhood. Also, more research is needed on how and when to integrate technology tools with instruction so they are not used only outside school for games, homework, and social networking.

USE OF TECHNOLOGY TOOLS AT SCHOOL AND OUTSIDE SCHOOL

Throughout schooling, all students should be taught safety precautions for the use of cell phones, headphones, and texting while crossing streets or walking anywhere there is car and bicycle traffic. When users are attending to the audio and visual stimuli or manual activity (while texting), they do not have sufficient attention capacity and resources to monitor the changing events in the external environment. Just as schools have traditionally provided safety education on paying attention to the color of signals in traffic lights for go, caution, and stop, safety issues regarding current technology also need to be taught. Beginning in early childhood, students need to learn to pay attention not only to what they hear through headphones or text messages on their cell phone screens, but also to drivers, vehicles, and other pedestrians when crossing the street.

Students benefit from discussion of socially appropriate and inappropriate use of technology. They need to learn what is and is not appropriate to "write" to others electronically. Appropriate and inappropriate content, tone, and language used should be addressed. Educators should spend more time teaching etiquette for online engagement, such as for opinion writing in blogs, discussion posts, and comment sections. These lessons can also be integrated into writing genre instruction at the secondary level (e.g., how to write business letters and e-mails).

One of the roadblocks to the increased integration of technology into the daily instructional program is the fear that students will use the Internet for bullying or be victims of predators who use it to contact minors. Schools face legal risks if such adverse events occur when students are using a computer with Internet access during class time. One way to prevent such events is to use only technology tools that do not require Internet or web access is turned off. Students may also benefit from ongoing instruction in appropriate and inappropriate ways of using the Internet for finding information and evaluating its authenticity.

Importantly, overuse of technology devices can undermine development of oral language including vocabulary skills for the social functions and use of language. The increasing use of handheld electronic devices may interfere with a student's development of making eye contact with the teacher and other students, experience in learning to read body language, and development of appropriate social interaction. Addiction to technology is becoming an increasing societal problem. Signs of addiction to texting, social media, or cell phones are that the technology user cannot disengage from technology, which in turn impairs the quality of functioning in life. One mother expressed how pleased she was when she set limits and did not allow her son to use his phone all the time; he started to focus more on school work and experienced greater academic success than in the past.

New Beginnings in Teaching Students with and without Specific Learning Disabilities

May the warm winds of heaven
Blow softly upon your house.
May the Great Spirit
Bless all who enter there.
May your moccasins
Make happy tracks
in many snows,
and may the rainbow
Always touch your shoulder.

Cherokee Prayer Blessing

Consistent with the systems solutions presented in Section III, multidisciplinary teams working with each other and the community outside the school can artfully and compassionately implement multiculturally sensitive and evidence-based oral, reading, writing, and math instruction with intellectually engaging, hands-on learning across the curriculum for all students in an increasingly diverse society. However, to do so, appropriate professional development is needed for teachers, members of the interdisciplinary team, educational policy makers, legislators, and government regulators of education.

Preservice and In-Service
Professional Development for
All Educationally Relevant Disciplines

This chapter addresses issues in preparing teachers at the preservice level, providing continuing professional development for in-service teachers, and providing professional development for members of other disciplines on interdisciplinary teams working with school-age children and youth at both the preservice and in-service levels. We will build on two longstanding models and propose new ones.

PREPARING TEACHERS AT THE PRESERVICE LEVEL

This book, along with resources listed in Appendix 12A, can be used as a textbook in a preservice teacher education course that prepares future teachers to work with students exhibiting multiple kinds of diversity, ranging from specific learning disabilities (SLDs) to diverse socioeconomic backgrounds, and multiple cultural, racial, language, and family differences. Foundational knowledge should cover cognitive science, neural science, psycholinguistics, developmental science, instructional science, and multicultural education so that teachers are well prepared to teach content areas in oral language, reading, writing, math, science, and social studies with grounding in the five domains of development/functional systems (sensory/motor, cognitive, language, social-emotional, attention/executive functions; see Chapters 2–6 and Appendix 12A). In addition to textbooks and basic foundational knowledge, preservice teachers need preparation in guiding students in their educational journeys in developmentally appropriate, individually tailored ways; helping students identify and develop their own unique capabilities; and developing teacher expertise in translation science, which means implementing research in educational practice.

Teaching is what teachers do—what they communicate with and without language, as well as how they structure learning activities and situations for teacher-directed explicit instruction and student-guided learning and discovery. Learning is what students do in response to teaching—what they communicate with and without language, and how they think and behave in learning activities that are teacher-directed, and their own self-regulated activities. Teaching and learning are related, but they are not the same. Preservice teachers must be prepared not only to teach but also to assess with assistance from the interdisciplinary team to the target, grade-appropriate skills, plan and implement differentiated instruction, and evaluate response to instruction.

Preservice teachers also need to understand conceptually what basic science has contributed to understanding the learning process, as well as what best professional practices (i.e., the voice of experience) have contributed to the implementation of research on teaching into teaching practices. Knowledge of the brain lays the foundation for understanding normal variation—no two brains are exactly alike (Berninger & Richards, 2008). Brain research has also identified hallmark characteristics of brain structures and functions associated with SLDs such as dysgraphia, dyslexia, oral and written language learning disability (OWL LD), and dyscalculia (Berninger & Richards, 2002). Knowledge of the brain, coupled with the growing body of research-supported, evidence-based instruction, may help teachers to design individualized instruction for students with SLDs in an era of educational accountability. At the preservice level, teachers should also have a clear understanding of the specialized instruction needed by students with dysgraphia, dyslexia, OWL LD, and dyscalculia. See Appendix 12A for proposed foundational knowledge for preservice teacher education professional development to prepare all teachers to teach students with SLDs in inclusionary settings with students without SLDs.

Preservice teachers should demonstrate their competence through coursework, tests, and other class assignments during their preservice education in foundational knowledge of the following:

- Development of cognition and memory; language by ear, mouth, eye, and hand; sensory, gross, and fine motor skills; attention and executive functions; social and emotional functions; and the functional brain systems that support them

- Brain development and the biological (brain and genetic) bases of individual and developmental differences

- Knowledge of content-specific curriculum for Grades K–12, the normal sequence of the development of content-specific knowledge, and research about effective instructional practices for typical learners and those with developmental and individual differences in learning content-specific curriculum

Preservice teachers also need beginning instruction in translation of the foundational knowledge into educational practice in collaboration with an interdisciplinary team. They need to understand characteristic developmental sequences; the normal ebb and flow with periodic plateaus, regressions, and advancement; and atypical variations within age or grade levels. They also need to learn about normal variations and the learning differences that are expected at any grade level. Such knowledge will allow teachers, once they are in their own classrooms, to accomplish the following:

1. Design and implement age- and grade-appropriate instruction.

2. Tailor instruction to individual students' unique profiles of strengths and weaknesses across developmental and academic domains.

3. Set reasonable levels of expected achievement in these domains of development and academic learning.

4. Evaluate whether response to instruction is appropriate for age and grade.

During preservice professional development, teachers will begin to learn how to assess individual students' response to instruction, evaluate when it is necessary to reteach, and provide scaffolding over hurdles.

Modeling and Coaching from Master Teachers and Practice in Translating Foundation Knowledge into Practice

Classes in basic science foundations and teaching methods do not alone prepare prospective teachers to be successful in helping all students learn; teachers also need supervised experiences in teaching and putting research and foundational knowledge into practice. Such tailored instruction is best learned under the guidance of a mentoring supervisor during preservice practica in 1) tutoring students with learning differences, including SLDs; 2) small-group instruction with typically developing students and those with learning differences, including SLDs; and 3) student teaching in classrooms in real world school settings. Also, with able supervision, preservice teachers will begin to learn about skillful implementation of foundational knowledge into teaching students who vary in their learning profiles. Skillful teachers stand out not only for their basic knowledge and teaching methods, but also for the art of teaching—the personal way they connect to students during the teaching process.

Model Preservice Teaching Preparation Program 1 Professors Diane Sawyer and Stuart Bernstein at Middle Tennessee State University developed one of the first models of exemplary preparation for future trainers of preservice educators. The interdisciplinary program developed by Sawyer and Bernstein provided a flexible framework of courses, field experiences, and opportunities for original research that will equip professionals with knowledge, insights, and skills essential to address effectively the lack of educators trained in evidence-based literacy instruction. Experienced faculty from the College of Education and Behavioral Sciences and the College of Liberal Arts provided the coursework and supervised the research of the graduate students who took core courses to provide a comprehensive understanding of literacy within biological, psychological, linguistic, social, developmental, learning, and motivation research. Students also took courses in one of the following four areas of specialization related to their dissertation research and electives: Literacy Instruction and Staff Development, Reading Disabilities/Dyslexia, Literacy Measurement and Analysis, and Administration/Policy. They also participated in course-based, supervised field practica that exposed them to a variety of environments in which research is put into practice.

These practica often involved participation in the assessment, consultation, and intervention activities of the Tennessee Center for the Study and Treatment of Dyslexia. This center was established by a grant from the Tennessee General Assembly in 1993 to help K–12 students with dyslexia, their teachers, and their families (Tennessee Center for the Study and Treatment of Dyslexia, n.d.). Prior to the Center being established in Tennessee, only four other states—Texas, Louisiana, California, and Mississippi—explicitly acknowledged dyslexia as an actual learning disability (Sawyer & Knight, 1997), despite the wealth of evidence worldwide confirming that dyslexia does exist. The Center operates as a unit attached to the College of Education and Behavioral Sciences at Middle Tennessee State University (MTSU). The Center offers assessment and progress monitoring for students receiving school-based intervention following Center assessment. In addition, the Center provided preservice and in-service professional development and consultation services. Professional development, which the Center implements statewide, is multifaceted and includes workshops that teach schools how to 1) conduct assessments, 2) implement detailed guidelines for interventions, 3) administer benchmarks for response to intervention, and 4) access curriculum resources.

Model Preservice Teaching Preparation Program 2   Malatesha Joshi has established a leading graduate-level teacher education program at Texas A&M. This teacher education program, which was ranked second in the United States in 2014, focuses on building preservice and in-service teachers' knowledge of research on reading and related skills. He and his colleagues gather evidence about how teacher knowledge changes as a function of formal coursework and professional development activities. For further information about evidence-based approaches to transmitting evidence-based knowledge and about the scale-up in Texas to provide continuing education professional development for all teachers, see Joshi et al. (2009). Although considerable research has been done on math development, assessment, and instruction such models for professional development in math would also make an important contribution.

In-Service Professional Development of Teachers

Transition to Early Career Teaching All too often supervised participation in assessment and instructional services ends in the preservice years for teachers. Consultation provided by guiding and supporting school-based personnel is also needed as beginning teachers transition to independence in designing individually tailored instruction, implementing it in group settings, and evaluating response to instruction. In the past, schools often had a reading specialist who was available building-wide to help with this. More recently, some schools have an instructional leader who works with classroom teachers and the building principal to provide this kind of ongoing mentoring. All too often the only in-service professional development beginning and continuing teachers receive, however, is the annual workshops they take for continuing education credits.

Slingerland® Model for In-Service Teaching The current version of Slingerland's professional development model consists of four sequential steps within a training session: 1) sharing of research-generated information on effective teaching practices; 2) modeling by a mentor teacher of these instructional strategies in teaching students with written language disability; 3) supervising by the mentor teacher who observes the participating teacher implement the same instructional strategies with the students; and finally 4) debriefing sessions in which the mentor teacher and participating teachers reflect on the process of translating research-supported strategies into practice and the mentor teacher provides constructive feedback to the teachers for improving the translation process. The opportunity for trainees to observe trainers model teaching strategies and for trainers to observe trainees implementing modeled teaching strategies with students, as well as the feedback session, are components that are often missing from most teacher training programs. See Appendix 12A for a representative syllabus from a Slingerland in-service professional development program.

International Dyslexia Association IDA, and previously the Orton Society from which it evolved (see Chapter 1), has long advocated for and supported professional development of educators working with students with dyslexia, speech disabilities, and associated language disorders. IDA encourages and promotes (a) research on the nature of such disabilities; (b) diagnosis and treatment of such disabilities; (c) efforts to prevent the academic and socio-emotional difficulties that may arise from such disabilities; and (d) training of personnel in the diagnosis and treatment of such disabilities. IDA has also been involved in *accreditation of teacher and therapist training program*s that meet criteria for appropriate instruction for students with dyslexia and associated language disorders. Further information is available at http://eida .org, the new IDA web site.

University of Colorado Learning Disabilities Center   Barbara Wise developed *Linguistic Remedies* as a professional development tool for teachers, which is based on research she and Richard Olson and others have conducted at the National Institute of Child and Human Development (NICHD)-funded University of Colorado, Boulder Learning Disabilities Center for about three decades. See Wise, Rogan, and Sessions (2009) for detailed information about how this pioneering professional development program, Linguistic Remedies, can be customized to bring research into the classroom and meet the needs of individual teachers in doing so.

Henry's (2005) Matrix for Choosing Among Training Programs
Framework for Informed Reading and Language Instruction compares similarities and differences among 12 approaches to reading and language instruction widely used in the United States. It enables teachers, school administrators, and parents to make educated choices among the various teacher training programs. The matrix is intended to help educators and parents evaluate and gain access to effective, sequential, multisensory, and structured language programs that have been successful in clinical and classroom settings. Though many programs are not included in the matrix because of space limitations, the IDA encourages use of programs that meet their listed standards. Among the program characteristics considered necessary for effective reading and written language instruction are those that include training in the following:

1. Phonological awareness: the ability to segment words into their component sounds

2. Phonics: sound–symbol association

3. Decoding: practice in word attack skills for reading based on phonics and understanding of the morphology of language

4. Encoding: practice in combining sounds for spelling in association with phonics and the understanding of the morphology of language

5. Fluency: the ability to read orally with speed, accuracy, and proper expression

6. Reading comprehension: instruction in vocabulary and the sentence and narrative levels of text

7. Written expression: instruction in handwriting, spelling, and constructing text

Professional Development for Multiple Professionals on Interdisciplinary Teams

Teachers are not the only ones who benefit from professional development for teaching students with SLDs. Professionals from a variety of disciplines other than classroom teaching are involved and need some way to design and implement appropriate education for students. Yet, often these professionals do not receive professional development related to SLDs or their roles on interdisciplinary teams. At the time of the first federal legislation in 1975 calling for free appropriate public education (FAPE) for students with SLDs, parents had the insight to call for multidisciplinary teams and participation of multiple professionals in assessments and recommendations for intervention. Yet, the field of education currently lacks professional development to prepare professionals from multiple disciplines for this important work. The next section introduces a model for such interdisciplinary preparation of educational professionals.

Proposed Preservice and In-Service Professional Development for Teachers and Other Professionals

Forty years after the original federal legislation guaranteeing FAPE, knowledge has exploded based on both research and teaching experience. Toward the goal of incorporating this knowledge into professional development of teachers and other educational professionals, in Appendix 12A we propose models for 1) preservice education of teachers and professionals in other educationally relevant disciplines, 2) in-service professional development of teachers, and 3) in-service professional development of professionals in other disciplines who work on multidisciplinary teams in regard to students with SLDs. A unique feature of these preservice and in-service models is the focus on what can be done effectively in the general education classroom, the least restrictive environment, for students with SLDs. Alternatives to referring students out to special education are considered, but these alternatives involve problem solving consultation and partnerships with special education teachers. Moreover, because parents are supposed to be part of those teams, we also propose guidelines for helping parents to parent children with SLDs. These guidelines make it clear that there are constructive ways to advocate for students with SLDs in the classroom. The legal route is not the only viable way to advocate for one's child.

Resources and Models to Prepare Preservice General Education Teachers and Other Educational Professionals for Teaching Students with Specific Learning Disabilities

PROFESSIONAL DEVELOPMENT FOR TEACHERS

Tennessee Center for the Study and Treatment of Dyslexia. 200 N. Baird Lane, Middle Tennessee State University, Box 397, Murfreesboro, TN 37132 (http://www.mtsu.edu/dyslexia)

Services for Teacher Educators, contact Ph.D. in Literacy Studies. College of Education and Behavioral Science, College of Liberal Arts. For further information see http://www.mtsu.edu/literacy.

COURSE SYLLABUS: INTRODUCTION TO INSTRUCTIONAL TECHNIQUES IN SPECIFIC LANGUAGE DISABILITY

This syllabus is from the Slingerland® adaptation for classroom use of the Orton-Gillingham Multisensory Approach for Children with Specific Language Disability (Dyslexia).

Requirements: Teaching experience or permission

Credits: 11 credits

Course Description

This course covers a 4-week period of intensive study. It is also offered over a period of several months during the school year. It offers training in the etiology and diagnosis of specific language disability (dyslexia) and provides training in the techniques designed for a preventive and/or remedial program for classroom use. These techniques were developed by Beth H. Slingerland as an adaptation of the approach originated by Dr. Samuel T. Orton and Anna Gillingham. They are based on sound neurological principles of learning. Multisensory in their organization, these techniques give the student the tools needed to function successfully in all areas of language arts, whether reading, writing, spelling, or speaking.

Course Objectives

To provide instruction in the introductory steps of handwriting, written language, decoding, and reading comprehension

To develop understanding of the etiology of dyslexia

To introduce phonic rules and their application to encoding and decoding

To provide understanding of the neurology of language and offer means of developing oral language skills

To provide information about history, philosophy, and current research in the field of dyslexia

To guide in the understanding of relationships of curriculum and classroom organization to the language arts program

Student Expectations

Participants will

Learn the Slingerland® Approach through multisensory strategies; they will see demonstrations and read their texts, hear lectures, and experience this way of teaching by practicing in class and working with students

Practice skills with other teachers in small groups

Participate in discussion of students and strategies used in the classroom

Read the text and materials chosen from the bibliography

Apply the approach to work in the practicum with students

Special Features: EDU and Special Education credits are available

Methods of Instruction

Each day is divided into the following components:

Observation of a group of students taught by a master teacher using Slingerland techniques

Guided practice in the use of multisensory techniques with student(s)

Lectures involving the areas listed below

Preparation of plans and materials

Individual and group conferences

Content/Topics and Outline for Each Session

The daily schedule consists of

8:00	Lecture
9:00	Assembly with students, working with oral language
9:15	Demonstration class—Slingerland techniques
10:30	Recess—observation of students in less-structured settings
10:30	Practicum—individual tutoring of one or two students
11:45	Story—observation of listening skills, further oral language experience
11:55	Prepare for lunch or dismissal
12:30	Evaluations of morning work
12:45	Lecture
	Additional explanation or practice with techniques

Preparation, under guidance, of lesson plans

The general outline may vary slightly according to the needs of the students and the participant teachers. Lecture topics are in italics, demonstration and planning take place from day 3 to the end of the course.

Day 1 (teachers only): *Get acquainted, review of syllabus, oral language development; definition of dyslexia; characteristics of dyslexia; phonological awareness; organization of tutoring station; Slingerland® Approach; demonstration and overview of the approach; planning for first day with students*

Day 2 (first day with students): *Format for instruction, demonstration, understanding of and writing of lesson plans*

Day 3: *Learning to write; demonstration, procedures for teaching new letters*

Day 4: *Phonological awareness, auditory alphabet review and encoding*

Day 5: *The reading process, preparation for reading*

Day 6: *Preparation for reading, teaching the structure of language*

Day 7: *Reading from the book step 1, relationship to language structure*

Day 8: *Phonics*

Days 9–10: *Reading from the book, steps 2 and 3*

Day 11: *Spelling, affixes, phrases*

Day 12: *Additional review as needed*

Day 13: *Rules*

Day 14: *Dictation, take-home examination*

Day 15: *Overview of screening*

Day 16: *Preparation for conferencing, continuum of instruction, assistance in evaluating students, conferencing strategies*

Day 17: *Questions and answers*

Day 18: *Grade-level curriculum K–2, 3–4, 5–6; creative activities; working as a tutor; planning independently*

Day 19: *Review of structure, basic principles, parent conferences*

Grading Criteria/System and Evaluation Activities

Criteria for *all participants* are as follows:

30%—A daily plan for work with individual pupils, to be turned in each day before leaving; plans are precise to ensure understanding and application of the Slingerland® Approach. Teacher participants will be guided by staff teacher. A daily, objective running account of a student's progress will include observed strengths and weaknesses and ways in which their performance will affect planning for the next day's lesson. Brief annotated notes on five books or articles related to the subject of dyslexia and/or oral or written language will include a brief synopsis and the purpose or value of the material. A summary of the conference with pupil's parents is submitted.

10%—Preparation of teaching materials and organization of space

10%—A willingness to be observed and to accept constructive criticism and guidance

35%—Participation in activities for students—use of the technique, directed play periods, story time, dismissal

15%—Test(s) covering demonstrations, lectures, and reading

Attendance affects all areas.

Texts

The following Slingerland texts/materials are included in course tuition:

Slingerland, B. (2013). *The Slingerland® Multisensory Approach: A practical guide for teaching reading, writing, and spelling* (2nd ed.). Bellevue, WA: The Slingerland® Institute for Literacy.

Slingerland, B., & Murray, C. (1987). *Teacher's word lists for reference.* Cambridge, MA: Educators Publishing Service.

Teacher's hand pack for classroom use

Manuscript alphabet cards

Yellow card pack

Wall cards or chart

Phonogram chart

Cursive wall cards (for Grades 3 and above)

PROPOSED PRESERVICE PROFESSIONAL DEVELOPMENT MODEL FOR PRESERVICE TEACHERS

Students will engage in learning activities that include professor-delivered instruction and supervised practica and pass written tests demonstrating knowledge of the following concepts:

1. *Because a learning problem has a biological basis (see Chapter 2), does it require medical treatment?* No. Nature–nurture interactions influence learning and students with dysgraphia, dyslexia, oral and written language learning disability (OWL LD), and dyscalculia respond to appropriate, specialized, individually tailored instruction (see Sections II and III).

2. *Can specific learning disabilities (SLDs) be defined on basis of what they are and what they are not?* Yes. Educationally relevant definitions address both what something is and how it is different from something else in a way that has educational applications. Research shows the heterogeneous nature of specific learning disabilities affecting reading and writing acquisition, but it has also identified common profiles within this heterogeneity that define what dysgraphia, dyslexia, OWL LD, and dyscalculia are. Thus, the general education teacher can meet many individual needs within group instruction in the general education classroom (see Chapters 2 and 3–8). Defining something also necessitates defining what it is not. The written language problems of individuals with dyslexia, for instance, cannot be explained on the basis of any other neurogenetic, developmental, or learning disorders. For example, such problems cannot be explained by intellectual disability across the five domains of development (cognitive,

oral language, motor, social emotional, attention/executive function), specific developmental disabilities in two or more developmental domains, autism, primary language disorder (developmental aphasia), fragile X syndrome, Down syndrome, Williams syndrome, Turner syndrome, Kleinfelter syndrome, brain injury or disease, psychiatric disorder, emotional trauma, or environmental issues (see Chapter 2). Students with these disorders also should receive free and appropriate public education (FAPE), but what they need instructionally is not the same as what students with SLDs need instructionally.

3. *Define dysgraphia.* Dysgraphia is an SLD that affects the legibility and automaticity of letter production (handwriting), which in turn may interfere with spelling and composition development. Contrary to widespread belief, dysgraphia is not purely a motor problem; rather, it is also due to an underlying problem with the orthographic loop that coordinates orthographic coding and grapho-motor output by the hands and fingers, and the executive functions involved in letter writing. Students with developmental motor disorders may also have handwriting problems, but for different reasons; these students may need different instructional approaches.

4. *Why is dysgraphia so often not identified and treated?* States do not use this term in the criteria for qualifying students for special education services, do not use this diagnostic term, and do not provide professional development for identifying and teaching students with dysgraphia. Thus, many students with dysgraphia are not identified and provided FAPE. Many government officials and educational professionals do not know the research showing that handwriting is still important for literacy development in the computer era.

5. *Why is it that many professionals think that students with dysgraphia who cannot complete written assignments that are legible, meet grade-appropriate standards for content and length, and/or finish assignments within time limits are lazy or not motivated?* They do not understand that dysgraphia is an invisible disability in which components of working memory needed for sustaining writing over time are not functioning normally. In fact, teaching, clinical, and research experiences suggest that many of these students are highly motivated to write but emotionally traumatized that others cannot read their writing or they cannot write adequately to succeed in school; many of these students also suffer from emotional problems (e.g., impaired self-esteem, self-efficacy, heightened anxiety) due to undiagnosed and untreated dysgraphia, rather than emotional or motivational problems causing incomplete work. After continually failing to keep up with written assignments or written tests at school, some students with dysgraphia will begin to avoid written work and are described as *writing avoidant* (for further discussion of these issues, see Berninger, Abbott, Whitaker, Sylvester,

& Nolen, 1995; Hidi & Boscolo, 2006). The important point is that emotional problems are often the consequence, not the cause, of writing disabilities. Gifted students with intellectual talent often have significant handwriting and/or spelling disabilities that compromise their abilities to express their ideas in writing and complete written assignments, even though they excel at learning with oral language (Yates, Berninger, & Abbott, 1994).

6. *Define dyslexia and explain why not all reading disabilities are dyslexia.* Some students have trouble only with word decoding and reading, but others have trouble with reading comprehension, even when they can decode. *Explain why dyslexia is also a writing disability.* Many students with dyslexia have persisting spelling problems. *Explain how dyslexia is an invisible disability.* One or more components of the multicomponent working memory system supporting language learning may be interfering with their written word learning, but this disability is not visible to others as a physical mobility or auditory or visual sensory deficit may be.

7. *Explain what OWL LD is and why it is an aural/oral language as well as written learning disability.* Some students have oral language learning problems that first surface in the preschool years, then continue during the school years and influence their learning to read and write. All too often, these students' oral and written language learning difficulties are not identified and appropriate, differentiated instruction is not provided.

8. *Why might students with dysgraphia, dyslexia, or OWL LD have difficulty with learning math?* Math learning draws on oral and written language skills.

9. *What does it mean to be twice exceptional?* A student has both an SLD and a talent (see Chapter 10).

10. *Why do most students with SLDs benefit from specialized, appropriate, differentiated instruction in the general education program?* They need specialized written and/or oral language and sometimes math instruction, but they also need access to the regular school curriculum because their SLDs are specific and do not affect every aspect of the curriculum. *How is it challenging yet professionally rewarding to teach students with SLDs in the general education classroom?* Providing FAPE initially requires more professional development, planning, and monitoring student progress, but with schoolwide staffing plans (see Chapter 7) it becomes quite manageable and very professionally rewarding.

11. *How has the debate about IQ–achievement discrepancy missed the real issue?* Although these students do not easily experience success in all aspects of academic learning, they really are intelligent and learn well in other areas of the curriculum. There is not a specific amount of discrepancy that differentiates SLD from non-SLD.

12. *Are there evidence-based ways to diagnose and teach students with dysgraphia, dyslexia, OWL LD, and dyscalculia?* Yes (see Chapters 2–11, 13).

PROPOSED IN-SERVICE PROFESSIONAL DEVELOPMENT MODEL FOR TEACHERS AND ALL MEMBERS OF AN INTERDISCIPLINARY TEAM

First, we raise issues for practitioners to think about as they carefully plan to incorporate in their teaching and individual education plans insights from evidence-based assessment. After raising the issue, we propose what we think is a reasonable answer. Second, in-service professional development should meet the same standards as preservice (see prior proposed model for preservice professional development).

1. *Why is it important to base instruction on careful diagnosis of whether a student may have oral language weaknesses beyond phonological processing that also need to be taken into account in planning and delivering written language instruction?* If the other oral language problems are not diagnosed, they will not be treated. Reading and written language problems may persist, even if the student improves in phonics and phonological decoding.

2. *Why is it important to understand that some students have only decoding problems, some have both decoding and reading comprehension problems, and some have only comprehension problems?* Because these individual differences exist, students differ in the nature of instruction they require in their general education reading and writing programs.

3. *Why is it important to understand that some students have a problem in decoding words despite good vocabulary knowledge and verbal reasoning, which may mask the decoding problems when reading words in context?* Students with this profile may survive in the early grades but often experience a great deal of difficulty in reading and writing in Grade 4 and above when curriculum requirements increase. Also, a student's talents, including verbal reasoning, may not be recognized and nurtured if not identified.

4. *Why is it important to understand that some students may have a problem in writing by hand that compromises their ability to communicate in written language as much as problems with speech do in communicating in oral language?* These students who have typical or better intelligence may fail at school, which requires successful completion of written work to pass content subjects; not be promoted to the next grade level; not graduate from high school; and/or not pass high-stakes tests given by the state. Students who cannot communicate in written language are also at risk for dropping out of school altogether. All of these unfortunate outcomes may also result in emotional problems such as anxiety, work avoidance, and depression.

5. *Why is it important to understand that dyslexia is both a writing and a reading disorder?* Teaching students with dyslexia to read is necessary but not sufficient. They also need to be able to spell and complete written assignments for reasons addressed previously. Otherwise, writing quality or length of compositions may be reduced.

6. *How do spelling problems of students with dyslexia interfere with their written composition?* Inability to spell words limits word choice. Nonautomatic retrieval of word spellings slows the speed of written composition and completing assignments in a reasonable amount of time.

7. *Why is it important to understand that some students have dysgraphia (writing problems) without reading problems or in addition to their reading problems?* Just because a student has trouble producing legible letters automatically does not mean that the student is not motivated, cannot think, or lacks vocabulary knowledge or high-quality ideas. The handwriting block problem interferes with spelling and thus the expression of that thinking ability, knowledge, and ideas.

8. *How do handwriting problems of students with dyslexia or dysgraphia interfere with their written composition?* Students with dyslexia and/or dysgraphia may forget what they planned to write while trying to remember how to form the letters. They might write the letters so slowly that they do not produce as much writing as classmates who can write letters automatically. Or, their handwriting may be so illegible that the reader cannot recognize the spelling and figure out the intended message.

Cross-Disciplinary
Communication and Collaboration

Serving students with dysgraphia, dyslexia, oral and written language learning disability (OWL LD), and dyscalculia requires the support services of an interdisciplinary team, coordination of general and special education teachers, and cooperation of school principals and district administrators. That is, an interdisciplinary team approach is required for systems-level education (see Section III of this volume and Berninger, 2015).

Scaling up to increase the number of students served by teams entails creating school- and district-level plans to serve the needs of students with dysgraphia, dyslexia, OWL LD, and/or dyscalculia in general education, but it does not necessarily mean more money is required. Rather, different strategies are needed. Special education laws call for the least restrictive environment and thus for general education teachers working in inclusive classrooms. However, all members of an interdisciplinary team should be involved in assessment (see Sections II and III) and support for general education classroom teachers in planning and implementing appropriate, individually tailored educational plans.

In fact, the whole school system needs to be involved. For an example of how one school district designed and implemented such a model, from the superintendent to school psychologist to classroom teachers in local school, see the story of Honor Role Models Seven and Eight in the Bellingham, Washington, Schools in Berninger (2015). At the district level, administrators should be updated frequently on recent research developments and unmet student needs in local buildings, despite federal education initiatives and state special education policies, of students with dysgraphia, dyslexia, OWL LD, and/ or dyscalculia and others with unmet educational needs. General education teachers who teach students with specific learning disabilities (SLDs) require instructional leadership support from their schools (building principals) and districts (district-level administrators as well as the director of special education) as well as ongoing professional development (see Chapter 12).

The principal, department head, or curriculum coordinator at the school needs to have the knowledge of students, staff, and curriculum for making administrative decisions about developmentally appropriate and individually tailored instruction encompassing a broad range of relevant variables. For example, special educators with the appropriate professional development at the preservice levels and teaching experience could become the instructional leaders described in Section II. These decisions affect scheduling, space assignments, budgeting, and placement of students with appropriate teachers. The Florida Center for Reading Research (http://www.fcrr.org) provides resources, which are continually updated, to assist administrators in making such decisions.

Implementation of school- and district-level plans requires adequate resources, including staff, time, space, materials, and financial support and plans for managing these. Provision of adequate time is dependent on decisions about student, teacher, support staff, and administrative schedules and allows for team meetings, in-service training time, progress monitoring, evaluation, and record keeping. Adequate time and support allows teachers and other members of an interdisciplinary team to concentrate their efforts on instruction rather than paperwork.

Space—or lack of it—often dictates the model or plan selected. There must be space for both whole-group and small-group intervention and tutoring. If technology is part of the intervention, the space must have provisions for the necessary electronic equipment. Parents and staff need space to confer and plan. Volunteers need space for materials and to carry out their work. Class configurations should also be considered in making space decisions. Some students, especially those with executive function problems, need highly structured teachers and classrooms, whereas other students respond more readily to an open-ended, less structured approach. Some students work well in small groups, but others do not. Matching teachers and learners on their tolerance of and need for highly structured versus open-ended learning environments can facilitate instruction and learning. However, space requirements may vary for these different learning environments for contrasting teacher–student interactions.

Schoolwide commitment is also needed. Serving students with dyslexia in the general education program requires that the entire staff recognizes the individual needs of each student and provides for those students at both ends of the spectrum—both those who are advanced and those who struggle to keep up with classmates. When each staff member accepts responsibility for the success of every student and participates in planning, opportunities increase for all students to succeed.

THREE-TIER MODELS

The assessment–instruction model in this book (see Section II) differs from the widely used three-tier approach to service delivery. In that model, the first two tiers are implemented within general education, and the third tier is implemented within pull-out special education. Within Tier 1, all students receive structured, sequential, multimodal instruction in the core curriculum. If the student does not respond at Tier 1, the same instructional approach is used more intensely. However, the instruction at Tier 1 and Tier 2 is not carefully linked to specific oral and written language and math skills in an individual students' learning profile; nor is response to instruction linked to the nature of an individual student's learning profile. Often it is assumed, there is one size that fits all (an intervention that is posted on a web site for What Works?) In contrast, in the model introduced in this book, evidence-based assessment–instruction links inform the systems approach to preventing SLDs based on What Works for Whom When?

Also, the model introduced in this book allows for comprehensive assessment to diagnose dysgraphia, dyslexia, OWL LD, or dyscalculia when warranted by a student's persisting problems, consistent with family history. The goal of this Tier 3 comprehensive assessment is to go beyond deciding if the student is eligible for pull-out services to instructionally relevant, differential diagnosis for possible dysgraphia, dyslexia, and OWL LD (see Berninger, 2007b) or dyscalculia and other specific math disabilities (Berninger, 2007a). The whole interdisciplinary team participates in the diagnostic process and supports the general education teacher in planning and implanting the appropriate instruction (see Berninger 2015 for frameworks for doing so).

There is precedent in some school districts of adopting a preventive approach in which students were screened in kindergarten or first grade and placed with a Slingerland-trained teacher. The goal was to identify and intervene before students failed. In this model, school collected data reviewed by the second author showed that from 25% to 30% of the students had mild to severe difficulties, but when they used the Slingerland® teaching approach (see Chapters 3–5) and the district-adopted curriculum in conventional class-size groupings, by the end of third grade, few students needed continued services. However, in some cases, classes had to continue in the intermediate grades. Most of the students in these classes had more severe problems or had entered the school districts after the early grades when prevention programs were offered. With early intervention, students avoided failure and fewer students were referred for individual testing. Some districts offered summer training for teachers but left implementation to school or teacher discretion. This approach did not provide the continuity of instruction from grade to grade, but it did benefit many of the students with whom they worked. Nevertheless, schoolwide professional development of teachers is critical to the success of prevention approach and schools need to collect data to evaluate the effectiveness of their translation of specific instructional methods into practice for their students.

Over many years of screening and evaluating students in many school districts, the second author has collected extensive screening data on 13,000 students in schools and consistently finds that 27 to 28% of the students have weaknesses in handwriting and oral and written language. These data show the importance of identifying these problems early so that instruction can be implemented to prevent SLDs not only in word reading but also in handwriting, spelling, composing, and oral language listening and oral expression.

DIFFERENTIAL DIAGNOSIS OF DYSGRAPHIA, DYSLEXIA, ORAL AND WRITTEN LANGUAGE LEARNING DISABILITY, AND DYSCALCULIA

As shown in Figure 13.1, learning is always a complex process influenced by the individual student, the teacher's instructional practices, and the curriculum (scope and sequence of skills to be taught and materials to use at specific grade levels). This model of multiple, interacting influences in the student's mind and the external learning environment—both teacher pedagogy and curriculum—applies to all the skills covered in Section II and Chapter 9. Diagnosis based on interdisciplinary team assessment can diagnose specific SLDs—dysgraphia, dyslexia, OWL LD, and dyscalculia—and related behavioral markers of genetically based SLDs, which are referred to as phenotypes (see Chapter 2 and Figures 13.2, 13.3, and 13.4), which are relevant to planning and implementing instruction tailored to the nature of the SLD.

Behavioral, genetics, and brain research studies have identified SLDs in individual students (see Chapter 2), which may affect how the three corners

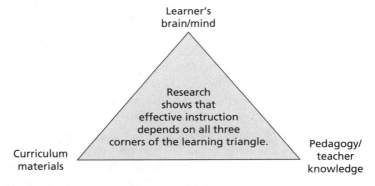

Figure 13.1. Learning triangle: interactions among the learning writer; the writing teacher; and the instructional materials, tools, and curriculum for writing. (Reprinted from *Handbook of Psychoeducational Assessment,* Jac J.W. Andrews, Alfredo Ardila, Virginia Berninger, Julie Busse, J.P. Das, George J. DuPaul, Ruben Echemendía, Colin D. Elliott, Bruce Gordon, Noel Gregg, Frank M. Gresham, Josette Harris, Denise Hildebrand, Henry L. Janzen, R.W. Kamphaus, Rex B. Kline et al., Assessment for reading and writing intervention: A three-tier model for prevention and intervention, pp. 198–218, Copyright 2001, with permission from Elsevier.)

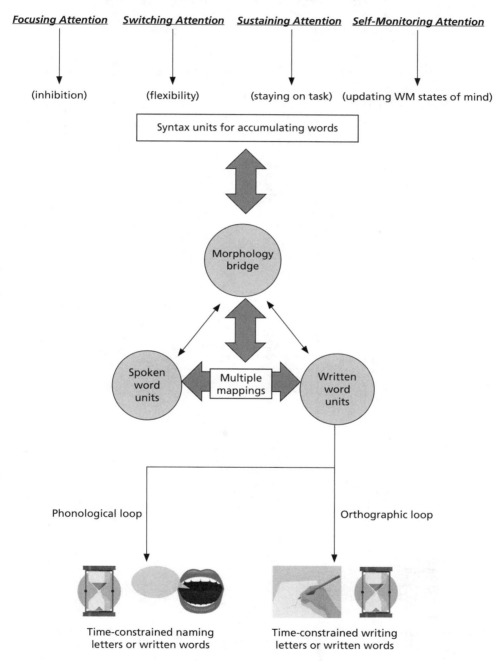

Cognitive Portal
Panel of Supervisory Attention
(Low-level executive functions of working memory, WM)

**Focusing Attention**   _**Switching Attention**_   _**Sustaining Attention**_   _**Self-Monitoring Attention**_

(inhibition)   (flexibility)   (staying on task)   (updating WM states of mind)

Syntax units for accumulating words

Morphology bridge

Spoken word units

Multiple mappings

Written word units

Phonological loop

Orthographic loop

Time-constrained naming letters or written words

Time-constrained writing letters or written words

Figure 13.2. Multicomponent working memory architecture supporting language learning. (Based on Berninger, 2007b and 2015.)

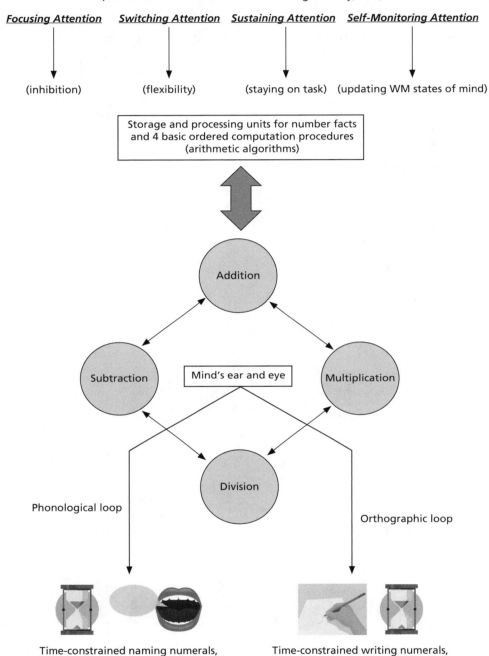

Panel of Supervisory Attention
(Low-level executive functions of working memory, WM)

Focusing Attention   *Switching Attention*   *Sustaining Attention*   *Self-Monitoring Attention*

(inhibition)   (flexibility)   (staying on task)   (updating WM states of mind)

Storage and processing units for number facts
and 4 basic ordered computation procedures
(arithmetic algorithms)

Addition

Subtraction   Mind's ear and eye   Multiplication

Division

Phonological loop   Orthographic loop

Time-constrained naming numerals,   Time-constrained writing numerals,
multi-place numbers, or number facts   multi-place numbers or number facts

Figure 13.3. Multicomponent working memory architecture supporting math learning. (Based on Berninger, 2007b and 2015.)

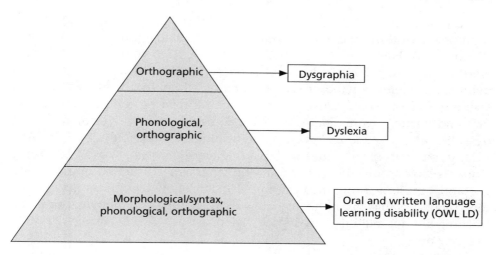

Figure 13.4. Relationship between word-form deficit and diagnosis. (*Process Assessment of the Learner, Second Edition: Diagnostics for Reading and Writing [PAL-II Reading and Writing]*. Copyright © 2007 NCS Pearson, Inc. Reproduced with permission. All rights reserved. "PAL" is a trademark, in the US and/or other countries, of Pearson Education, Inc. or its affiliates[s].)

of the learning triangle (Figure 13.1) interact in the learning of an individual student. As explained in Chapter 2, learning profiles can be identified that define SLDs: impaired handwriting (dysgraphia), impaired word reading and spelling (dyslexia), impaired listening and reading comprehension and oral and written expression (OWL LD), and impaired number concepts, math facts, and math computation (dyscalculia). Programmatic, multidisciplinary research (e.g., Berninger, Raskind, et al., 2008) has also identified phenotypes in multicomponent working memory architectures that support language learning (Figure 13.2) and math learning (Figure 13.3). Individual students may differ in which phenotypes of the multicomponent working memory architecture are impaired in their phenotype profile associated with their language learning profile (Figure 13.4):

- In Figure 13.2, note the three word-form coding units for storing and processing and linguistic reflection: phonological, orthographic, and morphological

- Syntactic buffer for storing and processing accumulating words

- Cross-code integration loops (time-sensitive phonological loop and orthographic loop)

- Panel of executive functions for focusing attention, switching attention, sustaining attention, and self-monitoring. In Figure 13.3, note the math fact storage and processing and units supporting math calculations that are specific to math. However, the working memory components supporting arithmetic also draw on phonological and orthographic loops (for numerals) and the same supervisory attention panel as for language in Figure 13.2.

Likewise, the SLDs may differ in which of the phenotypes of the multi-component working memory architecture supporting learning is impaired (Figure 13.4). For example, as shown in Figure 13.4, common and unique word-form coding skills (behavioral phenotypes) tend to be impaired in students with impaired handwriting (dysgraphia), impaired word reading and spelling (dyslexia), and impaired listening and reading comprehension and oral and written expression (OWL LD). Some of these may be shared with dyscalculia (e.g., students have trouble writing numerals), dyslexia or OWL LD (e.g., students have trouble with reading word problems), or OWL LD (e.g., students have trouble learning from oral language instruction in math). Importantly, these working memory impairments show how SLDs may be not directly observable, but rather are invisible disabilities, as they interfere with learning but not mobility, hearing, or vision, as "observable, visible" disabilities may do.

INSTRUCTIONAL RELEVANCE OF DIFFERENTIAL DIAGNOSES

An accurate diagnosis also has implications for treatment planning. In research conducted by the University of Washington Multidisciplinary Learning Disabilities Center (UW LDC), parents often expressed more interest in accurate diagnoses and understanding why their children struggled with reading or writing than in their children qualifying for pull-out special education services (i.e., meeting eligibility criteria; see Berninger, Nielsen, et al., 2008; Berninger, Raskind, et al., 2008). They believed that knowing why a student struggles more than classmates would provide instructional clues in the general education classroom.

Unfortunately, unlike medical and speech-language professionals who are given training in both diagnosis and treatment for the disorders they specialize in, teachers are prepared to teach and psychologists are prepared to assess. As a result, general and special education teachers need to partner with psychologists, speech-language specialists, and physical and occupational therapists in the school to link assessment and instruction in meaningful ways. Also, both teachers and psychologists need more preservice professional development in assessment–instruction links (see Chapter 12).

The distinctions among dysgraphia, dyslexia, and OWL LD, and dysgraphia have instructional implications. If a student has dysgraphia, he or she needs specialized instruction in handwriting (see Chapter 3 and related appendices). If a student has dyslexia, he or she needs specialized instruction in phonology, oral reading accuracy and fluency for single words and passages, and written spelling (see Chapter 3 and related appendices). If the student has OWL LD, the same kind of instruction as for dyslexia is necessary but is not sufficient. If students with OWL LD receive only instruction in phonological awareness and phonological decoding, they are likely to make progress in those areas but not necessarily in real-word reading or spelling skills, which also require morphological awareness treatment). Moreover, without morphological and syntactic awareness instruction, and sometimes explicit strategies for word retrieval they are unlikely to make progress in reading comprehension or in written expression of ideas (see Chapter 5 and related appendices).

A diagnosis of dyslexia, which is both a reading and writing disorder, is also instructionally relevant because students may need specialized instruction in spelling to compose and express ideas in writing (Berninger, Nielsen, et al., 2008b). In contrast, students with dysgraphia may have spelling and written composition problems, but they need specialized instruction in handwriting to overcome these difficulties. Even typically developing writers benefit from handwriting instruction. Although computer keyboards may make it easier to produce letters quickly, evidence shows that elementary school students write longer compositions and write them faster by pen than by keyboard (Berninger, Abbott, et al., 2009; Berninger, Richards, Stock, Trivedi, & Altemeier, 2007; Connelly, Gee, & Wal, 2007). Manuscript handwriting transfers to reading words because most written material is in manuscript fonts (Berninger et al., 1997). Cursive handwriting transfers to improved spelling and composing (Alstad et al., 2015).

Students with dysgraphia, dyslexia, and OWL LD benefit from specialized orthographic strategies and instruction because orthographic coding deficits may be shared phenotype deficits across these SLDs (see Figure 13.4). However, students with dyslexia and often OWL LD also need specialized instruction in making multiple connections between orthographic and phonological codes (see Chapter 4 and related appendices in this book; see also Berninger, 1998a, 2009; Berninger & Abbott, 2003; Berninger & Wolf, 2009a, 2009b).

The key to effective handwriting and spelling instruction is to draw attention to the orthographic word form and the constituent letters in the words for all students with dysgraphia, dyslexia, and OWL LD. Pretreatment in attention training (Kerns, Eso, & Thomson, 1999) was more effective than pretreatment in reading fluency on students' response to the same subsequent written composition instruction (Chenault, Thomson, Abbott, & Berninger, 2006). Another study found that rapid automatic naming (RAN) predicted transfer of taught spelling to one's own compositions (Amtmann, Abbott, & Berninger, 2008). This finding highlights the importance of teaching the alphabetic principle in the phoneme-to-grapheme direction until it is automatic and teaching specific, grade-appropriate spelling words through repeated, daily sentence dictation until spelling is automatic.

Although many students appear to have only dysgraphia, only dyslexia, or only OWL LD, others show signs of having more than one disability (see Chapter 10). They need individually tailored intervention to address all of their instructional needs.

QUESTIONS FOR TEACHERS TO ASK WHEN
REFERRING STUDENTS FOR MULTIDISCIPLINARY ASSESSMENT

Teachers should feel empowered to ask the following questions of the psychologists, speech-language therapists, and other members of the interdisciplinary team to whom they refer students for assessment of reading and writing problems:

1. Does this student have absolute or relative strengths or weaknesses in verbal or nonverbal reasoning that should be recognized and nurtured?

2. Does this student have a strength or weakness compared with grade or age peers in automatic letter writing, handwriting legibility, or handwriting speed?

3. Does this student have a strength or weakness compared with grade or age peers in phonological spelling (pseudowords), orthographic spelling (equated for phonology), or orthographic/morphological spelling (real words)?

4. Does this student have a strength or weakness compared with grade or age peers in accuracy or rate of pseudoword reading? Accuracy or rate of real-word reading on a list? Accuracy or rate of real-word reading in passages?

5. Does this student have a strength or weakness compared with grade or age peers in accuracy or rate of reading comprehension?

6. Does this student have a strength or weakness compared with grade or age peers in accuracy or rate of written composition for narrative or expository genre?

7. Does this student have a strength or weakness compared with grade or age peers in accuracy or rate of the following reading- and writing-related skills?

   - Phonological word-form storage (coding) and processing
   - Orthographic word-form storage (coding) and processing
   - Morphological word-form storage (coding) and processing
   - RAN—letters
   - Expressive orthographic coding—writing words and letters in them
   - Executive function for inhibition, rapid automatic switching, verbal fluency
   - Oral language syntax

Teachers should also feel empowered to ask the professionals who provide the assessment information for problem-solving consultation in planning instructional treatment based on the assessment results. The assessment should include teacher interview and classroom observation of the student during instruction (response to the planned and implemented instructional intervention) in order to assess the curriculum as well as the students' characteristics that mediate response to instruction. See the Teacher Resources in Appendices 3C, 4C, 5C, and 6C in Section II.

DISTINCTIONS BETWEEN RESPONSE TO INSTRUCTION AND DIFFERENTIAL DIAGNOSIS

All good instruction includes an assessment component (progress monitoring) to determine if a student is learning what the teacher is teaching or to set an educational goal. However, progress monitoring should not be confused with a diagnosis. The Individuals with Disabilities Education Improvement Act (IDEA) of 2004 (PL 108-446) stipulates that response to instruction may be a part of comprehensive assessment; it does not indicate, however, that response to instruction alone can replace comprehensive assessment. Moreover, qualifying students for special education services is not the same as evidence-based diagnosis grounded in science and best practices in relevant disciplines, such as psychology, speech and language, physical and occupational therapy, and specializations in medicine (see Berninger, 1998a; Berninger & Holdnack, 2008). Progress monitoring requires analysis by the teacher and the interdisciplinary team of the particular instructional needs of the student linked to assessment findings, not merely assessment of growth or lack of it. See Section II (chapters and related appendices).

Next, we raise issues for practitioners to think about as they carefully plan to incorporate insights from research into their teaching. First, we describe the issue and then propose a reasonable response.

- *Why is it important to base instruction on careful diagnosis of whether a student may have oral language weaknesses beyond phonological processing that also need to be taken into account in planning and delivering written language instruction?* If the other oral language problems are not diagnosed, they will not be treated, and the reading and written language problems may persist even if the student improves in phonics and phonological decoding.

- *Why is it important to understand that some students have only decoding problems, some have both decoding and reading comprehension problems, and some have only comprehension problems?* Due to these individual differences, students differ in the intensity and nature of instruction they require in their general education reading and writing programs in these skills.

- *Why is it important to understand that some students have a problem in decoding words despite good vocabulary knowledge and verbal reasoning, which may mask the decoding problems when reading words in context?* Students with this profile may survive in the early grades but often experience a great deal of difficulty in reading and writing in Grade 4 and above when curriculum requirements increase. Also, students' talents including verbal reasoning may not be recognized and nurtured if not identified.

- *Why is it important to understand that some students may have a problem in writing by hand that compromises their ability to communicate in written language as much as problems with speech do in communicating in oral language?* Students who have typical or even superior intelligence may fail at school, which requires successful completion of written work to pass content subjects; not be promoted to the next grade level; not graduate from high school; and not pass high-stakes tests given in the state. Students who cannot communicate in written language are also at risk for dropping out of school altogether. All of these unfortunate outcomes may also result in emotional problems such as anxiety, work avoidance, and depression.

- *Why is it important to understand that dyslexia is a writing as well as reading disorder?* Teaching students with dyslexia to read is necessary but not sufficient. They also need to be able to spell to complete written assignments for reasons addressed previously. Otherwise, writing quality or length of compositions may be reduced.

- *How do spelling problems of students with dyslexia interfere with their written composition?* Inability to spell words limits word choice. Nonautomatic retrieval of word spellings slows the speed of written composition.

- *Why is it important to understand that some students have dysgraphia (writing problems) without reading problems or in addition to their reading problems?* Just because a student has trouble producing legible letters automatically does not mean that the student is not motivated, cannot think, or lacks vocabulary knowledge or high-quality ideas. The handwriting interferes with spelling words and thus blocks the expression of that thinking ability, knowledge, and ideas.

- *How do handwriting problems of students with dyslexia or dysgraphia interfere with their written composition?* Students with dyslexia and/or dysgraphia may forget what they planned to write while trying to remember how to form the letters. Or, they might write the letters so slowly that they do not produce as much writing as classmates who can write letters automatically. Or, their handwriting may be so illegible that the reader cannot recognize the word spelling or figure out the intended message.

To summarize, some reasons for referral require comprehensive assessment using many different approaches to describe a student's profile. These profiles are unique for each individual. Nevertheless, researchers have identified patterns (configurations of phenotypes) in the writing, reading, and oral language profiles of school-age students that have diagnostic and instructional implications. The diagnoses of dyslexia, OWL LD, and dysgraphia are evidence based.

Regrettably, the federal legislation guaranteeing students a free appropriate public education (FAPE) does not guarantee them free evidence-based diagnosis and evidence-based instruction linked to said diagnoses. Thus, the special education categories used for students with disabilities are simply labels for qualifying students for services. Some students have a profile that enables them to receive pull-out or other kinds of special education services. Because education is under local control, students' profiles depend on the state and often the local school systems where students live. FAPE should be linked to evidence-based assessment–instruction links.

If the reader finds this perplexing, so do the authors, who believe the solution is for educational professionals to provide the best possible evidence-based assessment and instruction proactively. Nothing in state, federal, case, or legislative law prohibits that. Berninger and Holdnack (2008) provided further discussion of the differences among individual profiles (snowflakes), patterns of diagnostic phenotypes (constellations), and categories for providing services (labels) in assessment of learning disabilities.

To summarize, in most schools, the focus of interdisciplinary disciplinary assessment is on determining students' eligibility for special education services rather than diagnosing whether a student has a specific learning disability such as dyslexia, OWL LD, or dysgraphia. Accurate diagnosis is important because it has implications for which processes may be impaired and can explain a student's struggle in learning to read and/or write. An accurate diagnosis also has implications for instructional planning and implementation—how the regular instructional program may need to be modified with specialized instruction in the general or special education classroom.

IMPORTANCE, CHALLENGES, AND REWARDS OF AN INTERDISCIPLINARY APPROACH

Many students are dealing with family and/or other personal stressors outside school. Some students suffer from emotional problems (e.g., impaired self-esteem or self-efficacy, heightened anxiety, habits of avoiding tasks that are difficult); such emotional problems may occur with or without SLDs. The school psychologist on the interdisciplinary team has an important role to play in identifying these issues through reaching out to families, students at school, and colleagues on the team to address social, emotional, and motivational issues that play an important role in school learning. The speech-language therapist has important contributions to make in assessing and treating aural and oral language and speech problems, which (as emphasized in this book) play highly important roles in school learning. Some students have sensory and/or motor problems with or without SLDs that can affect their development both in and out of school. Some students have pervasive or specific developmental disabilities rather than SLDs, medical conditions, or other issues relevant to their education at school. Other students have intellectual talents, which require formal assessment to document, either with or without SLDs, and need to be considered in educational programming. No wonder it takes a whole team with different disciplinary expertise to address the needs of the whole student!

Members of interdisciplinary teams typically have very different kinds of training related to their disciplines and specializations. Such differences in expertise can pose challenges for communication—not only in terms of terminology but also in the possible variables that are considered relevant. Yet, with collaboration, professionals can learn to communicate and collaborate. *Interdisciplinary Frameworks for Schools* (Berninger, 2015) provides guidelines from multiple professional disciplines for such interdisciplinary communication and collaboration in working with students in K–12. Indeed, many professionals find the experience of cross-disciplinary collaboration to be rewarding when they see how previously struggling students become successful.

Free Appropriate Public Education for All Students, with and without Specific Learning Disabilities

A major goal of this book is to share with readers the results of programmatic research funded by federal grants made possible by the Interagency Initiative of 1989. This initiative was the result of parental requests for greater support of research on more effective educational services in public schools for students with learning disabilities. Federal initiatives at the beginning of the 21st century have emphasized the importance of grounding educational practice in scientific knowledge. At the same time, experienced teachers bring knowledge gained from practice in effective teaching that is also relevant to student learning outcomes. Effective teachers are scientist-practitioners—knowledgeable about the science of learning and the art of teaching.

Thus, the goal of this book is to share our current perspectives on translation science, that is, reduction of research into practice, related to four specific learning disabilities (SLDs)—dysgraphia, dyslexia, oral and written language learning disability (OWL LD), and dyscalculia. To accomplish this goal, Section I presented the history of the field, from the early pioneers who first raised awareness of students with reading and writing disabilities and began to develop educational treatments for them to current issues and a vision for the future (Chapter 1). Also, the target four SLDs were defined on basis of evidence-based, treatment-relevant differential diagnosis (Chapter 2). Section II focused on linking assessment to instruction for handwriting (Chapter 3), word reading and spelling (Chapter 4), listening and reading comprehension and oral and written expression (Chapter 5), and math (Chapter 6). The importance of explicit instruction that integrates listening, speaking, and reading in language arts and across the curriculum was emphasized in Chapter 8.

Section III addressed systems issues in classrooms and schools (Chapters 7 and 8) and in individual students' minds (Chapters 9 and 10), with consideration of the role of technology in the computer era for systems of human minds interacting with technology tools (Chapter 11). Finally, Section IV considered the role of preservice and in-service professional development (Chapter 12) and multidisciplinary teams (Chapter 13) in meeting the educational needs of all students, both with and without SLDs (Chapter 14). In this final chapter, we consider how teaching, teacher education, and research inform and enrich each other bidirectionally. Lillian Hellman (Hellman & Feibleman, 1984) pointed out that a child holding the hand of another child in a circle dance helps the other child dance well by dancing well him- or herself. Likewise, competent, dedicated teachers, teacher educators, and researchers collaborating with each other can help students with SLDs learn well in their educational journeys.

Teachers and teacher educators learn from the teachers with whom they work. At the same time, teachers want evidence-based strategies in an era that emphasizes evidence-based instruction. Thus, school–university partnerships are forming between teachers and researchers to explore the potential contributions of translational science. Such teacher–researcher partnerships are promising, as teaching is often a dance between science and practice. Experienced teachers seek connections between what they observe is effective in their own classroom and lessons from researchers. Therefore, this chapter highlights key themes that reflect this synthesis of lessons from science and teaching.

MULTIMODAL, LEVELED LANGUAGE

As discussed in Chapter 1, many professionals in the field of dyslexia emphasize the need for multisensory methods for teaching students with dyslexia. Others emphasize the language basis of reading. Based on research showing the role of motor output in language learning, the role of multimodal instruction in language learning was introduced—multisensory motor and four functional language systems with links to sensory and motor end organs: language by ear, language by mouth, language by eye, and language by hand. We refer to this approach as *multimodal functional language systems*. Indeed, sensorimotor learning may be important not only in the initial stage of cognitive development, as Piaget (1952) proposed, but also throughout the formative stages of oral and written language learning development throughout K–12. The phonological loop (linking the mouth in naming and internal codes for letters) and the orthographic loop (linking internal codes for letters and the hand) of working memory guide oral and written language learning through early and middle childhood and even adolescence.

Moreover, each of these functional language systems has multiple levels. The concept of analyzing levels of language is a basic tool of linguistics. Another important concept is the role of teaching to all the levels of language—in each of the four functional language systems—close in time to create functional language systems, especially in students who have impairments in specific components of the working memory system that support language learning. These levels of language include subword units, word units, syntactic units, and discourse schema composed of all the smaller units plus emergent text structures (see Chapters 1, 2, and 9). Many of the controversies between whole language and phonics approaches to teaching reading could have been avoided if teachers and reading experts had understood that all of these levels of language contribute to reading—subword correspondences between letters and sounds to decoding, written and spoken words to oral and silent reading word identification and vocabulary meaning, and syntax and discourse to oral and silent reading fluency and comprehension. Reading requires both identifying words, based on their links with speech and semantics (meaning), and constructing meaning based on syntax and discourse schema. To summarize, instruction should be aimed to all the levels of language to create a functional reading system, a functional writing system, a functional aural language system, and a functional oral language system that work independently as well as collaboratively.

SPOKEN–WRITTEN WORD CONNECTIONS

The subword level of both spoken/heard words and read/written words also has multiple levels or unit sizes that can be interrelated in multiple ways. Connections can be made at the whole-word level, the level of graphemes (one and two letters) and phonemes, and/or the level of syllables (whole syllables and onsets and rimes). Many National Institute of Child Health and Human Development (NICHD)–funded University of Washington research findings (e.g., Berninger, Abbott, et al., 2000; Berninger, Vaughan, et al., 1998) support multiple connections contributing to word reading and word spelling. Although many students can learn the whole-word connections from one or a few exposures (referred to as "fast mapping"), students with dyslexia or OWL LD cannot (see Chapters 4 and 9). Because they cannot rely on fast mapping, students with dyslexia must rely even more on slow mapping of subword units than do typically developing readers and spellers.

Slow mapping involves subword connections such as letters and phonemes (alphabetic principle), syllables, and onsets and rimes, which are sometimes referred to as word families. However, depending on the individual learning profile, students may have processing impairments that interfere with this slow mapping, such as impaired phoneme awareness (of phonemes in spoken words), orthographic awareness (of letters in written words), or rapid automatic naming (RAN). RAN, which requires oral naming of written symbols or pictures, assesses speed or accuracy of cross-code connections (e.g., a pictured object and its name or a letter or orthographic code and a whole oral word name code). Thus, RAN may be a marker of impaired time-sensitive cross-code mapping needed to learn to read and spell written words. Thus, students with dyslexia or OWL LD also benefit from instruction aimed at all the sublexical and lexical connections, as well as the related processes that may contribute to word decoding/reading and spelling.

MULTICOMPONENT WORKING MEMORY

Working memory is important in learning to read and write and in understanding the nature of dyslexia and other SLDs. First, both students and their parents with dyslexia showed impairments in multiple components of working memory—word form coding (storage and processing), phonological loop, and executive functions (supervisory attention) (see Chapter 9). When individuals with dyslexia have impaired phonological word from coding and/or phonological loop—that is, a phonological core deficit within a working memory architecture—and impaired accuracy of word decoding and reading, they have dyslexia (Berninger, Abbott, Thomson, et al., 2006). Fluency is often also impaired because the orchestration of all of the components of working memory in real time is impaired if one or more of the working memory components is impaired. Second, the widely used RAN task assesses phonological loop function in working memory for cross-code mapping; students who are fast and automatic in cross-code mapping are more likely to rely on fast mapping and learn slow mapping at different unit sizes more easily than those with dyslexia, as discussed previously.

These insights about working memory are relevant to how instruction should be packaged in time for students with dyslexia who have difficulty with temporal coordination of all the component processes in the functional systems (Luria, 1973) for reading and writing. In addition to the sequential, structured systematic instruction over time that students with dyslexia need, they also need a teaching approach that helps them to coordinate these multiple component processes simultaneously in time in working memory. Therefore, we investigated an instructional approach that combines subword, word, and text/discourse instruction close in time in the same lesson. This approach of aiming instruction to all levels of language close in time increases the probability that working memory will support all the levels of language to work in concert (see Chapter 9).

The impairment of working memory in dyslexia also explains why many students with dyslexia benefit from the teaching of procedural knowledge about the alphabetic principle and not just declarative knowledge about letter–sound correspondences. Simply verbalizing the phonics rules is often not enough; students need to apply them to decoding. Working memory capacity and resources are limited; therefore, the more that component processes such as word decoding, recognition, or spelling can be put on automatic pilot in implicit memory, the more capacity and resources will be available for the strategic, nonautomatic processes required for reading comprehension and written composition.

A children's book titled *The Vicar of Nibbleswicke* (Dahl, 1991) captures research findings about the role of working memory in dyslexia. In the book, the new pastor, when given his first assignment as vicar in a village church, suffers a reoccurrence of his childhood dyslexia—he begins to say words backward and often in hilarious ways. This symptom highlights the vulnerability of working memory in individuals with dyslexia, as the NICHD-funded University of Washington family genetics phenotyping studies had found (e.g. Berninger et al., 2006). Symptoms of dyslexia surface when working memory capacity is exceeded, which is likely to happen when one is learning a new task, such as new job responsibilities. The cure for the vicar's adult-onset dyslexia is walking backward—with a rearview mirror to see where he is going. Dahl was undoubtedly making fun of the widely held belief that dyslexia is a problem in reversals—writing letters or words backward. Although research has not shown that reversals cause dyslexia, this children's story makes the telling point that the order of language elements can be mixed up in spoken words as well as written words when working memory is taxed in individuals with dyslexia (Brooks, 2003; Brooks et al., 2011).

DYSGRAPHIA, DYSLEXIA, ORAL AND WRITTEN LANGUAGE LEARNING DISABILITY, AND DYSCALCULIA DO EXIST

Although researchers do not always agree on how to define each SLD, it is clear that many students have puzzling struggles in learning handwriting, word decoding/spelling, reading listening and reading comprehension, and oral/written expression. These struggles may occur despite all five domains of development being in the normal range or higher (see Chapter 2) and despite educational programs at school in which other students have learned these skills.

None of these SLDS are medical problems, even though they have a biological basis. They are educational problems. More often than not, students with SLDs respond well to appropriate instruction. If such instruction is not provided, they struggle.

INTEGRATING ASSESSMENT AND INSTRUCTION AND THE GRAMMAR OF TEACHING

Assessing profiles of reading and writing skills and related processes is important. By identifying impaired skills, it may be possible to explain why learning is difficult for some individuals and point to where teaching has to be individually tailored. Teachers who learn to plan and implement differentiated instruction that meets the needs of students with dysgraphia, dyslexia, OWL LD, and dyscalculia will abstract the grammar of teaching in the process—that is, instructional awareness. They become not only effective teachers for students and youth but also acquire expertise for mentoring other teachers. Although it is important to incorporate all of the necessary instructional components for teaching reading and writing, there is room for teacher creativity in the process. It is not necessary to teach the same way all the time, just as grammar of the language allows alternative ways of connecting words to express comparable ideas.

In instructional studies at the University of Washington, all the components for teaching and learning are included, but never in exactly the same way—yet the students respond to the instruction. The qualitative assessments based on experiences of affected individuals are informative. Below is an excerpt from one of the many e-mails and letters received from parents over the years. The student's name has been changed, but the e-mail is not edited for spelling or grammar; the Washington Assessment of Student Learning (WASL) test mentioned by the parent was the high-stakes test given in the past in Washington. These letters serve as reminders that the hope that is transmitted to struggling students is as important as the skills that are taught.

> I had to drop you an email to let you know how well Stephanie is doing in school now… She averaged a C to C+ in 7th grade last year. She really struggled and let her frustrations get to her. But this year she is maintaining a strong B–B+ and she is shooting for honor roll… Her WASL testing this last year were the closest she has come to "at grade level" ever. She is within 2 or 10 points of hitting them, as compared to last year being way below grade level, even her reading has come up significantly. But what I see the most is how much more she comprehends what she reads and is learning.…There is nothing greater then see your child go from feeling like the dumbest kid in the world to feeling pride in all her work.

The grammar of teaching and learning is not restricted to reading and writing skills. Rich classroom environments that integrate music, science, social studies, or math with language instruction make learning exciting and meaningful. By incorporating a variety of subject areas into language instruction, teachers can capture student interest and help them understand the value of learning.

One boy who was referred to us for severe reading problems had been threatened by his teacher if he could not pass his state's high-stakes test. The teacher's goal was to be the first in the state to have all students in her class pass all the sections of the test. Assessment showed that the boy had superior intelligence, severe dyslexia, and talent in science. At age 8, he was already collecting rare biological specimens and knew more about the phyla of the plant world than the psychologists assessing him. Moreover, he loved science. When he was asked what the class was learning in science, he replied that they did not have time to ever do science. They spent all of their time practicing for the test so that everyone could pass and not let the teacher down. Readers can form their own conclusion about what is wrong with this learning environment and why it was not appropriate for this boy, who was twice exceptional with superior verbal reasoning and an SLD—dyslexia (see Chapter 10).

Above all else, what any teacher can give to a student with SLDs is "compassionitivity"—a word coined by television show *Saturday Night Live Mother's Day 2001* to express the deep caring of one human being about another human being (see Berninger & Richards, 2002, Chapter 8). The term *compassionitivity* also illustrates the fundamental nature of English morphology, which supports transformations of words in playful ways to convey important messages in memorable ways. Compassionitivity is a blend of compassion and activity—mobilizing professionals with knowledge from research and teaching experience to care about each individual student as they implement that knowledge into professional practice. It serves as a reminder of the need for teachers to bring their hearts as well as their minds to teaching. Caring goes a long way for students who struggle with learning.

Although some teachers may feel they are not equipped to teach reading and writing to students with dysgraphia, dyslexia, or OWL LD or math to students with dyscalculia, they are probably very capable of providing intellectual engagement and joy in learning, which are equally important. In this grammar of teaching and learning, critical components include the following:

1. At the end of the school day each student—with or without an SLD—knows something he or she did not know when school started that day.

2. Each student experiences success in at least one activity each day.

3. Each student believes that the teacher cares about her or him as a learner.

Teachers who desire to learn more about the research on teaching reading and writing to students with and without dysgraphia, dyslexia, OWL LD and math to students with and without dyscalculia can contact the nearest college or university offering graduate courses on relevant topics or a systematic program in science-based literacy or numeracy preparation (see Chapter 12) or their alma mater. One principal, in frustration, suggested that teachers whose students did not pass high-stakes tests should sue their alma mater for not preparing them for the realities of teaching in the real world. A viable alternative is that teachers should consider contributing to the fundraising efforts of institutions that offer appropriate science- and practitioner-based preservice and in-service education that prepares teachers to serve all students, including those with SLDs. Increasingly, institutions of higher education are responsive to the interests and concerns of alumni and others who contribute to their fundraising efforts.

COMPENSATION VERSUS NORMALIZATION

Just because a student responds to instruction, it does not mean that he or she does not have an SLD or has completely overcome a biologically based SLD. Students brains may use alternate pathways, or all of the relevant brain regions may not be fully normalized or synchronized in time. If genetic or neural vulnerability is present, students may overcome problems at one stage of schooling only to confront new challenges as the nature of the curriculum and curriculum requirements change. Once diagnosed, students with SLDs should be monitored throughout schooling to make sure they are making progress and explicit instruction should be provided in skills in which they show impairment.

MULTIPLE SKILLS MATTER

Many researchers are seeking the single variable that explains causality and treatment of dyslexia. Teachers know, in contrast, that teaching and learning are complex and involve many variables. In addition to the components of effective instruction identified by the National Reading Panel (NICHD, 2000), research has shown that two additional linguistic awareness components are essential for learning to read and write—orthographic and morphological awareness. In addition, writing (handwriting, spelling, and composition) influences reading acquisition (see Chapters 3, 4, and 5), and successful school performance requires integrated reading-writing, reading-math, and writing-math, which also need to be integrated with oral language (see Chapter 8). Finally, executive functions (strategies for paying attention—focusing, staying on task, and switching tasks—and self-regulation of reading and writing processes) are critical. Learning to read and write involves many processes that have to be orchestrated in time in functional systems to achieve literacy goals. Individual differences in learners and their response to instruction across the life span are facts of life.

EXPANDING THE FIELD THROUGH CONNECTIONS AND COLLABORATIONS

The authors emphasize that educational practice is advanced through the collective, collaborative contributions of many professionals who build upon and extend the contributions of others. They hope that the message of this book has been clear. On the one hand, the increasing recognition of the importance of grounding educational practice in science and research is a good trend. On the other hand, researchers alone cannot generate all the knowledge necessary for effective teaching of students with dysgraphia, dyslexia, OWL LD, and/or dyscalculia. Teachers learn valuable knowledge from teaching experience that is also relevant. Teachers, who are closest to the ground, and can make the most difference and impact in the learning and quality of life of a student with an SLD. (See the excerpt from Pete Seeger's "Trouble at the Bottom" in the introduction to Section III.) Teachers' daily observations of student performance generate insights and questions of value to both their own teaching and to educating researchers about the issues that need to be investigated to deepen understanding for educational practice. Teacher interaction with students exhibiting a broad spectrum of strengths and weaknesses provides a perspective that places the information gained from research into the framework of the classroom.

Both science and teaching benefit from close connections and collaborations between researchers and teachers. Both students with and without SLDs can benefit from these researcher–teacher connections in translating research into practice in the general education classroom.

CHALLENGES IN MEETING THE NEEDS OF DIVERSE LEARNERS

In the authors' experience, educators want to teach all of the students in their classes, but they may not know how to deal with the individual differences among students in general. General education teachers often wonder whether devoting instructional time to those with SLDs will interfere with the teacher's ability to spend sufficient time with the other students in the class. Often, they report not feeling adequately prepared by their professional training programs for the daunting task of teaching students with SLDs or other impairments.

Why should general education teachers want to teach reading, writing, and math to students with dysgraphia, dyslexia, OWL LD, and/or dyscalculia? One reason is that these students are intelligent and can contribute to the intellectual climate of the classroom while benefiting from access to the general curriculum. They may excel in areas of the curriculum that are not as dependent on reading and writing, such as math, science, social studies, art, music, athletics, or drama. Some are even talented in the written expression of ideas despite severe handwriting or spelling problems. Research on adult outcomes has shown that many individuals with dyslexia become successful adults, especially if they had family and other social supports along the way (e.g., Goldberg, Higgins, Raskind, & Herman, 2003; Raskind, Goldberg, Higgins, & Herman, 1999). Despite the success stories that often appear in the media, however, not all students with dyslexia and related SLDs are successful as adults. If not treated effectively, learning disabilities can compromise quality of life in adulthood. Often, having a caring teacher who tries to understand a student's struggles can make a difference in the student's ability to deal with learning challenges both during and after school (Gilger & Wilkins, 2008).

Students with SLDs require access to the general curriculum to grow intellectually and develop in age-appropriate ways. Leaving the general program can disrupt their learning. Alternative ways exist to teach content of curriculum integrated with explicit reading, writing, and integrated reading-writing instruction. The authors hope that this book provides teachers with practical ideas for teaching not only writing, reading, oral language, and math but also other content subject areas of the curriculum to students with SLDs (see Chapter 8 and Berninger & Wolf, 2009a,b). Students with SLDs can learn from being in the general education classroom if teachers do not rely solely on lecturing, reading assignments, and writing assessments and draw on a variety of other instructional approaches to make learning interesting and fun.

NEW BEGINNINGS

The educational needs of students with SLDs can often be met in the general education classroom (the least restrictive environment, which should always be tried first). Teachers should be alert to the signs of dysgraphia, dyslexia, OWL LD, and dyscalculia and refer students for appropriate assessment to determine if such a diagnosis is warranted (see Chapter 13 for questions to pose to assessment specialists on the multidisciplinary team).

If a diagnosis is warranted, members of the multidisciplinary team should collaborate on making it and planning an appropriate educational program for the student. However, special education pull-out services are not always necessary to meet a student's instructional needs and should be considered a last resort. Nevertheless, diagnosis is needed if an educationally disabling condition exists so that necessary instructional interventions are identified and implemented to provide free appropriate public education (FAPE) under the Individuals with Disabilities Education Improvement Act of 2004 (PL 108-446). However, both FAPE and 504 accommodations in the Americans with Disabilities Act can be provided in general education.

Consider the words of a fifth-grade student who was thrilled to be moving from a school for students with dyslexia to a public school general education classroom:

> What I want in my new school is good teachers that explain things and take time to help. That would give me support if I'm stuck on something. I hope they have someone special to help with special needs. I want classes to be fun but educational.

Not all parents can afford to pay for private tutoring or private schools for their children with special learning needs. The federal law guaranteeing FAPE to all students with educational disabilities applies independent of parental level of income. Often, the learning needs of students with SLDs require more than pull-out services two or three times per week. These students need specialized learning environments throughout the school day every day (see Chapter 7), but it is possible to create such learning environments within general education classrooms if teachers are taught why and how.

According to Faust (2007), "Education is the engine that makes American democracy work. And it has to work, and that means people have to have access." Because Slingerland was motivated to help as many children as possible, she developed a classroom approach (see Chapter 1). A United Nations (1959) resolution says, "Mankind owes to the child the best it has to give." Schools owe students the same. Knowledge exists to provide the best education possible, which stems from the following:

1. Classroom experience in teaching students who differ in the ease of learning to listen, speak, read, write, and/or calculate

2. Research on how students learn these skills at specific grade levels throughout K–12 (developmental stepping stones)

3. Effective teaching methods for students with diverse learning profiles and instructional needs (individual differences)

Currently, the Common Core Standards are not informed by any of these three sources of knowledge. To do so would require modifying Common Core Standards so that they can be tailored to developmental and individual differences, as well as reflect research knowledge and the wisdom of experienced, effective teachers and other educational professionals. Such sorely needed modifications would benefit from policy makers, legislators, and government officials implementing educational laws and policies that also meet Common Core Standards to show they understand the lessons from science and teaching and the challenges of teaching diverse learners with and without SLDs in public school settings. Appendix 14A provides a proposed model of Common Core Standards for those who write the standards for teachers and students.

Former Washington State Governor Dan Evans, at a community breakfast where the first author presented the results of the first University of Washington study showing that instruction can normalize brain functions (Richards et al., 2000), observed that what research shows is effective instruction for students with dyslexia may work well for all students. Certainly, many of the approaches described in this book could be used with other students in general education, including English language learners, students from low-literacy home environments or culturally different backgrounds, and students with various SLDs. All of these students are likely to benefit from culturally sensitive (see Chapter 12 in Berninger, 2015), as well as sequential, structured, systematic reading, writing, math, and oral language instruction aimed at all levels of language and relevant math components close in time (see Chapters 3–10). Therefore, the teaching strategies covered in this book should have high utility for teaching a diverse student body in general education. Teachers should assess all students' responses to instruction, decide if the program in place is working for each student, and, if not, modify it flexibly for individuals.

At the same time, the authors caution that not all students struggle and need this kind of specialized instruction. However, all students may benefit from some common learning activities, such as word study (vocabulary development geared to phonological, orthographic, and morphological awareness and word origins) across the curriculum and word play (creating humor through language). We should not lose sight of the ultimate purpose of education, which is not only to optimize the achievement of individuals, but also to teach all individuals to function productively and peacefully in a diverse society. Ideally, we should provide FAPE for *all* students.

Common Core Standards
for Educational Policy Makers,
Lawyers, Legislators,
and Government Regulators

A Team Approach

To qualify for participation in creating Common Core Standards, common curriculum, and common annual assessments, participants should complete professional development (learning activities and written examination) and complete three supervised practica. Participants must be able to do the following:

1. Demonstrate knowledge of key concepts in modern genetics and epigenetics and environmental diversity (racial, multicultural, linguistic, and socioeconomic) that are relevant to understanding individual differences in learners

2. Demonstrate knowledge of key concepts in brain science that are relevant to understanding the developing brain and its role in learning aural and oral language, reading, writing, and math across early childhood, middle childhood, and adolescence—and thus developmental differences in learners

3. Demonstrate knowledge of developmental science and instructional science to articulate the normal developmental stepping stones in learning aural and oral language, reading, writing, and math from early childhood to middle childhood to adolescence

4. Define, explain how to diagnose, and be able to differentiate pervasive developmental disability, specific developmental disability, dysgraphia, dyslexia, oral and written language learning disability, and dyscalculia; summarize the appropriate instructional approaches for each of these disabilities from K–12; explain talents that students may have and educational programming needed to support and nurture these; and explain what *twice exceptional* is (how a student may have both talent and disability) and the kinds of educational programming needed to educate all these individuals

5. Explain why common core standards and assessment should be flexibly adapted to developmental and individual differences from K–12

6. Explain why all students deserve free appropriate public education

7. Explain why accounting practices in business (i.e., accountability) are not appropriate for evaluating teachers or students, why a more appropriate approach is grounded in best professional practices and biological and environmental diversity, and why the educational profession needs to have professional autonomy to optimize the achievement of all students

As part of supervised practica in public school settings serving diverse school populations, the individual must complete the following:

1. A 3-month supervised practicum in an early childhood classroom with at least 20 children per class

2. A 3-month supervised practicum in a middle childhood classroom with at least 20 children per class

3. A 3-month supervised practicum in an adolescent classroom with at least 20 students per class in sections across the day and across the content areas of the curriculum

References

Aaron, P.G. & Joshi, R.M. (2006). Written language is as natural as spoken language: A biolinguistic perspective. *Reading Psychology, 27,* 263–311.

Abbott, R., Berninger, V., & Fayol, M. (2010). Longitudinal relationships of levels of language in writing and between writing and reading in grades 1 to 7. *Journal of Educational Psychology, 102,* 281–298.

Adams, M.J. (1990). *Beginning to read: Thinking and learning about print.* Cambridge, MA: MIT Press.

Adams, M., Foorman, B., Lundberg, I., & Beeler, T. (1998). *Phonemic awareness in young children: A classroom curriculum.* Baltimore, MD: Paul H. Brookes Publishing Co.

Alstad, Z., Sanders, E., Abbott, R., Barnett, A., Hendersen, S., Connelly, V., & Berninger, V. (2015). Modes of alphabet letter production during middle childhood and adolescence: Interrelationships with each other and other writing skills. *Journal of Writing Research, 6*(3), 199–231. Retrieved from http://www.jowr.org/next.html #644747: NIHMS644747 [NCBI tracking system #16689920]

Altemeier, L., Abbott, R., & Berninger, V.W. (2008). Executive functions for reading and writing in typical literacy development and dyslexia. *Journal of Clinical and Experimental Neuropsychology, 30,* 588–606.

Amtmann, D., Abbott, R., & Berninger, V.W. (2007). Mixture growth models for RAN and RAS row by row: Insight into the reading system at work over time. *Reading and Writing: An Interdisciplinary Journal, 20,* 785–813.

Amtmann, D., Abbott, R., & Berninger, V. (2008). Identifying and predicting classes of response to explicit, phonological spelling instruction during independent composing. *Journal of Learning Disabilities, 41,* 218–234.

Apel, K., Oster, J., & Masterson, J. (2006). Effects of phonotactic and orthotactic probabilities during fast-mapping on five year-olds' learning to spell. *Developmental Neuropsychology, 29,* 21–42.

Aram, D., Ekelman, B., & Nation, J. (1984). Preschoolers with language disorders: 10 years later. *Journal of Speech and Hearing Research, 27,* 232–244.

Arfé, B. Personal communication, September 21, 2008.

Arieti, S. (1976). *Creativity: The magic synthesis.* New York, NY: Basic Books.

Auman, M. (2003). *Step up to writing* (2nd ed.). Longmont, CO: Sopris West.

Aylward, E., Richards, T., Berninger, V., Nagy, W., Field, K., Grimme, A., et al. (2003). Instructional treatment associated with changes in brain activation in children with dyslexia. *Neurology, 61,* 212–219.

Baddeley, A., & Hitch, G. (1974). Working memory. In G.A. Bower (Ed.), *Recent advances in learning and motivation* (pp. 47–90). New York, NY: Academic Press.

Bahr, R.H., Silliman, E.R., & Berninger, V. (2009). What spelling errors have to tell about vocabulary learning. In C. Wood & V. Connelly (Eds.). *Reading and spelling: Contemporary perspectives* (pp. 177–210). London, United Kingdom: Routledge.

Bailey, D.H., Hoard, M.K., Nugent, L., & Geary, D.C. (2012). Competence with fractions predicts gains in mathematics achievement. *Journal of Experimental Child Psychology, 113,* 447–455.

Balmuth, M. (2009). *The roots of phonics: A historical introduction* (Rev. ed.). Baltimore, MD: Paul H. Brookes Publishing Co.

Barbaresi, W., Katusic, S., Colligan, R., Weaver, A., & Jacobsen, S. (2005). Math learning disorder: Incidence in a population-based birth cohort, 1976–82. *Ambulatory Pediatrics, 5,* 281–289.

Barnett, A., Henderson, S., Scheib, B., & Schulz, J. (2007). *Detailed Assessment of Speed Handwriting, Second Edition (DASH-2).* London, United Kingdom: Pearson.

Batshaw, M., Roizen, N., & Lotrecchiano, G. (Eds.). (2013). *Children with disabilities* (7th ed.). Baltimore, MD: Paul H. Brookes Publishing Co.

Bear, D., Invernizzi, M., Templeton, S., & Johnston, F. (2000). *Words their way: Word study for phonics, vocabulary, and spelling instruction* (2nd ed.). Upper Saddle River, NJ: Prentice Hall.

Beck, I.L., & McKeown, M.G. (2001). Text talk: Capturing the benefits of reading aloud for young children. *The Reading Teacher, 55*(1), 10–19.

Beck, I.L., & McKeown, M.G. (2004). *Elements of reading: Vocabulary.* Austin, TX: Harcourt.

Beck, I.L., & McKeown, M.G. (2004). *Text talk.* New York, NY: Scholastic.

Beck, I.L., & McKeown, M.G. (2006). *Improving comprehension with questioning the author: A fresh and enhanced view of a proven approach.* New York, NY: Scholastic.

Beck, I.L., & McKeown, M.G. (2007). Increasing young low income children's oral vocabulary repertoires through rich and focused instruction. *Elementary School Journal, 107*(3), 251–271.

Beck, I.L., McKeown, M.G., & Kucan, L. (2008). *Creating robust vocabulary: Frequently asked questions and extended examples.* New York, NY: Guilford Press.

Beck, I.L, McKeown, M.G., & Kucan, L. (2013). *Bringing words to life: Robust vocabulary instruction* (2nd ed.). New York, NY: Guilford Press.

Beeler, D. (1988). *Book of roots: A full study of our family of words.* Homewood, IL: Union Representative.

Beery, K. (1982). *Administration, scoring, and teaching manual for the Developmental Test of Visual-Motor Integration* (Rev. ed.). Cleveland, OH: Modern Curriculum Press.

Benbow, M. (1990). *Loops and groups: A kinesthetic writing system.* San Antonio, TX: Therapy Skill Builders.

Berninger, V.W. (1998a). *Process Assessment of the Learner (PAL): Guides for intervention— Reading and writing.* San Antonio, TX: Pearson.

Berninger, V.W. (1998b). *Process Assessment of the Learner (PAL): Handwriting lessons.* San Antonio, TX: Pearson.

Berninger, V. (2000). Development of language by hand and its connections to language by ear, mouth, and eye. *Topics in Language Disorders, 20,* 65–84.

Berninger, V. (2002). Best practices in reading, writing, and math assessment-intervention links: A systems approach for schools, classrooms, and individuals. In A. Thomas & J. Grimes (Eds.), *Best practices in school psychology IV* (Vol. 1, pp. 851–865). Bethesda, MD: National Association of School Psychologists.

Berninger, V.W. (2007a). *Process Assessment of the Learner, Second Edition (PAL-II): Diagnostic for math* (PAL-II Math). San Antonio, TX: Pearson. [Contains CD with downloadable interventions to go with the assessment results.]

Berninger, V.W. (2007b). *Process Assessment of the Learner, Second Edition (PAL-II): Diagnostic for Reading and Writing (PAL-II RW).* San Antonio, TX: Pearson. [Contains CD with downloadable interventions to go with the assessment results.]

Berninger, V.W. (2008). Defining and differentiating dyslexia, dysgraphia, and language learning disability within a working memory model. In M. Mody & E.R. Silliman (Eds.), *Challenges in language and literacy: Brain, behavior, and learning in language and reading disorders* (pp. 103–134). New York, NY: Guilford Press.

Berninger, V. (2009). Highlights of programmatic, interdisciplinary research on writing. *Learning Disabilities Research and Practice, 24,* 68–79.

Berninger, V. (2012, May/June). Strengthening the mind's eye: The case for continued handwriting instruction in the 21st century (pp. 28–31). *Principal.* Alexandria, VA: National Association of Elementary School Principals.

Berninger, V. (2013, March). *Educating students in the computer age to be multilingual by hand*. Retrieved from National Association of State Boards of Education (NASBE) at http://www.nasbe.org/wp-content/uploads/Commentary-Handwriting-keyboarding-and-brain-development1.pdf

Berninger, V.W. (2015). *Interdisciplinary frameworks for schools: Best professional practices for serving the needs of all students*. Washington, DC: American Psychological Association. See Companion web sites for Readings and Resources closely aligned with hard copy and contributions of an Advisory Panel.

Berninger, V.W., & Abbott, S. (2003). *PAL research-supported reading and writing lessons and reproducibles*. San Antonio, TX: Pearson.

Berninger, V., & Abbott, R. (2010). Listening comprehension, oral expression, reading comprehension and written expression: Related yet unique language systems in grades 1, 3, 5, and 7. *Journal of Educational Psychology, 102*, 635–651.

Berninger, V., & Abbott, R. (2013). Children with dyslexia who are and are not gifted in verbal reasoning. *Gifted Child Quarterly, 57*, 223–233. doi: 10.1177/0016986213500342. Posted on PubMedCentral on 2013-09-22 15:41:46 for release August 30, 2014. NIHMSID #526583.

Berninger, V.W., Abbott, R., Abbott, S., Graham, S., & Richards, T. (2002). Writing and reading: Connections between language by hand and language by eye. *Journal of Learning Disabilities, 35*, 39–56.

Berninger, V., Abbott, R., Augsburger, A., & Garcia, N. (2009). Comparison of pen and keyboard transcription modes in children with and without learning disabilities affecting transcription. *Learning Disability Quarterly, 32*, 123–141.

Berninger, V.W., Abbott, R., Brooksher, R., Lemos, Z., Ogier, S., Zook, D., et al. (2000). A connectionist approach to making the predictability of English orthography explicit to at-risk beginning readers: Evidence for alternative, effective strategies. *Developmental Neuropsychology, 17*, 241–271.

Berninger, V., Abbott, R., Rogan, L., Reed, E, Abbott, S., Brooks, A., Vaughan, K., & Graham, S. (1998). Teaching spelling to children with specific learning disabilities: The mind's ear and eye beat the computer or pencil. *Learning Disability Quarterly, 21*, 106–122.

Berninger, V.W., Abbott, R., Thomson, J., Wagner, R., Swanson, H.L., Wijsman, E., et al. (2006). Modeling developmental phonological core deficits within a working-memory architecture in children and adults with developmental dyslexia. *Scientific Studies in Reading, 10*, 165–198.

Berninger, V., Abbott, R., Vermeulen, K., & Fulton, C. (2006). Paths to reading comprehension in at-risk second grade readers. *Journal of Learning Disabilities, 39*, 334–351.

Berninger, V.W., Abbott, R., Whitaker, D., Sylvester, L., & Nolen, S. (1995). Integrating low level skills and high-level skills in treatment protocols for writing disabilities. *Learning Disability Quarterly, 18*, 293–309.

Berninger, V., Abbott, R., Zook, D., Ogier, S., Lemos, Z., & Brooksher, R. (1999). Early intervention for reading disabilities: Teaching the alphabet principle within a connectionist framework. *Journal of Learning Disabilities, 32*(6), 491–503.

Berninger, V.W., & Amtmann, D. (2003). Preventing written expression disabilities through early and continuing assessment and intervention for handwriting and/or spelling problems: Research into practice. In H.L. Swanson, K.R. Harris, & S. Graham (Eds.), *Handbook of research on learning disabilities* (pp. 345–363). New York, NY: Guilford Press.

Berninger, V., & Dunn, M. (2012). Brain and behavioral response to intervention for specific reading, writing, and math disabilities: What works for whom? In B. Wong & D. Butler (Eds.). *Learning about Learning Disabilities* (4th ed., pp. 59–89). Philadelphia, PA: Academic Press.

Berninger, V., & Fuller, F. (1992). Gender differences in orthographic, verbal, and compositional fluency: Implications for diagnosis of writing disabilities in primary grade children. *Journal of School Psychology, 30*, 363–382.

Berninger, V.W., & Holdnack, J. (2008). Neuroscientific and clinical perspectives on the RTI initiative in learning disabilities diagnosis and intervention: Response to questions begging answers that see the forest and the trees. In C. Reynolds & E. Fletcher-Janzen (Eds.), *Neuroscientific and clinical perspectives on the RTI initiative in learning disabilities diagnosis and intervention* (pp. 66–81). New York, NY: Wiley.

Berninger, V., Nagy, W., & Beers, S. (2011). Child writers' construction and reconstruction of single sentences and construction of multi-sentence texts: Contributions of syntax and transcription to translation. *Reading and Writing: An Interdisciplinary Journal, 102,* 151–182. doi: 10.1007/s11145-010-9262-y PMC3048336.

Berninger, V., Nagy, W., Tanimoto, S., Thompson, R., & Abbott, R. (2015). Computer handwriting, spelling, and composing instruction for students with specific learning disabilities in grades 4 to 9. *Computers and Education, 81,* 154–168. doi: 10.1016/j.compedu.2014.10.00 Posted NIHMS636683 NIHMSID Publ.ID: CAE2713.

Berninger, V., & Niedo, J. (2014). Individualizing instruction for students with oral and written language difficulties. In J. Mascolo, D. Flanagan, and V. Alfonso (Eds.), *Essentials of planning, selecting and tailoring intervention: Addressing the needs of unique learners* (pp. 231–264). New York, NY: Wiley.

Berninger, V.W., Nielsen, K., Abbott, R., Wijsman, E., & Raskind, W. (2008). Writing problems in developmental dyslexia: Under-recognized and under-treated. *Journal of School Psychology, 46,* 1–21.

Berninger, V., & O'Malley May, M. (2011). Evidence-based diagnosis and treatment for specific learning disabilities involving impairments in written and/or oral language. *Journal of Learning Disabilities, 44,* 167–183.

Berninger, V.W., Raskind, W., Richards, T., Abbott, R., & Stock, P. (2008). A multidisciplinary approach to understanding developmental dyslexia within working-memory architecture: Genotypes, phenotypes, brain, and instruction. *Developmental Neuropsychology, 33,* 707–744.

Berninger, V., & Richards, T. (2002). *Brain literacy for educators and psychologists.* New York, NY: Academic Press.

Berninger, V.W., & Richards, T. (2008). How brain research informs reading, writing, and math instruction and learning. In E. Anderman, L. Anderman, C. Chinn, T. Murcock, & H.L. Swanson (Eds.), *Psychology of classroom learning: An encyclopedia* (pp. 15–22). Farmington Hills, MI: Gale Group.

Berninger, V., & Richards, T. (2010). Inter-relationships among behavioral markers, genes, brain, and treatment in dyslexia and dysgraphia. *Future Neurology, 5,* 597–617. doi: 10.2217/fnl.10.22.

Berninger, V.W., Richards, T., Stock, P., Trivedi, P., & Altemeier, L. (2007, June 28). *From idea generation to idea expression in language by hand in good and poor writers.* Keynote presented at the meeting of Learning and Teaching Writing: *British Journal of Educational Psychology* Psychological Aspects of Education Current Trends Conference, Oxford Brookes University, Oxford, UK.

Berninger, V.W., Rutberg, J., Abbott, R., Garcia, N., Anderson-Youngstrom, M., Brooks, A., et al. (2006). Tier 1 and Tier 2 early intervention for handwriting and composing. *Journal of School Psychology, 44,* 3–30.

Berninger, V., Stock, P., Lee, Y., Abbott, R., & Breznitz, Z. (2007, July). *Working memory enhancement through accelerated reading training.* Presentation in Symposium on Can the Dyslexic Brain Do Better? Enhancement of reading fluency (Z. Breznitz, organizer and chair). Society for the Scientific Study of Reading, Prague, Czech Republic.

Berninger, V., & Swanson, H.L. (2013). Diagnosing and treating specific learning disabilities in reference to the brain's working memory system. In H.L. Swanson, K. Harris, & S. Graham (Eds.), *Handbook of learning disabilities* (2nd ed., pp. 307–325). New York, NY: Guilford.

Berninger, V.W., Vaughan, K., Abbott, R., Abbott, S., Brooks, A., Rogan, L., et al. (1997). Treatment of handwriting fluency problems in beginning writing: Transfer from handwriting to composition. *Journal of Educational Psychology, 89,* 652–666.

Berninger, V.W., Vaughan, K., Abbott, R., Brooks, A., Abbott, S., Reed, E., et al. (1998). Early intervention for spelling problems: Teaching spelling units of varying size within a multiple connections framework. *Journal of Educational Psychology, 90,* 587–605.

Berninger, V., Vaughan, K., Abbott, R., Brooks, A., Begay, K., Curtin, G., Byrd, K., & Graham, S. (2000). Language-based spelling instruction: Teaching children to make multiple connections between spoken and written words. *Learning Disability Quarterly, 23,* 117–135.

Berninger, V.W., Winn, W., Stock, P., Abbott, R., Eschen, K., Lin, C., et al. (2008). Tier 3 specialized writing instruction for students with dyslexia. *Reading and Writing: An Interdisciplinary Journal, 21,* 95–129.

Berninger, V., & Wolf, B. (2009a). *Helping students with dyslexia and dysgraphia make connections: Differentiated instruction lesson plans in reading and writing.* Baltimore, MD: Paul H. Brookes Publishing Co.

Berninger, V., & Wolf, B. (2009b). *Teaching students with dyslexia and dysgraphia*: Lessons from *teaching and science.* Baltimore, MD: Paul H. Brookes Publishing Co.

Biemiller, A. (1977–1978). Relationship between oral reading rates for letters, words, and simple text in the development of reading achievement. *Reading Research Quarterly, 13,* 223–253.

Biemiller, A., & Siegel, L. (1997). A longitudinal study of the effects of the Bridge Reading Program for children at-risk for reading failure. *Learning Disability Quarterly, 20,* 83–92.

Birsh, J.R. (Ed.). (2011). *Multisensory teaching of basic language skills* (3rd ed.). Baltimore, MD: Paul H. Brookes Publishing Co.

Bishop, D.V.M., & Adams, C. (1990). A prospective study of the relationship between specific language impairment, phonological disorders and reading retardation. *Journal of Child Psychology and Psychiatry, 31,* 1027–1050.

Bishop, D.V.M., & Snowling, M. J. (2004). Developmental dyslexia and specific language impairment. *Psychological Bulletin, 130,* 858–886.

Blachman, B., & Tangleman, D. (2008). *Road to reading: A program for preventing and remediating reading difficulties.* Baltimore, MD: Paul H. Brookes Publishing Co.

Bond, G., & Tinker, T. (1967). *Reading difficulties: Their diagnosis and correction.* New York, NY: Appleton-Century-Crofts.

Bowers, P., & Wolf, M. (1993). Theoretical links between naming speed, precise timing mechanisms, and orthographic skill in dyslexia. *Reading and Writing: An Interdisciplinary Journal, 5,* 69–85.

Bradley, R., Danielson, L., & Hallahan, D. (2002). *Identification of learning disabilities: Research to practice.* Mahwah, NJ: Lawrence Erlbaum Associates.

Brady, S., Fowler, A., Stone, B., & Winebury, N. (1994). Training in phonological awareness: A study with inner city kindergarten children, *Annals of Dyslexia, 34,* 26–59.

Brandon, L. (2006). *Sentences at a glance.* Boston, MA: Houghton Mifflin.

Brkanac, Z., Chapman, N., Matsushita, M., Chun, L., Nielsen, K., Cochrane, E., et al. (2007). Evaluation of candidate genes for DYX1 and DYX2 in families with dyslexia. *American Journal of Medical Genetics Part B: Neuropsychiatric Genetics, 144B,* 556–560.

Brody, L., & Mills, C. (1997). Gifted children with learning disabilities: A review of the issues, *Journal of Learning Disabilities, 30,* 282–286.

Brooks, A.D. (2003). Neuropsychological processes related to persisting reversal errors in dyslexia and dysgraphia. *Dissertation Abstracts International, 63*(11-A), 3850.

Brooks, A., Berninger, V., Abbott, R., & Richards, T. (2011). Letter naming and letter writing reversals of some children with dyslexia: Symptoms of inefficient phonological and orthographic loops of working memory? *Developmental Neuropsychology, 36,* 847–868.

Bryant, B. (2015). Assistive and instructional technology. Posted on companion web site for Berninger, V.W. (2015). *Interdisciplinary frameworks for schools: Best professional practices for serving the needs of all students.* Washington, DC: American Psychological Association.

Bryant, B., Bryant, D., Kethley, C. Kim, S., Pool, C., & Seo, Y.-J. (2008). Preventing mathematics difficulties in the primary grades: The critical features of instruction in textbooks as part of the equation. *Learning Disabilities Quarterly, 31,* 21–36.

Bryant, B.R., Bryant, D.P., & Rieth, H.J. (2002). The use of assistive technology in postsecondary education settings. In L.C. Brinckerhoff, J.M. McGuire, and S.F. Shaw (Eds.), *Postsecondary education and transition for students with learning disabilities* (2nd ed., pp. 389–429). Austin, TX: PRO-ED.

Bryant, B.R., & Seay, P.C. (1998). The Technology-Related Assistance to Individuals with Disabilities Act: Relevance to individuals with learning disabilities and their advocates. *Journal of Learning Disabilities, 31*(1), 4–15.

Bryant, B.R., Seay, P.C., & Bryant, D.P. (1999). Assistive technology and adaptive behavior. In R. Schalock (Ed.), *Adaptive behavior and its measurement* (pp. 81–98). Washington, DC: American Association on Mental Retardation.

Bryant, B.R., Seok, S., Ok, M., & Bryant, D.P. (2012). Individuals with intellectual and/or developmental disabilities use of assistive technology devices in support provision. *Journal of Special Education Technology, 27*(2), 41–57.

Bryant, D., & Bryant, B. (2012). *Assistive technology for people with disabilities* (2nd ed.). San Antonio, TX: Pearson.

Busse, J., Berninger, V., Smith, D., & Hildebrand, D. (2001). Assessment for math talent and disability: A developmental model. (Eds.). In J. Andrews, H.D. Saklofske, & H. Janzen (Eds.), *Ability, achievement, and behavior assessment. A practical handbook.* (pp. 225–253). New York, NY: Academic Press.

Cain, K., & Oakhill, J. (2007). *Children's comprehension problems in oral and written language: A cognitive perspective.* New York, NY: Guilford Press.

Cardon, L., Smith, S., Fulker, D., Kimberling, W., Pennington, B., & DeFries, J. (1995). Quantitative trait locus for reading disability on chromosome 6. *Science, 266,* 276–279.

Carlisle, J. (1994). Morphological awareness, spelling, and story writing: Possible relationships for elementary-age children with and without learning disabilities. In N.C. Jordan & J. Goldsmith-Phillips (Eds.), *Learning disabilities: New directions for assessment and intervention* (pp. 123–145). Boston, MA: Allyn & Bacon.

Carlisle, J. (1996). *Models for writing: Levels A, B, and C.* Novato, CA: Academic Therapy.

Carlisle, J. (2000a). Awareness of the structure and meaning of morphologically complex words: Impact on reading. *Reading and Writing: An Interdisciplinary Journal, 12,* 169–190.

Carlisle, J. (2000b). *Beginning reasoning and reading, reasoning and reading level one, reasoning and reading level two.* Cambridge, MA: Educators Publishing Service.

Carlisle, J. (2003). *Vocabulary in reasoning and reading.* Cambridge, MA: Educators Publishing Services.

Carlisle, J., & Rice, M. (2002). *Improving reading comprehension: Research-based principles and practices.* Timonium, MD: York Press.

Carreker, S. (2006). The parts of speech: Foundation of writing. *Perspectives, 32*(2), 31–34.

Carter, F. (1990). *The education of Little Tree.* Albuquerque, NM: The University of New Mexico Press.

Cassiday, L. (2009). *Mapping the epigenome. New tools chart. Chemical modifications of DNA and its packaging proteins.* Retrieved from http://www.cen-online.org

Catts, H., Fey, M., Zhang, X., & Tomblin, B. (1999). Language basis of reading and reading disability: Evidence from a longitudinal investigation. *Scientific Studies in Reading, 3,* 331–361.

Catts, H., Fey, M., Zhang, X., & Tomblin, B. (2001). Estimating the risk of future reading difficulties in kindergarten children: A research-based model and its clinical implication. *Language, Speech, and Hearing Services in Schools, 32,* 38–50.

Catts, H., Hogan, T., & Adloff, S. (2005). Developmental changes in reading and reading disabilities. In H. Catts & A. Kamhi (Eds.), *The connections between language and reading disabilities* (pp. 25–40). Mahwah, NJ: Lawrence Erlbaum Associates.

Catts, H., & Kamhi, A. (Eds.) (2005). *The connections between language and reading disabilities.* Mahwah, NJ: Lawrence Erlbaum Associates.

Chapman, N., Igo, R., Thomson, J., Matsushita, M., Brkanac, Z., Hotzman, T., et al. (2004). Linkage analyses of four regions previously implicated in dyslexia: Confirmation of a locus on chromosome 15q. *American Journal of Medical Genetics/Neuropsychiatric Genetics, 131B,* 67–75.

Chenault, B., Thomson, J., Abbott, R., & Berninger, V.W. (2006). Effects of prior attention training on child dyslexics' response to composition instruction. *Developmental Neuropsychology, 29,* 243–260.

Childs, S. (1962). *Sound phonics.* Cambridge, MA: Educators Publishing Service.

Childs, S. (1968). *A biographical sketch: Education and specific language disability: The papers of Anna Gillingham, M.A.* Pomfret, CT: The Orton Society.

Colligan, R., & Katusic, S. (2015). Overview of epidemiological studies of incidence of learning disabilities with annotated research references from the Mayo Clinic, Rochester, MN. Posted on companion web site for resources under epidemiology for Chapter 9 for Berninger, V.W., (2015), *Interdisciplinary frameworks for schools: Best professional practices for serving the needs of all students.* Washington, DC: American Psychological Association.

Columbia University Health Sciences Library. (n.d.). *Personal papers and manuscripts: Samuel Torrey Orton, 1879–1948, and June Lyday Orton, 1898–1977.* Retrieved from http://library.cpmc.columbia.edu/hsl/archives/findingaids/ortoncasefiles.html

Connelly, V., Campbell, S., MacLean, M., & Barnes, J. (2006). Contribution of lower-order skills to the written composition of college students with and without dyslexia. *Developmental Neuropsychology, 29*, 175–196.

Connelly, V., Gee, D., & Wal, E. (2007). A comparison of keyboarded and handwritten compositions and the relationship with transcription speed. *British Journal of Educational Psychology, 77*, 479–492.

Connolly, A. (2008). *Key Math Third Edition (Key Math 3) Diagnostic Assessment.* Boston, MA: Pearson.

Connor, C., Morrison, F., & Katch, L. (2004). Beyond the reading wars: Exploring the effect of child-instruction interactions on growth in early reading. *Scientific Studies of Reading, 8*, 305–336.

Cox, A.R. (1992). *Foundations for literacy: Structures and techniques for multisensory teaching of basic written English language skills.* Cambridge, MA: Educators Publishing Service.

Craggs, J., Sanchez, J., Kibby, M., Gilger, J., & Hynd, G. (2006). Brain morphological neuropsychological profiles of a family displaying superior nonverbal intelligence and dyslexia. *Cortex, 42*, 1107–1118.

Crosnoe, R., Morrison, F., Burchinal, M., Pianta, R., Keating, D., Friedman, S. L., & Clarke-Stewart, K. (2010). Instruction, teacher–student relations, and math achievement trajectories in elementary school. *Journal of Educational Psychology, 102*(2), 407–417.

Culham, R. (2003). *6 + 1 traits of writing: The complete guide.* Teaching Resources. Scottsdale, AZ: Remedia.

Dawson, P., & Guare, R. (2010). *Executive skills in children and adolescents: A practical guide to assessment and intervention.* New York, NY: Guilford Press.

Deák, G.O. (2001). The development of cognitive flexibility and language abilities. *Advances in Child Development and Behavior, 31*, 271–327.

Dehaene, S. (2011). *The number sense: How the mind creates mathematics* (Rev. Ed.). New York, NY: Oxford University Press.

Delis, D., Kaplan, E., & Kramer, J. (2001). *Delis-Kaplan Executive Function System (D-KEFS).* San Antonio, TX: The Psychological Corporation/Pearson.

Delisle, J. (Ed.). (1984). *Gifted children speak out.* New York, NY: Walker & Company.

Denton, C., Vaughn, S., Wexler, J., Bryan, D., & Reed, D. (2012). *Effective instruction for middle school students with reading difficulties: The reading teacher's sourcebook.* Baltimore, MD: Paul H. Brookes Publishing Co.

Dickinson, D., & McCabe, A. (1991). The acquisition and development of language: A social interaction account of language and literacy development. In J. Kavanagh (Ed.), *The language continuum* (pp. 1–40). Timonium, MD: York Press.

Dixon, R.C., & Engelmann, S. (2001). *Spelling through morphographs: Teacher's guide.* Columbus, OH: SRA/McGraw-Hill.

Dowhower, S. (1987). Effects of repeated reading on second-grade transitional readers' fluency and comprehension. *Reading Research Quarterly, 22*, 389–406.

Dreyer, L., Luke, S., & Melican, E. (1995). Children's acquisition and retention of word spellings. In V.W. Berninger (Ed.), *The varieties of orthographic knowledge II: Relationships to phonology, reading, and writing* (pp. 291–320). Dordrecht, The Netherlands: Kluwer.

Eckert, M., Leonard, C., Richards, T., Aylward, E., Thomson, J., & Berninger, V.W. (2003). Anatomical correlates of dyslexia: Frontal and cerebellar findings. *Brain, 126*(2), 482–494.

Eckert, M., Leonard, C., Wilke, M., Eckert, M., Richards, T., Richards, A., et al. (2005). Anatomical signature of dyslexia in children: Unique information from manual-based and voxel-based morphometry brain measures. *Cortex, 41*, 304–315.

Eden, G., VanMeter, J., Rumsey, J., Maisog, J., Woods, R., & Zeffiro, T. (1996). Abnormal processing of visual motion in dyslexia revealed by functional brain imaging. *Nature, 382*, 66–69.

Education for All Handicapped Children Act of 1975, PL 94-142, 20 U.S.C. 3801 §§ *et seq.*

Ehrenworth, M., & Vinton, V. (2005). *The power of grammar: Unconventional approaches to the conventions of language.* Portsmouth, NH: Heinemann.

Ehri, L. (1992). Reconceptualizing the development of sight word reading and its relationship to recoding. In P. Gough, L. Ehri, & R. Treiman (Eds.), *Reading acquisition* (pp. 107–144). Mahwah, NJ: Lawrence Erlbaum Associates.

Ervin, J. (2001). *Reading comprehension in varied subject matter.* Cambridge, MA: Educators Publishing Service.

Faust, D.G. (2007, December 24). Notebook: Verbatim. *Time, 170*(26). Retrieved from http://www.time.com/time/magazine/article/0,9171,1694451,00.html

Fernald, G. (1943). *Remedial techniques in basic school subjects.* New York, NY: McGraw Hill.

Fey, M., Catts, H., Proctor-Williams, K., Tomblin, B., & Zhang, X. (2004). Oral and written story composition skills of children with language impairment. *Journal of Speech, Language, and Hearing Research, 47,* 1301–1318.

Fifer, M., & Flowers, N. (1993). *Vocabulary from classical roots: Strategic vocabulary instruction through Greek and Latin roots. Grades 7–11.* Cambridge, MA: Educators Publishing Service.

Fry, E. (1993). *Computer keyboarding for beginners.* Westminster, CA: Teacher Created Materials.

Fry, E. (1996). *Spelling book: Grades 1–6: Words most needed plus phonics.* Westminster, CA: Teacher Created Materials.

Fry, E. (1999). *Dr. Fry's computer keyboarding for beginners.* Westminster, CA: Teacher Created Materials.

Fuchs, L., Geary, D.C., Compton, D.L., et al. (2010). Do different types of school mathematics development depend on different constellations of numerical versus general cognitive abilities? *Developmental Psychology, 46,* 1731–1746.

Garcia, N., Abbott, R., & Berninger, V. (2010). Predicting poor, average, and superior spellers in grades 1 to 6 from phonological, orthographic, and morphological, spelling, or reading composites. *Written Language and Literacy, 13,* 61–99.

Gates, A. (1947). *The improvement of reading* (3rd ed.). New York, NY: Macmillan.

Geary, D. (1994). *Children's mathematical development: Research and practical applications.* Washington, DC: American Psychological Association.

Geary, D.C. (2010). Missouri longitudinal study of mathematical development and disability. In R. Cowan, M. Saxton, & A. Tolmie (Eds.), *Understanding number development and number difficulties.* Leicester, UK: British Psychological Society.

Geary, D.C., Hoard, M.K., & Bailey, D.H. (2012). Fact retrieval deficits in low achieving children and children with mathematical learning disability. *Journal of Learning Disabilities, 45,* 291–307.

Geary, D.C., Hoard, M.K., & Byrd-Craven, J. (2004). Strategy choices in simple and complex addition: Contributions of working memory and counting knowledge for children with mathematical disability. *Journal of Experimental Child Psychology, 88,* 121–151.

Geary, D.C., Hoard, M.K., Nugent, L., & Byrd-Craven, J. (2008). Development of number line representations in children with mathematical learning disability. *Developmental Neuropsychology, 33,* 277–299.

Gilger, J., & Wilkins, M. (2008). Atypical neurodevelopmental variation as basis for learning disorders. In M. Mody & E. Silliman (Eds.), *Language impairment and reading disability: Interactions among brain, behavior, and experience* (pp. 7–40). New York, NY: Guilford Press.

Gillingham, A., & Stillman, B. (1956). *Remedial training for children with specific disability in reading, spelling, and penmanship.* Cambridge, MA: Educators Publishing Service.

Goldberg, R., Higgins, E., Raskind, M., & Herman, K. (2003). Predictors of success in individuals with learning disabilities: A qualitative analysis of a 20-year longitudinal study. *Learning Disabilities Research & Practice, 18,* 222–236.

Goldstein, B., Waugh, J., & Linksky, K. (2004). *Grammar to go: How it works and how to use it.* Boston, MA: Houghton Mifflin.

Graham, S. (1997). Executive control in the revising of students with learning and writing difficulties. *Journal of Educational Psychology, 89,* 223–234.

Graham, S., Berninger, V.W., Abbott, R., Abbott, S., & Whitaker, D. (1997). The role of mechanics in composing of elementary school students: A new methodological approach. *Journal of Educational Psychology, 89*(1), 170–182.

Graham, S., Berninger, V.W., & Weintraub, N. (1998). But they use both manuscript and cursive letters—A study of the relationship of handwriting style with speed and quality. *Journal of Educational Psychology, 91,* 290–296.

Graham, S., & Harris, K.R. (1994). Implications of constructivism for teaching writing to students with special needs. *Journal of Special Education, 28,* 275–289.

Graham, S., & Harris, K.R. (2005). *Writing better: Effective strategies for teaching students with learning difficulties.* Baltimore, MD: Paul H. Brookes Publishing Co.

Graham, S., Harris, K.R., & Fink, B. (2000). Is handwriting causally related to learning to write? Treatment of handwriting problems in beginning writers. *Journal of Educational Psychology, 92,* 620–633.

Graham, S., Harris, K.R., & Loynachan, C. (1994). The spelling for writing list. *Journal of Learning Disabilities, 27,* 210–214.

Graham, S., & Perin, D. (2007a). A meta-analysis of writing instruction for adolescent students. *Journal of Educational Psychology, 99,* 445–476.

Graham, S., & Perin, D. (2007b). *Writing next: Effective strategies to improve writing of adolescents in middle and high schools—A report to Carnegie Corporation of New York.* Washington, DC: Alliance for Excellent Education.

Graham, S., & Weintraub, N. (1996). A review of handwriting research: Progress and prospects from 1980 to 1994. *Educational Psychology Review, 8,* 7–87.

Gray, W. (1956). *The teaching of reading and writing.* Chicago, IL: Scott Foresman.

Greene, J. & Coxhead, A. (2015). *Academic vocabulary for middle school students: Research-based lists and strategies for key content areas,* Baltimore, MD: Paul H. Brookes Publishing Co.

Greene, L.C. (1996). Jose Valdes Summer Math Institute. *Phi Delta Kappan, 77*(10), 692–693.

Grigorenko, E., Wood, F., Meyer, M., Pauls, J., Hart, A., & Pauls, D. (2001). Linkage studies suggest a possible locus for developmental dyslexia on chromosomes 6 and 15. *American Journal of Human Genetics, 105,* 120–129.

Gutiérrez, R. (1996). Practices, beliefs and cultures of high school mathematics departments: Understanding their influence on student advancement. *Journal of Curriculum Studies, 28,* 495–529.

Gutiérrez, R. (1999). Advancing urban Latina/o youth in mathematics: Lessons from an effective high school mathematics department. *Urban Review, 31*(3), 263–281.

Hall, S., & Moats, L. (2001). *Straight talk about reading and helping the struggling reader.* Chicago, IL: Contemporary Books.

Hammill, D., Widerholt, J., & Allen, E. (2006). *Test of Silent Contextual Reading Fluency (TOSCRF).* Austin, TX: PRO-ED.

Hart, T., Berninger, V.W., & Abbott, R. (1997). Comparison of teaching single or multiple orthographic-phonological connections for word recognition and spelling: Implications for instructional consultation. *School Psychology Review, 26,* 279–297.

Hayes, J.R., & Berninger, V. (2010). Relationships between idea generation and transcription: How act of writing shapes what children write. In C. Brazerman, R. Krut, K. Lunsford, S. McLeod, S. Null, P. Rogers, & A. Stansell (Eds.), *Traditions of Writing Research* (pp. 166–180). New York, NY: Taylor & Francis.

Hayes, J.R., & Flowers, L. (1980). Identifying the organization of the writing process. In L.W. Gregg & E.R. Sternberg (Eds.), *Cognitive processes in writing* (pp. 3–30). Mahwah, NJ: Lawrence Erlbaum Associates.

Haynes C., & Jennings, T. (2006). Listening and speaking: Essential ingredients for teaching struggling writers. *Perspectives, 32*(2), 12–16.

Heiligman, D. (author), & Pham, L. (illustrator). (2013). *The boy who loved math: The improbable life of Paul Erdős.* New York, NY: Roaring Brook.

Hellman, L., & Feibleman, P. (1984). *Eating together: Recipes and recollections.* Boston, MA: Little, Brown.

Henderson, S., Sugden, D., & Barnett, A. (2007). *Movement assessment battery for children* (2nd ed.). London, United Kingdom: Pearson.

Henry, M.K. (1988). Beyond phonics: Integrated decoding and spelling instruction based on word origin and structure. *Annals of Dyslexia, 38,* 259–275.

Henry, M.K. (1989). Children's word structure knowledge: Implications for decoding and spelling instruction. *Reading and Writing: An Interdisciplinary Journal, 2,* 135–152.

Henry, M. (1990). *Words: Integrated decoding and spelling instruction based on word origin and word structure.* Austin, TX: PRO-ED.

Henry, M.K. (1993). Morphological structure: Latin and Greek roots and affixes as upper grade code strategies. *Reading and Writing: An Interdisciplinary Journal, 5,* 227–241.

Henry, M. (1999). *Dyslexia: Samuel T. Orton and his legacy.* Baltimore, MD: International Dyslexia Association.

Henry, M.K. (2003). *Unlocking literacy: Effective decoding and spelling instruction.* Baltimore, MD: Paul H. Brookes Publishing Co.

Henry, M. (2005). *Framework for informed reading and language instruction.* Baltimore, MD: International Dyslexia Association.

Henry, M.K. (2010). *Unlocking literacy: Effective decoding and spelling instruction* (2nd ed.). Baltimore, MD: Paul H. Brookes Publishing Co.

Henry, M.K., & Redding, N.C. (1996). *Patterns for success in reading and spelling: A multisensory approach to teaching phonics and word analysis.* Austin, TX: PRO-ED.

Hidi, S., & Boscolo, P. (Eds.). (2006). *Motivation in writing.* Amsterdam, Netherlands: Elsevier.

Hiebert, E.H. (2003). *Quick reads.* Parsippany, NJ: Pearson Learning.

Hinsley, D., Hayes, J., & Simon, H. (1977). From words to equations: Meaning and representation in algebra word problems. In M. Just & P. Carpenter (Eds.). *Cognitive processes in comprehension* (pp. 89–106). Hillsdale, NJ: Lawrence Erlbaum Associates.

Hoard, M.K., Geary, D.C., Byrd-Craven, J., & Nugent, L. (2008). Mathematical cognition in intellectually precocious children. *Developmental Neuropsychology, 33,* 251–276.

Hodkinson, K., & Adams, S. (2000). *Wordly wise 3000: Systematic, sequential vocabulary development.* Cambridge, MA: Educators Publishing Service.

Hoffman, P. (1998). *The man who loved only numbers: The story of Paul Erdős and the search for mathematical truth.* New York, NY: Hyperion.

Honig, B. (1996). *How should we teach our children to read?* Thousand Oaks, CA: Corwin Press.

Hooper, S., Knuth, S., Yerby, D., Anderson, K., & Moore, C. (2009). Review of science supported writing instruction with implementation in mind. In S. Rosenfield & V.W. Berninger (Eds.), *Handbook on implementing evidence-based academic interventions.* New York, NY: Oxford University Press.

Hooper, S.R., Swartz, C.W., Wakely, M.B., de Kruif, R.E.L., & Montgomery, J.W. (2002). Executive functions in elementary school children with and without problems in written expression. *Journal of Learning Disabilities, 35,* 37–68.

Hooper, S.R., Wakely, M.B., de Kruif, R.E.L., & Swartz, C.W. (2006). Aptitude-treatment interactions revisited: Effect of metacognitive intervention on subtypes of written expression in elementary school students. *Developmental Neuropsychology, 29,* 217–241.

Hsu, L., Wijsman, E., Berninger, V.W., Thomson, J., & Raskind, W. (2002). Familial aggregation of dyslexia phenotypes: Paired correlated measures. *American Journal of Medical Genetics/Neuropsychiatric Genetics, 114,* 471–478.

Huey, E.B. (1968). *The psychology and pedagogy of reading.* Cambridge, MA: MIT Press. (Original work published 1908)

Igo, R., Chapman, N., Berninger, V.W., Matsushita, M., Brkanac, Z., Rothstein, J., et al. (2006). Genomewide scan for real-word reading subphenotypes of dyslexia: Novel chromosome 13 locus and genetic complexity. *American Journal of Medical Genetics/Neuropsychiatric Genetics, 141B,* 15–27.

Individuals with Disabilities Education Improvement Act (IDEA) of 2004, PL 108-446, 20 U.S.C. §§ 1400 *et seq.*

James, K., & Atwood, T. (2009). The role of sensorimotor learning in the perception of letter-like forms: Tracking the causes of neural specialization for letters. *Cognitive Neuropsychology, 26,* 91–110.

Jansky, J., & de Hirsch, K. (1966). *Predicting reading failure.* New York, NY: Harper Row.

Jansky, J., & de Hirsch, K. (1972). *Preventing reading failure,* New York, NY: Harper.

Johnson, D. (1991). Written language. In J. Kavanagh (Ed.), *The language continuum from infancy to literacy* (pp. 147–165). Timonium, MD: York Press.

Johnson, D. (2006). *Geschwind lecture.* Baltimore, MD: International Dyslexia Association.

Johnson, D., & Myklebust, H. (1967). *Learning disabilities.* New York, NY: Grune & Stratton.

Jones, D. (2004). *Automaticity of the transcription process in the production of written text* (Unpublished doctoral dissertation). Graduate School of Education, University of Queensland, Australia.

Jordan, N., Hanich, L., & Kaplan, D. (2003). A longitudinal study of mathematical competencies in children with specific mathematics difficulties versus children with co-morbid mathematics and reading difficulties. *Child Development, 74,* 834–850.

Joshi, R.M., Binks, E., Hougen, M., Dean, E., Graham, L., & Smith, D. (2009). The role of teacher education programs in preparing teachers for implementing evidence-based reading practices. In S. Rosenfield & V.W. Berninger (Eds.), *Handbook on implementing evidence-based academic interventions* (pp. 605–625). New York, NY: Oxford University Press.

Juarez, B., Parks, S., & Black, H. (2000). *Learning on purpose: A self-management approach to study skills.* North Bend, OR: Critical Thinking Co.

Juel, C. (1994). *Learning to read and write in one elementary school.* New York, NY: Springer Verlag.

Julnes, R.E., & Brown, S.E. (1993). Assistive technology and special education programs: Legal mandates and practice implications. *West Education Law Reporter, 82,* 737–748.

Katusic, S., Barbaresi, W., Colligan, R., Weaver, A., Leibson, C., & Jacobsen, S. (2005). Case definition in epidemiologic studies of AD/HD. *Annals Epidemiology, 15,* 430–437.

Kaufman, A., & Kaufman, N. (2012). *Kaufman Test of Educational Achievement, Third Edition (KTEA-3).* San Antonio, TX: Pearson.

Kaufman, L. (1995, November). *Phonological awareness training and Orton-Gillingham.* Presented at the meeting of the International Dyslexia Association, Houston, TX.

Kerns, K.A., Eso, K., & Thomson, J. (1999). Investigation of a direct intervention for improving attention in young children. *Developmental Neuropsychology, 16*(2), 273–295.

King, D. (2005). *Keyboarding skills* (Rev. ed.). Cambridge, MA: Educators Publishing Service.

Kirk, S., & Kirk, D. (1971). *Psycholinguistic learning disabilities: Diagnosis and remediation.* Chicago, IL: University of Chicago Press.

Kovas, Y., Haworth, C., Dale, P., & Plomin, R. (2007). The genetic and environmental origins of learning abilities and disabilities in the early school years. *Monographs of the Society for Research in Child Development, 72*(3).

Lefly, D., & Pennington, B. (1991). Spelling errors and reading fluency in dyslexics. *Annals of Dyslexia. 41,* 143–162.

Leslie, L., & Caldwell, J. (2011). *Qualitative Reading Inventory -5 (QRI-5).* Boston, MA: Pearson.

Levine, M. (1987). *Developmental variation and learning disorders.* Cambridge, MA: Educators Publishing Service.

Levine, M. (1990). *Keeping a head in school: A student's book about learning abilities and learning disorders.* Cambridge, MA: Educators Publishing Service.

Levy, B., Abello, B., & Lysynchuk, L. (1997). Transfer from word training to reading in context: Gains in reading fluency and comprehension. *Learning Disability Quarterly, 20,* 173–188.

Liberman, A. (1999). The reading researcher and the reading teacher need the right theory of speech. *Scientific Studies of Reading, 3,* 95–111.

Liberman, I., Shankweiler, D., Fischer, F., & Carter, B. (1974). Explicit syllable and phoneme segmentation in the young child. *Journal of Experimental Child Psychology, 18,* 201–212.

Logan, R. (1986). *The alphabet effect.* New York, NY: William Morrow and Company.

Lovett, M. (1987). A developmental perspective on reading dysfunction: Accuracy and speed criteria of normal and deficient reading skill. *Child Development, 58,* 234–260.

Lubliner, S. (2005). *Getting into words: Vocabulary instruction that strengthens comprehension.* Baltimore, MD: Paul H. Brookes Publishing Co.

Luria, A.R. (1973). *The working brain.* New York, NY: Basic Books.

Lyon, G.R., & Krasnegor, N.A. (Eds.). (1996). *Attention, memory, and executive function.* Baltimore, MD: Paul H. Brookes Publishing Co.

Lyytinen, H., Aro, M., Elklund, K., Erskine, J., Gottorm, T., Laakso, M.-L., et al. (2004). The development of children at familial risk for dyslexia: Birth to early school age. *Annals of Dyslexia, 54,* 184–220.

Ma, X. (1999). A meta-analysis of the relationship between anxiety toward mathematics and achievement in mathematics. *Journal for Research in Mathematics Education, 30,* 520–540.

MacArthur, C.A. (2000). New tools for writing: Assistive technology for students with writing difficulties. *Topics in Language Disorders, 20,* 85–100.

MacArthur, C.A. (2006). Assistive technology for writing: Tools for struggling writers. In L.V. Waes, M. Leijten, & C. Neuwirth (Eds.), *Writing and digital media* (pp. 11–20). Amsterdam, Netherlands: Kluwer.

MacArthur, C.A. (2008). Using technology to teach composing to struggling writers. In G. Troia (Ed.), *Writing instruction and assessment for struggling writers: From theory to evidence-based practices* (pp. 243–265). New York, NY: Guilford Press.

MacArthur, C.A. (2009). Technology and struggling writers: A review of research. *Teaching and Learning Writing: Psychological Aspects of Education—Current Trends: British Journal of Educational Psychology Monograph Series II, 6,* 159–174.

MacArthur, C.A., & Cavalier, A. (2004). Dictation and speech recognition technology as accommodations in large-scale assessments for students with learning disabilities. *Exceptional Children, 71,* 43–58.

MacArthur, C.A., Ferretti, R. P., Okolo, C. M., Cavalier, A. R. (2001). Technology applications for students with literacy problems: A critical review. *Elementary School Journal, 101,* 273–301.

Mace, R. (2010). *Center for universal design.* Retrieved from http://www.ncsu.edu/project /design-projects/udi/center-for-universal-design/ron-mace

MacGinitie, W., MacGinitie, R., Maria, K., Dreyer, L., & Hughes, K. (2000, norms updated 2006). *Gates-MacGinitie Reading Tests (GMRT), Fourth Edition.* Rolling Meadows, IL: Riverside.

Masland, R. (1979). Subgroups in dyslexia. Issues of definition. *Bulletin of the Orton Society: Current Issues in Dyslexia.* Towson, MD: The Orton Society.

Masterson, J., Apel, K., & Wasowicz, J. (2006). *Spelling Performance Evaluation for Language and Literacy (SPELL 2).* Evanston, IL: Learning by Design.

Mather, N., Hammill, D., Allen, E., & Roberts, R. (2004). *Test of Silent Word Reading Fluency (TOSWRF).* Austin, TX: PRO-ED.

Mather, N., Roberts, R., Hammill, D., & Allen, E. (2008). *Test of Orthographic Competence (TOC).* Austin, TX: PRO-ED.

Mattingly, I. (1972). Reading, the linguistic process, and linguistic awareness. In J. Kavanagh & I. Mattingly (Eds.), *Language by ear and by eye: The relationships between speech and reading* (pp. 133–147). Cambridge, MA: MIT Press.

Mayer, R. (2005). Should there be a three-strikes rule against pure discovery learning? *American Psychologist, 59,* 14–19.

Mayer, R.E. (2009). *Multimedia learning* (2nd ed.). New York, NY: Cambridge University Press.

Mazzocco, M., & Devlin, K. (2008). Parts and "holes": Gaps in rational number sense among children with vs without mathematical learning disabilities. *Developmental Science, 11,* 681–691.

Mazzocco, M., Feigenson, L., & Halberda, J. (2001). Impaired acuity of the approximate number system underlies mathematical learning disability (dyscalculia). *Child Development, 82,* 1224–1237.

McGregor, K.K. (2004). Developmental dependencies between lexical semantics and reading. In C.A. Stone, E. Silliman, B. Ehren, & K. Apel (Eds.), *Handbook of language literacy: Development and disorders* (pp. 302–317). New York, NY: Guilford Press.

Mesulam, M. (1990). Large-scale neurocognitive networks and distributed processing for attention, language, and memory. *Annals of Neurology, 28,* 597–613.

Meyer, M., & Felton, R. (1999). Repeated reading to enhance fluency: Old approaches and new directions. *Annals of Dyslexia, 49,* 283–306.

Meyer, M.L., Salimpoor, V.N., Wu, S.S., Geary, D.C., & Menon, V. (2010). Differential contribution of specific working memory components to mathematical skills in 2nd and 3rd graders. *Learning and Individual Differences, 20,* 101–109.

Midgley, C., Feldlaufer, H., & Eccles, J.S. (1989). Change in teacher efficacy and student self- and task-related beliefs in mathematics during the transition to junior high school. *Journal of Educational Psychology, 81*(2), 247–258.

Moats, L.C. (2000). *Speech to print: Language essentials for teachers.* Baltimore, MD: Paul H. Brookes Publishing Co.

Monroe, M. (1936). *Reading aptitude tests.* New York, NY: Houghton Mifflin.

Morris, R., Stuebing, K., Fletcher, J., Shaywitz, S., Lyon, G.R., Shakweiler, D., et al. (1998). Subtypes of reading disability: Variability around a phonological core. *Journal of Educational Psychology, 90,* 347–373.

Nagy, W. (2007). Metalinguistic awareness and the vocabulary-comprehension connection. In R.K. Wagner, A. Muse, & K. Tannenbaum (Eds.), *Vocabulary acquisition and its implications for reading comprehension* (pp. 52–77). New York, NY: Guilford Press.

Nagy, W., & Anderson, R.C. (1999). Metalinguistic awareness and literacy acquisition in different languages. In D. Wagner, B. Street, & R. Venezky (Eds.), *Literacy: An international handbook* (pp. 155–160). New York, NY: Garland Publishing.

Nagy, W., Berninger, V.W., Abbott, R., Vaughan, K., & Vermeulen, K. (2003). Relationship of morphology and other language skills to literacy skills in at-risk second graders and at-risk fourth grade writers. *Journal of Educational Psychology, 95,* 730–742.

Nagy, W., Osborn, J., Winsor, P., & O'Flahavan, J. (1994). Structural analysis: Some guidelines for instruction. In F. Lehr & J. Osborn (Eds.), *Reading, language, and literacy* (pp. 45–58). Mahwah, NJ: Lawrence Erlbaum Associates.

Nation, K., & Snowling, M. (2004). Beyond phonological skills: Broader language skills contribute to the development of reading. *Journal of Research in Reading, 27,* 342–356.

National Institute of Child Health and Human Development. (2000). Report of the National Reading Panel. *Teaching children to read: An evidence-based assessment of the scientific research literature on reading and its implications for reading instruction—Reports of the subgroups* (NIH Publication No. 00-4754). Washington, DC: U.S. Government Printing Office.

National Mathematics Advisory Panel. (2008). *Foundations for success: Final report of the National Mathematics Advisory Panel.* Washington, DC: U.S. Department of Education.

Nelson, N.W., Bahr, C., & Van Meter, A. (2004). *The writing lab approach to language instruction and intervention.* Baltimore, MD: Paul H. Brookes Publishing Co.

Nelson, N.W., Plante, E., Helm-Estabrooks, N., & Hotz, G. (2016). *Test of Integrated Language and Literacy Skills™ (TILLS™).* Baltimore, MD: Paul H. Brookes Publishing Co.

Neuhaus, G. (2002). What does it take to read a letter? *Perspectives, 28*(1), 6–8.

Niedo, J., Lee, Y.L., Breznitz, Z., & Berninger, V. (2014). Computerized silent reading rate and strategy instruction for fourth graders at risk in silent reading rate. *Learning Disability Quarterly, 37*(2), 100–110. doi: 10.1177/0731948713507263. NIHMSID 526584.

Nunes, T., & Bryant, P.E. (1996). Children doing mathematics. Oxford, England: Basil Blackwell.

Nunes, T., & Bryant, P. (2006). *Improving literacy by teaching morphemes (Improving Learning Series).* New York, NY: Routledge.

Nussbaum, E.M. (2002). Appropriate appropriation: Functionality of student arguments and support requests during small-group classroom discussions. *Journal of Literacy Research, 34,* 501–544.

Oliphant, G. (1976). The lens of language. *Bulletin of the Orton Society,* 49–62.

Olson, R., Wise, B., Connors, F., Rack, J., & Fulker, D. (1989). Specific deficits in component reading and language skills: Genetic and environmental influences. *Journal of Learning Disabilities, 22,* 339–348.

Opitz, M., & Zbarachki, M. (2004). *Listen hear! 25 effective listening comprehension strategies.* Portsmouth, NH: Heinemann.

Orton, S. (1989). *Reading, writing, and speech problems in children and selected papers.* Austin, TX: PRO-ED. (Original work published 1937)

Pacton, S., Fayol, M., & Perruchet, P. (2005). Children's implicit learning of graphotactic and morphological regularities. *Child Development, 76,* 324–329.

Pacton, S., Perruchet, P., Fayol, M., & Cleeremans, A. (2001). Implicit learning in real world context: The case of orthographic regularities. *Journal of Experimental Psychology: General, 130,* 401–426.

Peverly, S.T. (2006). The importance of handwriting speed in adult writing. *Developmental Neuropsychology, 29,* 197–216.

Peverly, S.T., Ramaswamy, V., Brown, C., Sumowski, J., Alidoost, M., & Garner, J. (2007). Skill in lecture note-taking: What predicts? *Journal of Educational Psychology, 99,* 167–180.

Phelps, J., & Stempel, L. (1987). *CHES's Handwriting Improvement Program (CHIP).* Dallas, TX: Children's Handwriting Evaluation Scale.

Phelps-Terasaki, D. & Phelps-Gunn, T. (2007). *Test of Pragmatic Language, Second Edition (TOPL-2).* Austin, TX: PRO-ED.

Piaget, J. (1952). *The origins of intelligence in children.* New York, NY: International Universities Press.

Posner, M., Petersen, S., Fox, P., & Raichle, M. (1988). Localization of cognitive operations in the human brain. *Science, 240,* 1627–1631.

Posner, P., & Rothbart, M. (2007). *Educating the human brain.* Washington, DC: American Psychological Association.

Prescott-Griffin, M., & Witherell, N. (2004). *Fluency in focus: Comprehension strategies for all young readers.* Portsmouth, NH: Heinemann.

Pugh, K., Shaywitz, B., Shaywitz, S., Constable, T., Skudlarski, P., Fullbright, R., et al. (1996). Cerebral organization of component processes in reading. *Brain, 119,* 1221–1238.

Rack, J., Snowling, M., & Olson, R. (1992). The nonword reading deficit in developmental dyslexia: A review. *Reading Research Quarterly, 27,* 28–53.

Raskind, M., Goldberg, R., Higgins, E., & Herman, K. (1999). Patterns of change and predictors of success in individuals with learning disabilities: Results from a twenty-year longitudinal study. *Learning Disabilities Research and Practice, 14,* 35–49.

Raskind, W., Hsu, L., Thomson, J., Berninger, V.W., & Wijsman, E. (2000). Familial aggregation of phenotypic subtypes in dyslexia. *Behavior Genetics, 30,* 385–396.

Raskind, W., Igo, R., Chapman, N., Berninger, V.W., Thomson, J., Matsushita, M., et al. (2005). A genome scan in multigenerational families with dyslexia: Identification of a novel locus on chromosome 2q that contributes to phonological decoding efficiency. *Molecular Psychiatry, 10*(7), 699–711.

Raskind, W., Peters, B., Richards, T., Eckert, M., & Berninger, V. (2012). The genetics of reading disabilities: From phenotype to candidate genes. *Frontiers in Psychology, 3,* 601. Published online 2013 January 7. doi: 10.3389/fpsyg.2012.00601. PMCID: PMC3538356.

Rawson, M. (1973). Semantics—diagnostic categories: Their use and misuse. *Bulletin of the Orton Society,* 143–144.

Read Naturally. (2006). *Read Naturally Masters Edition.* Saint Paul, MN: Author.

Reznitskaya, A., Anderson, R., McNurlen, B., Nguyen-Jahiel, K., Archodidou, A., & Kim, S. (2001). Influence of oral discussion on written argument. *Discourse Processes, 32,* 155–175.

Rice, J.M. (1897). The futility of the spelling grind. *Forum, 23,* 163–172, 409–419.

Richards, T., Aylward, E., Raskind, W., Abbott, R., Field, K., Parsons, A., et al. (2006). Converging evidence for triple word form theory in child dyslexics. *Developmental Neuropsychology, 30,* 547–589.

Richards, T., Berninger, V., Aylward, E., Richards, A., Thomson, J., Nagy, W., Carlisle, J., Dager, S., & Abbott, R. (2002). Reproducibility of proton MR spectroscopic imaging (PEPSI): Comparison of dyslexic and normal reading children and effects of treatment on brain lactate levels during language tasks. *American Journal of Neuroradiology. 23,* 1678–1685.

Richards, T., Berninger, V.W., Nagy, W., Parsons, A., Field, K., & Richards, A. (2005). Dynamic assessment of child dyslexics' brain response to alternative spelling treatments. *Educational and Child Psychology, 22*(2), 62–80.

Richards, T., Berninger, V.W., Winn, W., Stock, P., Wagner, R., Muse, A., et al. (2007). fMRI activation in children with dyslexia during pseudoword aural repeat and visual decode: Before and after instruction. *Neuropsychology, 21,* 732–747.

Richards, T., Corina, D., Serafini, S., Steury, K., Dager, S., Marro, K., Abbott, R., Maravilla, K., & Berninger, V. (2000). Effects of phonologically-driven treatment for dyslexia on lactate levels as measured by proton MRSI. *American Journal of Neuroradiology, 21,* 916–922.

Richardson, S. (1989). Specific developmental dyslexia: Retrospective and prospective views. *Annals of Dyslexia, 39,* 3–24.

Rivera, S., Reiss, A., Eckert, M., & Menon, V. (2005). Developmental changes in mental arithmetic: Evidence for increased functional specialization in the left inferior parietal cortex. *Cerebral Cortex, 15,* 1779–1790.

Robinson, N., Abbott, R., Berninger, V., & Busse, J. (1996). Structure of precocious mathematical abilities: Gender similarities and differences. *Journal of Educational Psychology, 88,* 341–352.

Robinson, N., Abbott, R., Berninger, V., Busse, J., & Mukhopadhyay, S. (1997). Developmental changes in mathematically precocious young children: Longitudinal and gender effects. *Gifted Child Quarterly, 41,* 145–158.

Roeske, D., Ludwig, K.U., Neuhoff, N., Becker, J., Bartling, J., Bruder, J., et al. (2011). First genome-wide association scan on neurophysiological 1729 endophenotypes points to trans-regulation effects on SLC2A3 in dyslexic children. *Molecular Psychiatry, 16,* 97–107.

Rosenberg-Lee, M., Chang, T., Young, C., Wu, S., & Menon, V. (2011). Functional dissociations between four basic arithmetic operations in the human posterior parietal cortex: A cytoarchitectonic mapping study. *Neuropsychologia, 49,* 2592–2608.

Rubel, B. (1995). *Big strokes for little folks.* Tucson, AZ: Therapy Skill Builders.

Samuels, S. (1985). Automaticity and repeated reading. In J. Osborn, P. Wilson, & R. Anderson (Eds.), *Reading education: Foundations for a literate America* (pp. 215–230). Lexington, MA: Lexington Books.

Samuelsson, S., Byrne, B., Olson, R., Hulslander, J., Wadsworth, S., Corley, R., et al. (2008). Response to early literacy instruction in the United States, Australia, and Scandinavia: A behavioral-genetic analysis. *Learning and Individual Differences, 18,* 289–295.

Sanderson, C. (1985). *Hands on phonics, book I.* Edmonds, WA: CLS Enterprises.

Sanderson, C. (1988). *Hands on phonics, book II.* Edmonds, WA: CLS Enterprises.

Sawyer, D., & Knight, D. (1997, Spring). Tennessee meets the challenge of dyslexia. *Perspectives.* Towson, MD: International Dyslexia Association.

Scarborough, H.S. (2005). Developmental relationships between language and reading: Reconciling a beautiful hypothesis with some ugly facts. In H.W. Catts & A.G. Kamhi (Eds.), *The connections between language and reading abilities* (pp. 3–24). Mahwah, NJ: Lawrence Erlbaum Associates.

Schneider, W., & Chein, J. (2003). Controlled & automatic processing: Behavior, theory, and biological mechanisms. *Cognitive Science, 27,* 525–559.

Schneider, W., & Shiffrin, R.M. (1977). Controlled and automatic human information processing: 1. Detection, search, and attention. *Psychological Review, 84,* 1–66.

Schulte-Korne, G., Grimm, T., Nothen, M.M., Muller-Myhsok, B., Cichon, S., Vogt, I.R., et al. (1998). Evidence for linkage of spelling disability to chromosome 15. *American Journal of Human Genetics, 63,* 279–282.

Science. (2010, October 29). Epigenetics [special issue] *Science, 330.*

Scott, C. (2004). Syntactic contributions to literacy learning. In C.A. Stone, E.R. Silliman, B.J. Ehren, & K. Apel (Eds.), *Handbook of language and literacy: Development and disorders* (pp. 340–362). New York, NY: Guilford Press.

Scott, C., & Winsor, J. (2000). General language performance measures in spoken and written narrative and expository discourse of school-age children with language learning disabilities. *Journal of Speech, Language, and Hearing Research, 43,* 324–333.

Seeger, P. (1998). *Trouble at the bottom.* Beverly Hills, CA: Sanga Music.

Share, D.L. (2008). Orthographic learning, phonology, and the self-teaching hypothesis. In R.V. Kail (Ed.), *Advances in child development and behavior* (Vol. 36, pp. 31–82). Amsterdam, Netherlands: Elsevier.

Shiffrin, R., & Schneider, W. (1977). Controlled and automatic human information processing II: Perceptual learning, automatic attending, and a general theory. *Psychological Review, 84,* 127–190.

Shurtleff, H., Faye, G., Abbott, R., & Berninger, V. (1988). Neuropsychological and cognitive correlates of academic skills: A levels of analysis assessment model. *Journal of Psychoeducational Assessment, 6,* 298–308.

Sian, B., Gunderson, E., Ramirez, G., & Levine, S. (2010). Female teachers' math anxiety affects girls' math achievement. *Proceedings of the National Academy of Science, 107,* 1860–1863.

Siegel, L. (1994). Working memory and reading: A life span perspective. *International Journal of Behavioral Development, 17,* 109–124.

Siegler, R.S., & Lortie Forgues, H. (2014). An integrative theory of numerical development. *Child Development Perspectives, 8,* 144–150.

Siegler, R.S., & Ramani, G. (2011). Improving low-income children's number sense. In S. Dehaene & E. Brannon (Eds.), *Space, time, and number in the brain: Searching for the foundations of mathematical thought* (pp. 343–354). New York, NY: Oxford University Press.

Silliman, E., & Berninger, V. (2011). Cross-disciplinary dialogue about the nature of oral and written language problems in the context of developmental, academic, and phenotypic profiles. *Topics in Language Disorders, 31,* 6–23. Available at http://journals.lww.com/topicsinlanguagedisorders/Fulltext/2011/01000/Cross_Disciplinary_Dialogue_about_the_Nature_of.3.aspx

Silliman, E., & Scott, C. (2009). Research-based oral language intervention routes to the academic language of literacy: Finding the right road. In S. Rosenfield & V. Berninger (Eds.), *Implementing evidence-based academic interventions in school settings* (pp. 107–145). New York, NY: Oxford University Press.

Slavica, K., Colligan, R., Barbaresi, W., Schaid, D., & Jacobsen, S. (2001). Incidence of reading disability in a population-based birth cohort, 1976–1982, Rochester, Minn. *Mayo Clinic Proceedings, 76,* 1081–1092.

Slavica, K., Colligan, R., Katusic, S., Colligan, R., Weaver, A., & Barbaresi, W. (2009). The forgotten learning disability: Epidemiology of written-language disorder in a population-based birth cohort (1976-1982), Rochester, Minnesota. *Pediatrics, 123,* 1306–1313.

Slavin, R. (1987, Autumn). Ability grouping and student achievement in elementary schools: A best-evidence synthesis. *Review of Educational Research, 57,* 293–336.

Slingerland, B. (1967). *Training in some prerequisites for beginning reading.* Cambridge, MA: Educators Publishing Service.

Slingerland, B. (1971). *A multisensory approach to language arts for specific language disability children: A guide for primary teachers.* Cambridge, MA: Educators Publishing Service.

Slingerland, B. (1976). *Basics in scope and sequence of a multisensory approach to language arts for specific language disability children.* Cambridge, MA: Educators Publishing Service.

Slingerland, B. (1980). Unpublished personal papers.

Slingerland, B. (1997). *Prereading screening procedures to identify first grade academic needs,* Cambridge, MA: Educators Publishing Service.

Slingerland, B. (2005). *Slingerland® screening tests for identifying children with specific language disability.* Cambridge, MA: Educators Publishing Service.

Slingerland, B. (2013). *The Slingerland® Multisensory Approach: A practical guide for teaching reading, writing, and spelling* (2nd ed.). Bellevue, WA: The Slingerland® Institute.

Slingerland, B. (2014a). *Cursive writing instructional packet.* Bellevue, WA: The Slingerland® Institute for Literacy.

Slingerland, B. (2014b). *Manuscript writing instructional packet.* Bellevue, WA: The Slingerland® Institute for Literacy.

Slingerland, B., & Murray, C. (2008). *Revised teacher word lists for reference.* Bellevue, WA: The Slingerland® Institute for Literacy.

Snowling, M.J., & Hayiou-Thomas, M.E. (2006). The dyslexia spectrum: Continuities between reading, speech, and language impairments. *Topics in Language Disorders, 26*(2), 110–126.

Spector, C. (2009). *As far as words go: Activities for understanding ambiguous language and humor* (Rev. ed.). Baltimore, MD: Paul H. Brookes Publishing Co.

Stahl, S., & Nagy, W. (2005). *Teaching word meaning.* Mahwah, NJ: Lawrence Erlbaum Associates.

Stanovich, K.E., & Siegel, L.S. (1994). Phenotypic performance profile of children with reading disabilities: A regression-based test of the phonological-core variable-difference model. *Journal of Educational Psychology, 86,* 24–53.

Steffler, D., Varnhagen, C., Friesen, C., & Treiman, R. (1998). There's more to children's spelling than the errors they make: Strategic and automatic processes for one-syllable words. *Journal of Educational Psychology, 90,* 492–505.

Steinbeck, J. (1976). *The acts of king Arthur and his noble knights.* New York, NY: Farrar, Straus and Giroux.

Stoecke, R., Colligan, R., Barbaresi, W., Weaver, A., Killian J.M., & Katusic, S. (2013). Early speech-language impairment and risk for written language disorder: a population-based study. *Journal Developmental and Behavioral Pediatrics, 34,* 38–44.

Swanson, H.L. (1999). Reading comprehension and working memory in learning disabled readers: Is the phonological loop more important than the executive system? *Journal of Experimental Child Psychology, 72,* 1–31.

Swanson, H.L. (2006). Working memory and reading disabilities: Both phonological and executive processing deficits are important. In T. Alloway & S. Gathercole (Eds.), *Working memory and neurodevelopmental conditions* (pp. 59–88). London, United Kingdom: Psychology Press.

Swanson, H.L. (2011, August 22). Working memory, attention, and mathematical problem solving: A longitudinal study of elementary school children. *Journal of Educational Psychology, 103*(4), 821–837.

Swanson, H.L. (2014). Does cognitive strategy training on word problems compensate for working memory capacity in children with math difficulties? *Journal of Educational Psychology, 106,* 831–848.

Swanson, H.L., & Ashbaker, M. (2000). Working memory, short-term memory, speech rate, word recognition, and reading comprehension in learning disabled readers: Does the executive system have a role? *Intelligence, 28,* 1–30.

Swanson, H.L., & Beebe-Frankenberger, M. (2004). The relationship between working memory and mathematical problem solving in children at risk and not at risk for serious math difficulties. *Journal of Educational Psychology, 96,* 471–491.

Swanson, H.L., Jerman, O., & Zheng, X. (2008). Growth in working memory and mathematic problem solving in children at risk and not at risk for serious math difficulties. *Journal of Educational Psychology, 100,* 343–379.

Swanson, H.L. & Sachse-Lee, C. (2001). Mathematical problem solving and working memory in children with learning disabilities: Both executive and phonological processes are important. *Journal of Experimental Child Psychology, 79,* 294–321.

Tanimoto, S., Thompson, R., Berninger, V., Nagy W., Abbott, R. (in press, April 26, 2015). Computerized writing and reading instruction for students in grades 4 to 9 with specific learning disabilities affecting written language. *Journal of Computer Assisted Learning.*

Templeton, S., & Bear, D. (1992). *Development of orthographic knowledge and the foundations of literacy: A memorial Feltschrift for Edmund Henderson.* Mahwah, NJ: Lawrence Erlbaum Associates.

Texas Scottish Rite Hospital for Children, Child Development Division. (1990). *Dyslexia training program developed in the Dyslexia Laboratory, Texas Scottish Rite Hospital* [Videotape]. Cambridge, MA: Educators Publishing Service.

Texas Scottish Rite Hospital for Children, Child Development Division. (1996). *Teaching cursive writing* [Brochure]. Dallas, TX: Author.

Thomson, J., Chenault, B., Abbott, R., Raskind, W., Richards, T., Aylward, E., et al. (2005). Converging evidence for attentional influences on the orthographic word form in child dyslexics. *Journal of Neurolinguistics, 18,* 93–126.

Tomblin, J.B., Zhang, X., Weiss, A., Catts, H., & Ellis Weismer, S. (2004). Dimensions of individual differences in communication skills among primary grade children. In M.L. Rice & S.F. Warren (Eds.), *Developmental language disorders* (pp. 53–76). Mahwah, NJ: Lawrence Erlbaum Associates.

Torgesen, J.K. (1996). *Phonological awareness: A critical factor in dyslexia.* Baltimore, MD: The International Dyslexia Association.

Torgesen, J.K. (2004). Learning disabilities: An historical and conceptual overview. In B. Wong (Ed.), *Learning about learning disabilities* (3rd ed., pp. 3–40). San Diego, CA: Academic Press.

Torgesen, J., Wagner, R., & Rashotte, C. (1999). *Test of Word Reading Efficiency, Second Edition (TOWRE 2).* Austin, TX: PRO-ED.

Torrance, E. (1963). *Education and the creative potential.* Minneapolis, MN: University of Minnesota Press.

Treiman, R. (1993). *Beginning to spell: A study of first grade children.* New York, NY: Oxford University Press.

Treiman, R., Kessler, B., Knewasser, S., Tincoff, R., & Bowman, M. (2000). English speakers' sensitivity to phonotactic patterns. In M.B. Broe & J.B. Pierrehumbert (Eds.), *Papers in laboratory phonology V: Acquisition and the lexicon* (pp. 269–282). Cambridge, UK: Cambridge University Press.

Troia, G.A. (Ed.) (2009). *Instruction and assessment for struggling writers. Evidence-based practices.* New York, NY: Guilford Press.

United Nations. (1959). *Declaration of the rights of the child.* Retrieved from http://www.humanium.org/en/childrens-rights-history/references-on-child-rights/declaration-rights-child/

Vaughn, S., Moody, S., & Schumm, J. (1998). Broken promises: Reading instruction in the resource room. *Exceptional Children, 64,* 211–225.

Vellutino, F. (1979). *Dyslexia, theory, and research.* Cambridge, MA: MIT Press.

Venezky, R. (1970). *The structure of English orthography.* The Hague, Netherlands: Mouton.

Venezky, R. (1999). *The American way of spelling.* New York, NY: Guilford Press.

Wagner, R.K., Torgesen, J.K., & Rashotte, C.A. (1999). *The Comprehensive Test of Phonological Processing (CTOPP).* Austin, TX: PRO-ED.

Wagner, R.K., Torgesen, J., Rashotte, C.A., & Pearson, N. (2010). *Test of Silent Reading Efficiency and Comprehension (TOSREC).* Austin, TX: PRO-ED.

Wasowicz, J., Apel, K., Masterson, J., & Whitney, A. (2004). *SPELL-links to reading and writing: A word study curriculum and supplemental program for K–adult.* Evanston, IL: Learning by Design.

Watts, T.W., Duncan, G.J., Siegler, R.S., & Davis-Kean, P.E. (2014). What's past is prologue: Relations between early mathematics knowledge and high school achievement. *Educational Researcher, 43,* 352–360.

Wechsler, D. (1991). *Wechsler Individual Achievement Test, Third Edition (WIAT III)*. San Antonio, TX: Harcourt Assessment.

Wechsler, D. (2003). *Wechsler Intelligence Scale for Children, Fourth Edition (WISC-4)*. San Antonio, TX: Pearson.

Whitehurst, G., Falco, F., Lonigan, C., Fischel, J., DeBaryshe, B., Valdez,-Menchaca, M., & Caulfied, M. (1988). Accelerating language development through picture book reading. *Developmental Psychology, 24*, 552–559.

Wiederholt, L., & Bryant, B. (2011). *Gray Oral Reading Test, Fifth Edition*. San Antonio, TX: Pearson.

Wiig, E.H., Semel, E., & Secord, W.A. (2013). *Clinical Evaluations of Language Fundamentals, Fifth Edition (CELF-5)*. San Antonio, TX: Pearson Education, Inc.

Wijsman, E., Peterson, D., Leutennegger, A., Thomson, J., Goddard, K., Hsu, L., et al. (2000). Segregation analysis of phenotypic components of learning disabilities I: Nonword memory and digit span. *American Journal of Human Genetics, 67*, 631–646.

Willcutt, E., Pennington, B., & DeFries, J. (2000). Twin study of the etiology and comorbidity between reading disability and attention deficit/hyperactivity disorder. *American Journal of Medical Genetics, 54*, 122–131.

Wingert, K., Del Campo, R., & Berninger, V. (2015). Person behind the written language learning disability. In Bahr, R., & Silliman, E. (Eds.). *Handbook of Communication Disorders* (pp. 226–236). London, UK: Routledge.

Winn, W., Berninger V., Richards, T., Aylward, E., Stock, P., Lee, Y., & Lovitt D. (2006). Effects of nonverbal problem solving treatment on skills for externalizing visual representation in upper elementary grade students with and without dyslexia. *Journal of Educational Computing Research, 34*, 395–418.

Wise, B., Rogan, L., & Sessions, L. (2009). Training teachers in evidence-based intervention: The story of linguistic remedies. In S. Rosenfield & V.W. Berninger (Eds.), *Handbook on implementing evidence based academic interventions* (pp. 443–477). New York, NY: Oxford University Press.

Wolf, B.J. (2011). Teaching handwriting. In J. Birsh (Ed.), *Multisensory teaching of basic language skills: Theory and practice* (3rd ed., pp. 179–206). Baltimore, MD: Paul H. Brookes Publishing Co.

Wolf, M., & Denckla, M. (2005). *RAN/RAS Rapid Automatized Naming and Rapid Alternating Stimulus Tests*. Austin, TX: PRO-ED.

Wong, B., & Berninger, V.W. (2004). Cognitive processes of teachers in implementing composition research in elementary, middle, and high school classrooms. In B. Shulman, K. Apel, B. Ehren, E. Silliman, & A. Stone (Eds.), *Handbook of language and literacy: Development and disorders* (pp. 600–624). New York, NY: Guilford Press.

Wong, L. (2002). *Sentence essentials: A grammar guide*. Boston, MA: Houghton Mifflin.

Wood, F.B., Flowers, L., & Grigorenko, E. (2001). *On the functional neuroanatomy of fluency or why walking is just as important to reading as talking is*. In M. Wolf (Ed.), *Dyslexia, fluency and the brain* (pp. 235–244). Timonium, MD: York Press.

Woodcock, R.W., Mather, N., & McGrew, K. (2008). *Woodcock-Johnson III Tests of Achievement (WJ III ACH)*. Rolling Meadows, IL: Riverside.

Woods, M.L., & Moe, A. (2003). *Analytical Reading Inventory* (7th ed.). Upper Saddle River, NJ: Merrill.

Yates, C. (May, 1996). *Screening for math abilities and disabilities in first and second graders* (Unpublished doctoral dissertation). Seattle, WA: University of Washington.

Yates, C., Berninger, V., & Abbott, R. (1994). Writing problems in intellectually gifted children. *Journal for the Education of the Gifted, 18*, 131–155.

Zhou, Z., Peverly, S.T., & Xin, T. (2006). Knowing and teaching fractions: A cross-cultural study of American and Chinese mathematics teachers. *Contemporary Educational Psychology, 31*, 438–457.

Index

Page numbers followed by *f* and *t* indicate figures and tables, respectively.